WITHDRAWN
L. R. COLLEGE LIBRARY

W9-BBH-222

WITHDRAWN

University of Michigan Publications

LANGUAGE AND LITERATURE

VOLUME III

THE SOCIAL MODE
OF RESTORATION COMEDY

CARL A. RUDISILL LIBRARY
LENOIR RHYNE COLLEGE

THE SOCIAL MODE OF RESTORATION COMEDY

BY

KATHLEEN M. LYNCH

"La mode nous oblige à cette complaisance."
PIERRE CORNEILLE

OCTAGON BOOKS

A DIVISION OF FARRAR, STRAUS AND GIROUX

New York   1975

822.409
L99s
95301
nov. 1975

Originally published 1926 by The Macmillan Company

Reprinted 1965
by special arrangement with The University of Michigan Press

Second Octagon printing 1975

OCTAGON BOOKS
A DIVISION OF FARRAR, STRAUS & GIROUX, INC.
19 Union Square West
New York, N. Y. 10003

LIBRARY OF CONGRESS CATALOG CARD NUMBER: 65-25569
ISBN 0-374-95207-8

Manufactured by Braun-Brumfield, Inc.
Ann Arbor, Michigan

Printed in the United States of America

To

MARY FRENCH LYNCH

FOREWORD

THIS study was originally undertaken in partial fulfillment of the requirements for the degree of Doctor of Philosophy at the University of Michigan. For purposes of publication it has been considerably enlarged and altered. I have been much assisted in the work of revision by the kind advice and criticism of Professor Hyder E. Rollins of Harvard University and Professor Henry Ten Eyck Perry of the University of Wisconsin.

My chief indebtedness is to Professor Oscar James Campbell of the University of Michigan, who suggested the subject of my dissertation and under whose direction the entire investigation has proceeded. It is quite impossible for me to express at all adequately my gratitude for Professor Campbell's ever generous faith in the work and exceptionally stimulating guidance. To him this volume owes whatever significance it may possess as a study of the Restoration comic mode.

KATHLEEN M. LYNCH

CONTENTS

THE SOCIAL MODE
OF RESTORATION COMEDY

CHAPTER I

A SURVEY OF RESTORATION COMEDY

TWO outstanding points of view have been advanced by literary critics regarding the sources of Restoration comedy of manners. One opinion has been that the work of the Restoration comic dramatists is largely to be accounted for as an English adaptation of Molière's comedy, enforcing his dramatic method and, to a considerable extent, exhibiting his comic temper.[1] A number of prominent critics, on the other hand, have insisted just as strongly that, although the Restoration dramatists often made generous use of material derived from Molière's drama, their work differs markedly from his in purpose and in spirit,[2] and should be judged simply as "an independent growth springing spontaneously from the impulse of English Restoration Society to view itself in reflexion upon the stage."[3] Both groups are agreed that the new comedy marks "rather a revolution than a development"[4] in English comedy and that its indebtedness to earlier English comedy is of very slight importance.

[1] Cf. especially Sir Edmund Gosse, *Seventeenth Century Studies* (1897 edition), "Sir George Etheredge," pp. 259–298, and D. H. Miles, *The Influence of Molière on Restoration Comedy.*

[2] Cf. especially Sir A. W. Ward, *A History of English Dramatic Literature to the Death of Queen Anne*, III, pp. 318–320; F. E. Schelling, "The Restoration Drama," in *Cambridge History of English Literature*, VIII, pp. 137–139; and John Palmer, *The Comedy of Manners*, pp. 64–66.

[3] Palmer, *The Comedy of Manners*, p. 66.

[4] *Ibid.*, p. 65.

Occasional arguments, it is true, have been suggested in support of the influence of English dramatic tradition on Restoration comedy.[5] Specific borrowings from the late Elizabethans have been noted in the drama of Etherege and his contemporaries. But no systematic study of such material has heretofore been attempted. Nor do the casual references to Jonson and Fletcher on the part of critics who have urged the English influence imply that a deliberate examination of this field might yield results sufficiently definite to be of distinct value. Beyond the period of Jonson and Fletcher, moreover, these critical reminiscences have not extended. Apparently none of our critics of Restoration comedy have been interested in the possibility of a gradual shift in comic standards, slowly asserting itself in late Elizabethan comedy, gathering energy in the court drama of the reign of Charles I, and becoming imperfectly defined in the work of Etherege's immediate predecessors, who may have anticipated, we are privileged to surmise, the admirably finished expression of the new spirit in Etherege's own comedy. In the pages which follow, an attempt has been made to trace the development and expansion of this English dramatic tradition.

The continued satisfaction of critics of Restoration comedy in sweeping assertions as to its origins has probably resulted from the conventional absorption of these critics in one conspicuous problem which such comedy suggests. Most critics of Restoration comedy have been vehemently concerned with the problem of evaluating it in accordance with the moral standards of their time. They have shown little interest in the problem of ascertaining whether or not Restoration comedy enforces harmonious standards of its own. Consequently, the accurate defining of Restoration comedy has proved a singularly slow and painful

[5] Cf. especially G. H. Nettleton, *English Drama of the Restoration and Eighteenth Century*, pp. 47–48; Allardyce Nicoll, *A History of Restoration Drama*, pp. 68–81; and Bonamy Dobrée, *Restoration Comedy, 1660–1720*, pp. 31–47.

process. Yet it has been a very significant process, and we can hardly afford to overlook its history.

Unfortunately, the mood of Jeremy Collier's contemporary outbursts against "the immorality and profaneness" of Restoration comedy has been an all too dominant mood in much of the later criticism of this drama. It was Collier's lament, supported by profuse and passionate citation from the comedies:

> On what unhappy Times are we fallen! The Oracles of Truth, the Laws of Omnipotence, and the Fate of Eternity are Laught at and despis'd.[6]

Of course, succeeding eighteenth century critics no longer felt called upon to assume the function of lonely prophets of the Lord in perilous times, for the peril was past. But they continued to apply severely Collier's test of morality to plays obviously lacking in the rudiments of such morality. In summing up Congreve's achievement, Dr. Johnson insisted that "the general tenour and tendency of his plays must always be condemned. It is acknowledged with universal conviction that the perusal of his works will make no man better; and that their ultimate effect is to represent pleasure in alliance with vice, and to relax those obligations by which life ought to be regulated." [7] Steele professed horror at Etherege's conception of an ideal gentleman in a Dorimant who talked vulgarly to an orange-woman and behaved barbarously to a lady, and an ideal gentlewoman in a Harriet who laughed at the notion of obedience to an absent mother! [8] *The Man of Mode*, as a whole, in accordance with the typical moralistic criticism of his age, Steele denounced as "a perfect Contradiction to good Manners, good Sense, and common Honesty." [8]

Among nineteenth century critics, to be sure, Lamb, Hazlitt, and Leigh Hunt rebelled, in varying degrees, against this sort of

[6] Jeremy Collier, *A Short View of the Immorality and Profaneness of the English Stage*, p. 80.

[7] Samuel Johnson, *Lives of the English Poets*, ed. G. B. Hill, II; "Congreve," p. 22.

[8] *The Spectator*, ed. Henry Morley (1868), p. 107.

criticism. Lamb properly maintained that the fashions of Restoration comedy should not be subjected to the test of more recent custom. His point of view is open to question, however,
through his quaint release of the whole world of Restoration
society from all laws of time and space, and his whimsical recon-
struction of this society as an "Utopia of gallantry," "a specula-
tive scene of things, which has no reference whatever to the
world that is." [9] Within this fairy country, "beyond the diocese
of the strict conscience," [10] Lamb extended his poetic musings in
a most engaging maner. But of the fact that this was once the
society which men like Etherege and Rochester had known and
loved, Lamb took no account. He avoided the reasonable reality
of Restoration comedy as an interpretation of the *beau monde* of
seventeenth century England. Hazlitt had a much firmer reali-
zation of the historical importance of this manners comedy. He
readily relived in imagination that "gala day of wit and pleasure,
of gallantry and Charles II." [11] He became seriously interested
in the standards of Restoration comedy, as apart from all super-
imposed standards of criticism of a later era. Here is a world
where "sense makes strange havoc with nonsense. Refinement
acts as a foil to affectation, and affectation to ignorance." [11]
Leigh Hunt wisely commended Hazlitt's sanity in viewing the
whole group of Restoration comic dramatists "as nature and society (short of the exaggerations of art) threw them forward during the progress of civilization." [12] Leigh Hunt himself was
genial, although not very searching, in his own criticism of the
Restoration mode. He urged that intelligent comprehension of
the manners of an earlier period must inevitably enrich the

[9] Charles Lamb, *Works*, ed. E. V. Lucas, IV; *Elia*, "On the Artificial
Comedy of the Last Century," p. 143.

[10] *Ibid.*, p. 142.

[11] William Hazlitt, *Works*, ed. Waller and Glover, VIII; *Lectures on the
English Comic Writers*, p. 70.

[12] *The Dramatic Works of Wycherley, Congreve, Vanbrugh, and Farquhar*,
ed. Leigh Hunt, Preface, p. lxx.

thought of the present age and serve to stimulate, rather than dismay, all minds "candidly and healthily trained." [13]

Victorian moral earnestness effectually extinguished these more generous and gracious moods of the critical spirit. Notably, Macaulay, even while parading his liberalism, brilliantly disparaged the "exceedingly bad" [14] morality of a Restoration society which he found "a great deal too real" [15] in "every thing ridiculous and degrading." [16] George Meredith, in the very act of assailing our unlovely English propensity for moralistic judgments, heartily decried "our so-called Comedy of Manners" as "comedy of the manners of South-Sea islanders under city veneer; and, as to comic idea, vacuous as the mask without the face behind it." [17] *The Way of the World*, indeed, he proposed to treat as an exceptional case, liberated from his general condemnation of these Restoration comedies. That proposal perhaps raises a question as to the intimateness of his study of a comic mode of which *The Way of the World* is no more than a very perfect illustration. In any case, Meredith's dismissal of this type of comedy is one of the most puzzling and disappointing of critical verdicts. Some of his penetrating comments on the nature of the Comic Spirit, apply admirably to Restoration comedy, despite the fact that he did not choose so to apply them.

From these discouraging indictments of Restoration comedy we may turn with gratitude to a recent court of appeal. A great service to aesthetic criticism has been rendered by that keen modern critic of manners comedy, Mr. John Palmer. In *The Comedy of Manners* (1913), Palmer has made it his primary concern to vindicate the integrity of Restoration comedy as a

[13] *Ibid.*, p. lxiii.
[14] Thomas Babington Macaulay, *Critical and Historical Essays*, ed. F. C. Montague, III; "Leigh Hunt," p. 11.
[15] *Ibid.*, p. 12.   [16] *Ibid.*, p. 7.
[17] George Meredith, *An Essay on Comedy and the Uses of the Comic Spirit*, ed. Lane Cooper, p. 83.

sincere form of art, when judged, as it should be judged, "according to the laws of the imagination." [18]   His method of approach to his subject has resulted, as might have been foreseen with a critic naturally gifted for the task, in his defining Restoration comedy with a new precision and accuracy.   Restoration comedy introduces us, he admits, to a strange country, yet a country where "the laws are harmonious and just" within its bounds and where we are privileged to realize "a mood of the human spirit which is in every age, though in this particular age it was more conspicuous." [19]   He asserts with confidence: "The comedies of Etherege are the natural product of an age for which life was an accepted pageant, incuriously observed, uncritically accepted, stuff for a finished epigram. . . . There was form; and there was bad form.   The whole duty of man was to find the one, and to eschew the other." [20]   Two types of persons move in this society, people of "true wit and perfect fashion," and people who merely "ape the smartness of the time." [21]   In the opposition of these two types the most striking effects in the comedy of Etherege, Wycherley, and Congreve are attained.   On the people of "true wit and perfect fashion" in this drama Palmer comments again, and in more detail, in a later essay on *Comedy*.   His discussion of Millamant's relations with Mirabell in *The Way of the World* leads him to the significant conclusion:

. . . In the comedy of manners men and women are seen holding the reality of life away or letting it appear only as an unruffled thing of attitudes. Life is here made up of exquisite demeanour. Its comedy grows from the incongruity of human passion with its cool, dispassionate and studied expression. Laughter does not here burst rudely forth at a vision of people housed in the flesh, aiming to scale the Empyrean. It ripples forth in ironic contemplation of people born to passion high and low, posing in the social mirror. This is the real justification of the term "artificial comedy" as applied to the plays of Etherege and Congreve. We are born naked into nature. In the comedies of Congreve we are born again into civilization and clothes. We are no

---

[18] Palmer, *The Comedy of Manners*, p. 29.   [19] *Ibid.*, pp. 292–293.
[20] *Ibid.*, p. 91.   [21] *Ibid.*, p. 86.

longer men; we are wits and a peruke. We are no longer women; we are ladies of the tea-table. . . . [22] The comedy of manners, in a word, is the natural flower of the civilized life of leisured and clever people as it reveals itself upon the surface. There must be no loud passion or emphasis; but a harmony of agreeable voices "congreeing to a full and natural close." [23]

In the foregoing quotations, accumulated from various sections of Palmer's essays, we are virtually given a working definition of Restoration comedy. In order to avail ourselves of that definition, all that we need to do is to unite and to some extent amplify its isolated elements. Palmer rightly emphasizes the fact that Restoration comedy portrays a specialized society, which enforces a standard of its own, quite opposed to the standards of the normal outside world. He rightly emphasizes the contrast within this society of two types of individuals, those who intelligently support its standard and those who are ludicrous through failing to do so. He certainly implies, without precisely stating the case, that these two sorts of people are to be judged by two different comic standards. The social posing of a Millamant, which this critic so admirably describes, obviously produces a different sort of comic effect from the social posing of a Sir Fopling Flutter. Millamant represents good form, Sir Fopling bad form; her group can appropriately laugh at the follies of his, while the outsider can laugh, besides, at the affectations of hers. Here, surely, is a variety of comic outlook possible only in the highly sophisticated society which this type of comedy represents. One may search in vain in Elizabethan drama and in the drama of Molière for a similar consistent contrast of comic standards. It is the unfailing identification mark of all Restoration comedy, and clearly serves to distinguish the type from all related forms.

What there is of satirical emphasis in this Restoration comedy is pretty plainly confined to the presentation of such social pretenders as Etherege's Sir Fopling in *The Man of Mode* and Con-

[22] Palmer, *Comedy*, pp. 32–33.   [23] *Ibid.*, p. 35.

greve's Witwoud in *The Way of the World*. The nonsense of the fools and half-wits, who so clumsily try to be persons of fashion, properly exposes them to the scornful or at least patronizing laughter of the enlightened few. And how are we to regard the enlightened few? Palmer's suggestion of a mood of "ironic contemplation" concerning such personages may seem misleading.

Congreve's Millamant cannot behave naturally, even when she becomes agitated by the normal experience of being in love; her predicament is consequently amusing. Yet if Millamant could behave naturally, she would not be nearly so charming. Congreve was well aware of the fact that the social world in which she moves has its limitations. Its standard allows only a very incomplete expression of the real Millamant's personality. Still, this society is exquisitely polite and agreeable. Congreve himself would surely not have wished it more candid at the cost of being less refined. He smiles at its ideal heroine with the most gracious and affable of smiles. He anticipates the conviction of Meredith:

> Contempt is a sentiment that cannot be entertained by comic intelligence. What is it but an excuse to be idly-minded, or personally lofty, or comfortably narrow, not perfectly humane? [24]

Congreve's laughter at Millamant is perfectly humane; it is actually friendly. In the same manner, his fellow-dramatists acknowledge the charm of their accomplished heroes and heroines. Restoration comedy owes its distinctive comic harmony to the genial and sympathetic laughter which its finer characters inspire.

To Meredith the comedy of Molière represented the highest level of pure comedy. He profoundly admired Molière's insistence upon the single comic standard of common sense. But Meredith never perceived that Molière's comedy is less provoc-

[24] Meredith, *Essay on Comedy*, p. 140.

ative than Restoration comedy of the humane laughter of the
Comic Spirit. By virtue of the standard which they set, Molière's ideal characters are never comic. They belong to no artificial coterie, which demands the regulation of conduct by an
artificial social code. They are models of common sense. Some
of Molière's ridiculed characters, of course, have no special fail-
ings, except in the way of a youthful indiscretion and impetuous-
ness which they will probably outgrow. Valère and Marianne
in *Tartuffe* absurdly quarrel, and Dorine exclaims indulgently:

A vous dire le vrai, les amants sont bien fous! [25]

And Célimène in *Le Misanthrope* is sympathetically presented as
a shrewd and witty, yet foolishly capricious, coquette. Nevertheless, Molière is mainly interested in the opposition of affected,
insincere people, who are positive fools, and candid, sensible
people, who have attained maturity of wisdom like his own. Because, on the other hand, the Restoration comic dramatists uti-
lize a double comic standard, it is possible for their finer sort of
affected characters to be uniformly intelligent and gracious, and
so more lovable and more capable of arousing friendly laughter
than nearly all corresponding affected characters in Molière's
comedy. This fact in no way discredits Molière's dramatic program, which proposes a much more vital interpretation of human
experience than that with which any of the Restoration comic
dramatists have been concerned. This divergence in standards
simply emphasizes the special source of comic effectiveness in
Restoration comedy, to which its essential triumphs are due, and
which isolates it in a very distinct fashion from such comedy as
that of Molière.

The dominance of Molière's influence on Restoration comedy
may thus legitimately be questioned. We may question even
more decidedly, perhaps, the view, conspicuously maintained by

---

[25] *Tartuffe* (*Oeuvres*, ed. Despois et Mesnard, IV) II, 4, p. 453.

Palmer, that the stereotyped comic pattern just reviewed was a new feature in the plays of Etherege. In Etherege's second and third comedies, we may observe, this pattern was already firmly impressed and perfectly outlined. It is at least plausible to suppose that a gradual change, rather than a sudden revolution in dramatic conventions, was responsible for Etherege's highly perfected comedies of manners. Palmer is plainly not interested in the subject of the development of Restoration comedy. He is keenly interested in its masterpieces, from a wise and eager study of which he successfully interprets the temper of the entire period. He is impatient of the chronological method. He comments carelessly, for example, that Wycherley's Dapperwit is "the successor of Sir Fopling," [26] a chronological impossibility, provoking the false notion that Etherege wrote all his plays as the first chapter in Restoration comedy and Wycherley all his as the second. A more uninspired task than that fulfilled by this brilliant critic, a less rewarding labor, though still rewarding, becomes suggested through Palmer's disregard of all problems connected with the origin and growth of the manners tradition.

Before us opens a field of exploration which has the fascination of any untried way. Late Elizabethan comedy, court comedy under Charles I, and the comedy of the Commonwealth period, when perceived as a background for Restoration comedy, acquire a new interest and a new unity. Hazardous guesses need not be indulged in. Restoration plays, in considerable abundance, are available for confirming each step of our proof. It may be hoped that, as the process of comparison is pursued, we may speak with an ever increasing sense of conviction of the development of the social mode of Restoration comedy.

[26] Palmer, *The Comedy of Manners*, p. 122.

CHAPTER II

THE TREND OF REALISTIC COMEDY FROM
JONSON TO SHIRLEY

A T THE outset of the seventeenth century the task of re-
leasing comedy from its "romantic entanglements" [1] still
remained unfulfilled. It was Ben Jonson's distinction to create a
new realistic comedy and to build up in its behalf a stout defense
of dramatic theory. Jonson's method persisted with his disciples,
more and more directed, however, by important new motives and
principles which Jonson could hardly have foreseen. Without its
Elizabethan background, it would be hard to visualize Restoration realistic drama. Whatever other influences played an important part in its evolution, Restoration comedy owed much, after
all, to the realistic pattern of comedy, with its steadily expanding
social emphasis, developed within the Elizabethan tradition.

It must not be forgotten that in the two decades before the
beginning of Jonson's dramatic career, John Lyly was already
writing a new kind of comedy, which often suggested, but never
realized, the program of comedy of manners. The Euphuistic
habit of speech, with all its ingenious tricks of style, afforded a
novel social language for comedy. Deities, kings, philosophers,
courtiers and court ladies, servants and clowns all exist, in
Lyly's plays, for the pleasurable diversion of Euphuistic fencing.
Wit counts for everything, humanity for nothing. Lyly gives a
special prominence to artificial courtship scenes, in which the
nimble-witted contestants exchange facile arguments in love casu-
istry. The same arguments appear in a more elaborated and

[1] A. H. Thorndike, "Ben Jonson," in *Cambridge History of English
Literature*, VI, p. 15.

stereotyped form in the prose narratives of *Euphues, The Anat-
omy of Wit* (1578) and *Euphues and His England* (1580).   Yet
this social language, the bond of a common purpose among his
characters, fails to contribute any true realism of effect to Lyly's
portrayal of social custom.   The actors on Lyly's stage are without substance.   The lady Caelia, debating on constancy with her
courtly lover Eristus in *Midas* (c. 1590),[2] has no peculiar features
which differentiate her from Niobe, a nymph of Ceres, skilfully
disputing a similar theme with the forester Silvestris in *Love's
Metamorphosis* (c. 1588–1589).   Lyly's court characters might well
have belonged to contemporary court society; yet such reality as
they have through their Euphuistic sophistication they share
with quaint personages of classical mythology.   The pressure of
that precise social code, with all its comic implications, which was
to determine the fashionable proprieties of Restoration comedy of
manners, is nowhere illustrated in Lyly's fragile and fanciful
drama.

Lyly founded no dramatic school.   Euphuistic conceits
strongly flavor the dialogue of Shakespeare's early comedy.   To
Shakespeare, however, the Euphuistic habit signified merely attractive ornamentation of discourse, not a social manner through
which alone his characters might reflect their thoughts and emotions.   Perhaps more consistently than most plays of the period,
John Day's graceful comedies, *The Isle of Gulls* (1606) and
Humour out of Breath (c. 1607–1608), continue, in their courtship
scenes, the verbal triumphs of Lyly, sometimes heightened by
Day's own poetic insight.   But Day was only a minor dramatist,
and more a poet than a dramatist, and he seems to have made
little impression on the more robust personalities of his brother
playwrights.

---

[2] Unless otherwise specified, for all plays produced before 1642 the dates
cited are those accepted by F. G. Fleay, *A Biographical Chronicle of the
English Drama*, vols. I and II.

Throughout its history, even at its strongest impulse, Euphuistic drama failed to achieve a realistic portrayal of life. Opposing prevailing fashions in comedy, Ben Jonson set himself the task of exhibiting in his drama

> . . . deeds and language, such as men do use,
> And persons, such as comedy would choose.[3]

He chose to effect a dramatic treatment of character on the gray level of habitual modes of thought and conduct. Into Shakespeare's vivid universe, where experience becomes so supremely transmuted through lyrical intensities of youthful loves or tempestuous sovereignty of mature passions, he had no legitimate entrance. Nor could Jonson view an actual workaday world in the romantic mood of Dekker. In Dekker's world a joyous-hearted shoemaker rates himself "princely born," and a basket-maker's challenge to the riddle of life becomes the song on the, lips:

> Art thou poor, yet hast thou golden slumbers? [4]

Jonson, on the other hand, emphasizes no such elastic laws of adjustment. He replaces the sweet irresponsibility of Elizabethan day-dreaming by a tone of measured discipline, resulting from his even grasp on the firm facts of experience. As one of his critics has declared, it became Jonson's task "to define and guide the shaping forces which a declining romanticism was setting free." [5]

The relation of Jonson's comedy to the realistic comedy of the Restoration period is a matter of considerable interest. In his deliberate and unsentimental scrutiny of human conduct, Jonson plainly foreshadows the Restoration comic dramatists. He also anticipates these dramatists, to some extent, in his

[3] *Every Man in His Humour* (*Works*, ed. Gifford and Cunningham, I), Prologue, p. 4.
[4] *Patient Grissil*, I, p. 8.
[5] G. Gregory Smith, *Ben Jonson*, p. 290.

general methods of characterization. All students of Restoration comedy are aware that Jonsonian "humours," however lightly and superficially reconstructed, remained a saving inspiration with lesser Restoration dramatists and the readiest means for procuring broad comic effects with the masters.

As to the chief contrast between Jonson's comedy and Restoration comedy, critics have not agreed. Palmer insists: "Molière and Jonson write the comedy of morals; Etherege the comedy of manners." [6] Such a contrast the Restoration dramatists themselves would have been the last persons to admit. Dryden, for example, excused his taste for extolling unscrupulous cleverness and failing to punish vice on the basis of Jonson's excellent example in *The Alchemist* and *Epicoene*.[7] In modern times, a more serious challenge to Palmer's statement, in the case of Jonson, has been voiced by Elisabeth Woodbridge, whose essay on Jonson's dramatic theory offers the most elaborate exposition of this subject to date. Miss Woodbridge urges the danger of perpetually judging Jonson's plays by his theories about them, and concludes: "Jonson's comedy . . . is judicial but not always moral, that is, it always subjects its persons to a judgment according to some standard, but this standard is quite as apt to be an intellectual one as a moral one." [8] To many minds, this verdict dwarfs the moral energy of Jonson's comedy, always pervasive if not always enforced, and minimizes the very real opposition between his fundamental intolerance of sin and folly and the urbane acceptance of both on the part of the Restoration dramatists. Some of us, however, are disposed to agree with Miss Woodbridge that, within the actual limits of his comedies, Jonson maintains an intellectual standard more often than a moral standard.

[6] Palmer, *The Comedy of Manners*, p. 16.

[7] *An Evening's Love* (*Works*, ed. Scott and Saintsbury, III), Preface, pp. 246–247.

[8] Elisabeth Woodbridge [Morris], *Studies in Jonson's Comedy*, pp. 30–31.

As far as Jonson's essential connection with Restoration comedy is concerned, are we not still begging the question? It is unfortunate that no critic has examined this relationship in detail. In the interests of the present study, such an examination can no longer be postponed.

In comparing Jonson with the Restoration comic dramatists, we have occasion to bear in mind a few well-known facts regarding Jonson's dramatic method. In his early plays, more strictly than ever again, Jonson is preoccupied with the problem of portraying and curing the "humours" resulting from variously disordered mental states. The secret of each disorder he detects as the preponderance of some one element in the victim's nature, to such an extent as to absorb all the forces of his personality in its own special channel. Not until the individual has recovered harmoniously balanced faculties is the norm of conduct achieved. The theory imposes grave dramatic limitations. In *Every Man in His Humour* (1598) the plot issues, such as they are, are directed by a small group of intriguers who do not have to be cured of humours. On the other hand, in *Every Man out of His Humour* (1599), where the fullest exposition of this theory occurs, the characters with humours dominate the entire action, all of them living so completely within these humours that only through a process of clumsy nudges on the part of their creator do they stop shouting their obsessions and become interested in the corrective program essential for the dénouement. So dominant in this play is the emphasis on humours that even the intrinsic unifying qualities of a dramatic fable disappear.

After the ventures in personal satire of *Cynthia's Revels* (1600) and *The Poetaster* (1601), in the period of the four great masterpieces in comedy, *Volpone* (1606),[9] *Epicoene* (1609),

---

[9] For date see Sir E. K. Chambers, *The Elizabethan Stage*, III, pp. 368–369, and C. H. Herford and Percy Simpson, *Ben Jonson*, I, pp. 43–44.

The Alchemist (1610), and *Bartholomew Fair* (1614), we may observe Jonson's apparently conscious attempt to strengthen the dramatic fibre of his comedy. In the main, the rigidity of the humours gives way before new demands of intrigue. The dupers and duped, whom Jonson habitually opposes, become pitted against each other in a clash of eccentric mental forces. The dupes become fools or foolish rascals in a broad sense and are thus open to ways of attack not possible according to the narrower conception of the humours. The dupers are more emphasized in their rôles of clever intriguers and are usually unscrupulous in their trickery. Whenever the habits of over-intellectualized cunning are most in evidence, perhaps more conspicuously in *The Alchemist* than elsewhere, the actual curing of humours ceases to be a vital part of the dramatist's program, and the corrective intention is pursued with greater subtlety.

In his late plays Jonson appears engaged in a process of drawing heavily upon various dramatic expedients, in order to prop up comedies which have no sure foundations and no real unity of design. He turns lovingly to some of the old humours, which had once served him well, but he vacillates in their use. Thus, Fitzdottrel in *The Devil is an Ass* (1616) appears in the curiously shifting lights of weak dupe of a "projector," morbidly jealous husband, and brazen intriguer. To bolster a weak intrigue, Jonson has recourse in this play to supernatural machinery, as in *The Staple of News* (1625) he uses the questionable support of allegory, and as in *The Magnetic Lady* (1632) he depends extravagantly on a device of mistaken identity.

It is surely significant that through all these shifts in dramatic method Jonson consistently evaluates human conduct by an absolute comic standard. With the Restoration dramatists, who regarded the realities of life with an equal steadiness of vision, a carefully determined comic standard is again of supreme importance. But to the Restoration standard, enforcing the peculiar social fashions of that age, Jonson's standard is radically opposed.[10] Long ago, Dryden felt the marked hostility between the two modes. He took pains to comment that Truewit, "the best character of a gentleman which Jonson ever made," [11] is nothing more than "a fine gentleman in an university." [12] The essential "meanness" of most of Jonson's characters Dryden decried as unmannerly, remarking: "Gentlemen will now be entertained with the follies of each other; and, though they allow Cob and Tib to speak properly, yet they are not much pleased with their tankard, or with their rags: And surely their conversation can be no jest to them on the theatre, when they would avoid it in the street." [13] Such comments indicate Dryden's very definite perception of the unsocial emphasis of Jonson's comic standard.

The case is clearly this. Nearly all of Jonson's characters manifest an extraordinary self-sufficiency. The earlier characters are closely bound up in humours, which have comic value quite apart from any social implications. Kitely in *Every Man in His Humour* is absorbed in a thoroughly unwarranted humour of jealousy. He rushes frantically back and forth from his place of business to his house, nursing his suspicions. He has no integral relations with a social order, although he is made to have outward and accidental ones, imposed by the dramatist. The boaster Bobadill and the poetaster Matthew are quite devoid of social consciousness. They are exhibited and put through their paces for the amusement of persons with whom they have and desire to have nothing in common. The foppish Brisk in *Every Man out of His Humour* declares the typical independence of the

---

[10] Dobrée, *op. cit.*, pp. 31–35, mentions this contrast, but is much more interested in the fact that Restoration humours are more lightly developed than their Jonsonian originals.

[11] *An Evening's Love* (*Works*, III), Preface, p. 247.

[12] *The Conquest of Granada*, Part II (*Works*, IV), *Defence of the Epilogue*, p. 239.   [13] *Ibid.*, p. 243.

Jonsonian character when he announces swaggeringly to Fungoso:

> Why, do you see, sir, they say I am fantastical; why, true, I know it, and I pursue my humour still, in contempt of this censorious age. . . . For my own part, so I please mine own appetite, I am careless what the fusty world speaks of me.[14]

In the later comedies the same unsocial attitudes are continued. In *Epicoene*, to be sure, certain characters are governed by a special social code. Mrs. Otter boasts:

> I am the servant of the court and courtiers.[15]

Her two great aims in life are indubitably social: to keep her husband "under correction" as the best etiquette prescribes, and to get herself admitted advantageously into a choice coterie of fashionable ladies. The collegiate ladies themselves follow a precise social code, of which Truewit gives a confident exposition. Yet the scenes in which this code is defined have only a secondary interest in the play and show a marked divergence from Jonson's usual manner. They proceeded from the pen of a dramatist who was more at home even in picturing such eccentrics as a Morose fleeing from society with his nightcaps tied over his ears or a mad Pennyboy senior sitting "like an old worm of the peace"[16] wrapped up in furs, holding a court of justice over his two dogs. As a rule, in the later plays the characters are absorbed in careers of intrigue. The rogues use the fools for individual ends, which are not affected by social sanctions. No one tries to adapt himself to his surroundings. The cozenage of the quacks in a London house or of the tricksters at Bartholomew Fair does not have to be modified to suit class distinctions; it simply has to be clever.

Generally speaking, then, it may be conceded that Jonson's realism does not include a relation of his characters to social

[14] *Every Man out of His Humour* (*Works*, II), III, 1, pp. 99–100.
[15] *Epicoene, or The Silent Woman* (*Works*, III), III, 1, p. 183.
[16] *The Staple of News* (*Works*, V), V, 1, p. 283.

standards. According to his program, adjustments are to be effected within the consciousness of the individual, not in his relations with others, and are made possible only through certain hard knocks of experience. Meanwhile, the individual himself accepts no guide but that of his own intelligence and goes his way, sturdily indifferent to the way of the world.

When in Restoration comedy, most often in second-rate comedy and in farce, but now and again in the best plays of the period, the old Jonsonian humours live again, they live with a distinct difference. Many of the humours are those of affected fops and would-be fine ladies, who make their blunders because they are unsuccessfully aping the social refinements of the day. It is true that some individuals still stubbornly refuse to comply with the rules of contemporary etiquette. These persons, however, unlike Jonson's eccentrics, are comic merely through their lack of social faith. Victims of "the old Elizabeth way in all things," [17] they contend in a futile and often ludicrous battle against the dominance of a new and supremely powerful social order.

A number of the plays of Jonson's contemporary, John Fletcher, are usually termed "comedies of manners." That comparatively few of Fletcher's comedies belong to this group even his most enthusiastic critics have been willing to admit. Yet it is not infrequently asserted that these plays did serve as models to the Restoration comic dramatists.[18] Strangely enough, the exact nature of this debt has never been investigated. Evidence has not been assembled. We are still confronted with the interesting problem: Did Fletcher's comedies of manners determine, as perhaps Jonson's comedies could not, the essential mode of Restoration comedy of manners?

[17] Dryden, *Sir Martin Mar-all* (*Works*, III), I, 8, p. 7.
[18] Cf. especially Orie L. Hatcher, *John Fletcher, A Study in Dramatic Method*, p. 36, and Nicoll, *op. cit.*, p. 170.

It is generally considered that Fletcher displays no higher artistic aim in his drama than facile mastery of "immediate stage effect." [19] We need only inspect the comedies, from this point of view, to observe how seriously this artistic handicap affects Fletcher's study of manners. In submission to the demands of successfully varied intrigue, whatever interests he has in consistent characterization break down sooner or later.

Although at times Fletcher employs Jonsonian humours, he can never be depended upon to maintain these whenever a right-about-face in his characters will help on his intrigue more effectively. In *The Humorous Lieutenant* (1619) the lieutenant himself ceases to be exhibited in his whimsical martial humour from the point in the action where he happens to be conveniently on hand to drink by mistake a certain love potion. Henceforth the original humour is forgotten; in his new affliction he dotes on his king like a love-sick girl. In *The Elder Brother* (revised after 1626) [20] Charles' humour of pedantry is carefully elaborated, but is abandoned for love and sagacious schemes for self-advancement as soon as he meets the heroine. It remains Fletcher's primary concern, in support of his cleverly contrived intrigue, to keep his characters sufficiently flexible for prompt response to surprising situations.

Fletcher's women are particularly vacillating. His typical heroine, to use a phrase of his own, is "as cunning as she is sweet." [21] In *The Spanish Curate* (1626) [22] Amaranta gives her lover a smart rap on the head with a chess-board in one mood, in the next offers him kindly encouragement, and in a third expresses amazed displeasure at the wantonness of his thoughts. Rosalura and Lillia-Bianca in *The Wild-Goose Chase* (1621),

[19] G. C. Macaulay, "Beaumont and Fletcher," in *Cambridge History of English Literature*, VI, p. 121.

[20] For date see F. E. Schelling, *Elizabethan Drama*, II, p. 249.

[21] *The Spanish Curate* (*Works*, ed. Dyce, VIII), IV, 7, p. 472.

[22] Certain scenes are by Massinger. Cf. Fleay, *op. cit.*, I, p. 217.

Celia in *The Humorous Lieutenant,* and the nameless heroine in *The Scornful Lady* (with Beaumont, 1613–1616) [23] present conspicuous illustrations of the same fickle genius for spinning out lovers' quarrels. The instability of Fletcher's heroines naturally confuses their lovers and works havoc with the study of manners.

Fletcher's best-drawn characters are undoubtedly the young libertines who, from the earliest plays to the latest, throng the pages of his comedy. In his portrayal of these sentimental and lively gentlemen Fletcher takes a genuine interest, it appears, in featuring certain social fashions of the day. Indolence and prodigality are fashionable habits with all young gallants. In *The Scornful Lady* the Younger Loveless succeeds gloriously in his project to

> live upon others as others have lived upon me.[24]

He enjoys his brother's estate with the utmost unscrupulousness. The Elder Loveless, in return, persuades a rich widow to marry the boy, then good-humoredly brushes aside the matter of his brother's follies, with the comment:

> . . . Now brother, I should chide;
> But I'll give no distaste to your fair mistress.
> .   .   .   .   .   .
> You have been wild and ignorant, pray mend it.

And the happy young rascal concedes:

> Sir, every day, now spring comes on.[25]

In impudence, cynicism, and taste for witty speech and for unscrupulous intrigue, Fletcher's gallants predict, in a general way, the heroes of Restoration comedy. But Fletcher's heroes do not understand the meaning of compliance with strict rules of etiquette, such as govern the Restoration *beau monde.*

The boisterous Wildbrain in *The Nightwalker* (revised by Shirley,

---

[23] For date see Chambers, *op. cit.,* III, pp. 229–230.
[24] *The Scornful Lady* (*Works,* II), I, 1, p. 13.
[25] *Ibid.,* III, 2, p. 66.

1633) is a thoroughly irresponsible rogue, who steals his aunt's spoons and goes bell-ringing with her coachman. Often sheer abundance of intrigue opposes any emphasis on the study of social attitudes, as in *Monsieur Thomas* (1610–1616),[26] where the hero speeds from one trick to another, the play concluding when his fantastic ingenuity gives out. That "outfacing fellow Mirabel" in *The Wild-Goose Chase* is probably the most whimsical gallant of them all. In the height of his caprice, Mirabel jubilantly shows the heroine the book in which he chronicles the names of his conquests — girls to whom, as to her, he has sworn marriage. His behavior is determined less by social standards than by an eccentric personal whim.

A study of all his comedies enforces the verdict that *Wit without Money* (1614) is certainly "the best essay of Fletcher in the comedy of London life." [27] It is a play entirely free from that romantic machinery to which in the form of lover's madness, feigned deaths, duels, night robberies, and the like, Fletcher normally has recourse, even in realistic comedy. Here, at last, Fletcher describes a definitely organized social group. Most of the characters are absorbed in the pleasures of London society. When the widow, alarmed by her sister's love affair, gives orders for going down into the country, a whole household is in despair, from the sister herself to the servant who prays for "a trickling storm, to last ten days." [28] The two gallants are typical young men of fashion, cherished in their follies by the indulgent heroines. But even in this play the study of manners is far more circumscribed than the type of comedy would lead us to expect. We learn relatively little about the London fashions in which the characters profess such an interest. The action moves swiftly, artfully varied by the schemes of the wise old uncle. None of

26 For date see Chambers, *op. cit.*, III, p. 228.
27 Schelling, *op. cit.*, I, p. 527.
28 *Wit without Money* (*Works*, IV), II, 5, p. 135.

the characters have either freedom or disposition to practise faithfully the poses of fashionable gallantry.

In *The Noble Gentleman* (left unfinished by Fletcher, licensed in 1626) [29] Fletcher had perhaps even better opportunities for a well-rounded study of fashionable society. Madame Marine's great object in life is to enjoy a social career in Paris, in pursuance of which aim she carries out a preposterous scheme for keeping her husband in town. She has also sufficient spare time on her hands to dupe the husband's cousin and teach his wife to become a lady — that is, to cuckold her husband. The cousin's wife is a country innocent but is apt in learning city ways. After a couple of gallants have paid her attentions, she announces that she can no longer bear the thought of the country. With great eagerness she sits at the feet of Madame Marine and drinks in that lady's up-to-date matrimonial suggestions:

> As I was telling you, your husband must be
> No more commander; look to that; be several
> At meat and lodging; let him have board wages,
> And diet 'mongst his men i' the town; for pleasure
> If he be given to it, let him have it;
> Else as your own fancy shall direct you. [30]

Unfortunately, the social situations of the play are only sketched in. The dramatist's main interest is in his comparatively dull program for keeping a foolish country gentleman in the conceit that he is a duke. Only at brief intervals does Fletcher take a rapid survey of the far more interesting social follies of Madame Marine and her select circle.

It is to be regretted that Fletcher's taste for social portraiture never impressed upon his comedy that unity of design which Jonson's comedy, through another emphasis, usually displays. In Fletcher's few "comedies of manners" the spirit of Eliza-

---

[29] Fleay, *op. cit.*, I, p. 222, attributes the completion of the play to Rowley, aided probably by Middleton.
[30] *The Noble Gentleman* (*Works*, X), IV, 4, p. 173.

bethan exuberance, unsteadied by any firm perception of character, still dominates the action and makes even the wearing of
fashions more a matter of buoyant and wayward self-expression
than of conscious self-discipline. In *Wit without Money* and *The
Noble Gentleman* there are hints, to be sure, of the excellent comic
possibilities inherent in any socially homogeneous society, where
the personages of the drama become united in their kindred
aspirations and interests. Yet these persons of fashion still have
an incurable zest for random adventure and farcical intrigue. At
all times, Fletcher cares too much for rapid variation of stage
effects to have more than passing sympathy with the conventionalized attitudes of fashionable society.

A much more thorough-going realism than Fletcher's is represented in the London comedies of that "unduly neglected
author," [31] Thomas Middleton. Indeed, Middleton has been
declared "the most absolute realist in the Elizabethan drama." [32]
The coarse quality of this realism has undoubtedly told against
its master in the judgment of most of our critics. Even the occasional lovers of Middleton's "random brilliance" [33] have felt
obliged to adopt an apologetic tone in his defense. Repelled from
Middleton in the conventional manner, critics of Restoration
comedy have been more indifferent to his influence on later
comedy than to the influence of Jonson and Fletcher.

It has been all too convenient to dispose of Middleton by
comparing him with Jonson. It is plain enough that in his un-
scholarly, rough-and-ready fashion Middleton often avails himself
of Jonsonian humours, as a convenient expedient in rapidly defining character or blocking out action. He sets forth in true
Jonsonian style such types as the wrangler in law-suits, the jealous husband, the credulous astrologer, the prodigal host. With

---

[31] Ward, *op. cit.*, II, p. 538.　　　　[32] Schelling, *op. cit.*, I, p. 516.
[33] Arthur Symons, "Middleton and Rowley," in *Cambridge History of
English Literature*, VI, p. 70.

Middleton, again, as with Jonson, the relations of the intriguing parties often become of primary dramatic interest. Dupers and duped contend against each other, sometimes shifting their positions, as a play progresses, through the natural tendency of rascality to overreach itself. Often in the last act of a play, in the manner affected by Jonson, Middleton has one of the characters assume a judicial position, unravel the tangle of intrigue, and assign rewards and punishments. These resemblances are rather striking. On the other hand, Middleton never illustrates Jonsonian principles with any evident conviction of their philosophical supremacy. He seizes upon them, as his fancy pleases, to give variety to his dramatic pattern. As the greatest realist in Elizabethan drama, Middleton is a hearty observer of life at first hand. For the joyous animation of most of his scenes, Jonson's studiously evolved theories could hardly have furnished the essential stimulus.

The peculiar quality of Middleton's realism appears to be largely due to his keen perception, resulting from direct observation, of certain social aspects of character. The social unrest of contemporary London life attracts his eager attention, as it had never attracted Jonson's. The trafficking which goes on between different social classes offers him picturesque and telling contrasts. His scenes take life from the bustling intercourse of knights and citizens, gallants and citizens, country clowns and cony-catchers. His comic intrigue is directed by the psychology of class relationships.

Middleton enjoys the social spectacle from a variety of angles, satirizing all groups with good-natured impartiality. His conception of a lord is somewhat shadowy, and he never emphasizes the social mannerisms of the upper classes. But his realism is quite adequate for his favorite situations, in which a preference for a bourgeois setting is marked. When his gentlemen and tradesmen parley over a shop-counter, the realism of portrayal is admirably convincing.

Middleton's town gallants frequently cut a figure at the expense of well-to-do citizens or dull country rustics. Sometimes the intriguers are actual cony-catchers, as in *Your Five Gallants* (*c.* 1607). Again, they content themselves with playing fairly harmless pranks on tradesmen, as in *Anything for a Quiet Life* (*c.* 1623). Witgood announces the initial status of them all at the beginning of *A Trick to Catch the Old One* (*c.* 1605): " All's gone! still thou'rt a gentleman, that's all; but a poor one, that's nothing." [34] A match with a rich widow is the salvation of any gallant; an intrigue with a citizen's wife is his next best expedient. The suspicious attitude with which the average citizen naturally regards these shrewd schemers is well expressed by Mistress Purge, the apothecary's wife, in *The Family of Love* (1604–1607?): [35]

. . . Of all men I love not these gallants; they'll prate much but do little: they are people most uncertain; they use great words, but little sense; great beards, but little wit; great breeches, but no money. [36]

The social attitudes which Middleton best describes are those of exceptionally prosperous and correspondingly ambitious London citizens who aspire to the privileges of people of fashion. Discontented with their drab station in life, these capable city merchants traffic warily with unsuspecting country gentlemen for the estates and titles which the latter possess by hereditary right. Quomodo in *Michaelmas Term* (1606 ?) [35] cleverly avails himself of the financial distresses of Easy in order to get control of Easy's estate in Essex. In glowing terms the citizen pictures to himself his future magnificent progress to this desired abode:

. . . A fine journey in the Whitsun holydays, i' faith, to ride down with a number of citizens and their wives, some upon pillions, some upon side-saddles, I and little Thomasine i' the middle, our son and heir, Sim Quomodo, in a peach-colour taffeta jacket, some horse-length, or a long yard before us — there will be a fine show on's I can tell you. [37]

[34] *A Trick to Catch the Old One* (*Works*, ed. Bullen, II), I, 1. p. 251.
[35] For date see Chambers, *op. cit.*, III, p. 440.
[36] *The Family of Love* (*Works*, III), I, 3, p. 22.
[37] *Michaelmas Term* (*Works*, I), IV, 1, p. 299.

Similarly, in *A Trick to Catch the Old One*, Hoard exults in the prospect of a spectacular journey down to the widow's country estate, in his vision of having ten men ride after him "in watchet liveries, with orange-tawny capes," and in his anticipation of hunting-sports in the new home, conducted on so imposing a scale that "all the gentlemen a' th' country shall be beholding to us and our pastimes." [38]

The play in which Middleton most elaborately and most successfully portrays the relations of country knight and city merchant is *A Chaste Maid in Cheapside* (c. 1612). In this comedy Sir Walter Whorehound comes up to London with his courtesan, whom he tries to dispose of as his Welsh niece in a convenient match with Tim, son of the rich goldsmith Yellowhammer. Yellowhammer, in return, is charmed at the notion that his Tim shall wed a girl "heir to some nineteen mountains." [39] On the side, the goldsmith attempts to negotiate a match between his daughter Moll and Sir Walter himself, enticing the latter by a promised dowry of two thousand pounds. All Yellowhammer's attitudes are colored by his ambition to raise his social standing. He privately prides himself on his manner of educating his son, and describes to Sir Walter, with feigned depreciation, Tim's agreeable prospects in life. Tim, as his father explains modestly, is

> A poor, plain boy, an university man;
> Proceeds next Lent to a bachelor of art;
> He will be call'd a Yellowhammer then
> Over all Cambridge, and that's half a knight.[40]

Although a merchant, the goldsmith will have it known that he comes from the Yellowhammers of Oxfordshire. His wife Maudlin is afflicted with the same social malady. At the very moment when she receives the news of her daughter's death, she can con-

---

[38] *A Trick to Catch the Old One* (*Works*, II), IV, 4, pp. 323–324.
[39] *A Chaste Maid in Cheapside* (*Works*, V), I, 1, p. 12.
[40] *Ibid.*, I, 1, p. 13.

tinue placidly planning her son's fine marriage, for, as she declares with composure:

> We'll not lose all at once, somewhat we'll catch.[41]

Middleton's keen concentration on the spectacle of the interplay of different social classes marks an important development in realistic comedy. With Middleton the uniform test of efficiency for the individual becomes his sensitiveness of response to the code of his special social group in its relationship to other groups. Class barriers, at last, are breaking down. Success is spelled in terms of social advancement. Ambitious London tradesmen eagerly seek for themselves the privileges and immunities enjoyed by gentlemen. It is true that fashionable manners, for their own sake, still mean practically nothing to Middleton's bluff and downright citizens. Yet already in Middleton's drama, the fashionable leisure class, which was to dominate later comedy so completely, assumes at times, through its crude but vigorous pressure on middle class life, a social authority hitherto unrealized on the comic stage.[42]

Richard Brome is usually regarded as an extraordinarily conscientious follower of Ben Jonson.[43] "His plays," it is declared, "are the work of a man who learned playwriting by being apprenticed to it as a trade, just as he might have learned carpentry. He followed his master's methods, and applied them to his own pieces of work with much skill and intelligence, but without

---

[41] *Ibid.*, V, 2, p. 106.

[42] In the choice of material for this chapter a carefully selective method has necessarily been followed. It is hoped that the main currents in realistic comedy may be sufficiently illustrated in the work of five thoroughly representative dramatists. For example, Massinger has not been discussed, as his achievement in realistic comedy offers no marked contrast to Middleton's, save in the former's vehemence of moral satire.

[43] Cf. especially C. E. Andrews, *Richard Brome: A Study of His Life and Works*, pp. 64–65 and 81–98; and Mina Kerr, *Influence of Ben Jonson on English Comedy, 1598–1642*, pp. 57–75.

much literal plagiarism and without any originality." [44] Such a statement accounts admirably for Brome's picturesque portrayal of a long line of Jonsonian humours and for his clever elaboration and variation of the Jonsonian system of intrigue. On the other hand, it is incontestable that the student of comedy will find much to interest him in Brome's work that is not borrowed from Jonson. Brome's plays exhibit a study of class relationships which is more detailed and more impressive than Middleton's. It is only just that Brome should be given credit for whatever originality he achieved in the study of contemporary manners.

Brome approaches the study of social attitudes with a definite mental bias. Perhaps because of the homeliness of his early environment and training, he never chose to assume the manners of a courtier. In his dedication to *The Northern Lasse* (c. 1630) [45] he warns his patron that he is "one of the last rank, and therefore cannot do like the first." [46] In his dedication to his last play, *A Joviall Crew* (1641), the same temper is stated as the proud prerogative of age: "You know, Sir, I am old and cannot cringe, nor Court with the powder'd and ribbanded Wits of our daies." [47] Individual prejudices seem to have forced Brome's concentration, in his plays, on the concerns of citizen life. He habitually regards from the outside the manners of fashionable society, gaining his comic effects through their caricature and distortion when aped by curious citizens who perceive them only as mannerisms.

The chief concern of Brome's citizens is to become gentlemen, not only in name, but also in all the refinements of life. The character which Widgine gives of Sir Paul Squelch in *The Northern Lasse* indicates a typical frame of mind:

[44] Andrews, *op. cit.*, p. 98.
[45] The dates accepted for Brome's plays are those (revised from Fleay's dates) used in the chronological table of Andrews, *op. cit.*, p. 36.
[46] *The Northern Lasse* (*Works*, III), p. vii.
[47] *A Joviall Crew: or, The Merry Beggars* (*Works*, III), p. 344.

. . . I have heard Sir Paul Squelch protest he was a Gentleman, and might quarter a Coat by his wives side. Yet I know he was but a Grasier when he left the Country; and my Lord his father whistled to a Team of Horses (they were his own indeed.) But now he is Right Worshipful. . . .[48]

In like fashion, the citizen's widow will leave no stone unturned in her schemes to become a lady. The essential plot interest in *The Northern Lasse* centers about the cunning attempts of Mistress Fitchow, a "city-widow," to ensnare a young gentleman in a match with her. With the wedding in prospect, her brother goes about on tiptoe, exclaiming: "My Ladie that shall be! how sweetlie it chimes! . . ."[49] In the same interval, she herself concentrates on the problem of transforming her man Howdee into a gentleman-usher. She succeeds in getting him to address her as "madam," but the process of instruction proves laborious, and the exclamation is forced from her in one moment of desperation: "Shall I ever mould thee into a Gentleman Usher?"[50] One is relieved to learn that in time Howdee becomes quite proficient in the art and is able to discourse with the best of them on the "eight parts" of behaving as a member of the fraternity. He explains in confidence: "I learnt all of a good old Ladies man in the Strand . . . that must be nameless."[51]

The citizen's wife, debarred from the pleasure of aspiring to a ladyship, has still agreeable social diversions open to her in her fashionable relations with town gallants. The gallants accept these relations as a matter of course. In *The New Academy* (c. 1628) one of them queries: "O Tradesmen, why do you marry?" And his friend gives the prompt rejoinder: "Why? to make Tradeswomen For Gentlemen that want money and commodity."[52] The citizen usually tries to make the best of this well-recognized situation. Camelion in *The New Academy* proves such a compliant husband that he precipitately runs out of his shop, leav-

---

[48] *The Northern Lasse* (*Works*, III), II, 1, p. 23.
[49] *Ibid.*, I, 3, p. 7.   [50] *Ibid.*, I, 6, p. 13.   [51] *Ibid.*, IV, 1, p. 72.
[52] *The New Academy, Or, the New Exchange* (*Works*, II), II, 1, p. 29.

ing Hannah alone there, when he observes "one of the Blades" [53]
approaching. In *A Mad Couple well Match'd* (1636?) Alicia,
wife of Saleware, a silk merchant, persuades her husband to an
actual pride in her supposed acquisition of court manners. She
instructs him carefully in her exaggerated notions of Platonic
friendship:

> *Al.* Will you never be governd by my judgment, and receive that onely
> fit for you to understand, which I deliver to you undemanded? Doe not I
> know the weight of your floore thinke you? Or doe it you on purpose to
> infringe friendship, or breake the peace you live in?
>
> *Sal.* Never the sooner for a hasty word, I hope Friend.
>
> *Al.* Did you not Covenant with mee that I should weare what I
> pleased, and what my Lord lik'd, that I should be as Lady-like as I would,
> or as my Lord desir'd; that I should come, and go at mine own pleasure,
> or as my Lord requir'd; and that we should be alwayes friends and call so,
> not after the sillie manner of Citizen and Wife, but in the high courtly way?
>
> *Sal.* All this, and what you please sweete Courtly-friend I grant as I
> love Court-ship, it becomes thee bravely.[54]

After some further discussion, the wife brings her advice to a
close with the comfortable decision: "Bee you a Cittizen still
Friend, 'tis enough I am courtly." [55] Alicia's Platonic enthusiasms are ultimately rather cooled by the discovery that she has
been carrying on an intrigue with a girl in a boy's attire;
and she is content to adopt her husband's mild suggestion that
"by your favour friend, we will be friends no more, but loving
man and wife henceforward." [56] The dialogue quoted above may
seem reminiscent of the conversations between Mistress Otter and
her husband in *Epicoene*. But such scenes are rare in Jonson's
comedy.

Not so courtly as Alicia's love adventures, but none the less
eager, are those of Josina, the merchant's wife, in *The City Wit*
(c. 1629). No sooner has her husband undertaken a journey and

---

[53] *Ibid.*, II, 1, p. 24.
[54] *A Mad Couple well Match'd* (*Works*, I), III, 1, p. 58.
[55] *Ibid.*, III, 1, p. 60.   [56] *Ibid.*, V, 2, p. 97.

left Josina to her own devices than she sets about illustrating her private conviction: "Lord, what a thing a woman is in her husband's absence!"⁵⁷ Any lover will do, if only he is a gentleman. When her husband in disguise begs an interview, Josina questions her maid earnestly: "But are you sure he is a true Gentleman? does he weare clean Linnen, and lack Money?"⁵⁸ In *The Sparagus Garden* (1635) Rebecca, wife of a china-shop merchant, expresses similar attitudes. Her conduct in the play is regulated on the basis of her conviction: "I see what shift soever a woman makes with her husband at home, a friend does best abroad."⁵⁹ Although all these intrigues turn out harmlessly enough, the wife's customary calm admission of honest motives at the end of her holiday comes with a distinct shock of surprise. A good moral is pointed at the expense of consistent characterization.

The zest of the average citizen for playing a fashionable rôle at any price is naturally taken advantage of, in Brome's world, by unprincipled sharpers. In a number of striking cases, Brome heightens his comic effects by allowing tricksters to gull his ambitious fools through the influence of some preposterous school of manners. Such schemes triumph in *The New Academy* and *The Damoiselle* (1637–1638 ?). In *The Sparagus Garden* this system of cozenage is emphasized with special detail. Tim Hoyden, a country fellow, son of a yeoman, is cozened of four hundred pounds in the process of being made a gentleman and acquiring what he is pleased to term "a finical City wit, and a superfinicall Court wit."⁶⁰ He undergoes a painful discipline, which includes bleeding until he is purged of his father's peasant blood, followed by a diet of delicacies until he is nearly starved. Finally, he has to memorize laboriously the "principles" for being a gentleman

⁵⁷ *The City Wit, or The Woman Wears the Breeches* (*Works*, I), I, 1, p. 287.
⁵⁸ *Ibid.*, II, 2, p. 300.
⁵⁹ *The Sparagus Garden* (*Works*, III), III, 9, p. 172.
⁶⁰ *Ibid.*, II, 3, p. 141.

and attend and take notes on an exhibition of "single Rapier" and "Back-sword Complement foyle." [61]

In this final stage of Hoyden's training the satire is directed against the affected language of courtly compliment and is highly amusing. Springe and Brittleware, two of the dupers, set forth "single Rapier" in "three bouts." Approaching each other in the manner of gallants who are hardly acquainted, they engage in the following elegant conversation:

Spr. Noble Master Fine-wit, the single example of Court-ceremony, if my apprehension deals fairly with me.

Brit. Sir, how auspiciously have I falne upon the knowledge of you by vertue of the same apprehension.

Spr. Sir, I shall ever blesse the promptnesse of my memory, in being so fortunate to collect the fallicious acquaintance of so compleat a goodnesse.

Brit. Oh you are pleas'd out of that noble worth which can convert all things to the forme and image of its owne perfection to make your selfe glorious, with that which is miserably impoverish'd in it selfe.

Spr. Sir, you have such a conquering way in humility, that he shall be sure to come off vanquish'd that offers to contend with you.

Brit. This is the noblest of all humanity to peece up the defect of your friend with a glory of your owne.[62]

The "Back-sword," next illustrated, presents a startling contrast. Moneylacks, another duper, is master of ceremonies.

Mon. So much for single Rapier: now for your secret wipe at Back-sword.

Hoy. I that I would see, like the hackling of the Millers leggs: now for a delicate back-blow.

Spr. See you yon fellow I held complement with?

Hoy. Yes sir, a well-spoken gentleman and a lovely.

Spr. The arrantst trifle in a Kingdome.

Hoy. What he is not, is he?

---

[61] *Ibid.*, IV, 9, p. 195.

[62] *Ibid.*, IV, 9 and 10, pp. 195–196. I have omitted the comments of the spectators.

Spr. . . . a very lumpe of laughter.

Hoy. Ha, ha, ha.

Mon. You have done well, now you sir.

Brit. Doe you note him yonder that past from you?

Hoy. That gallant sir.

Brit. The very scorne at Court;
So empty not one passable part about him.

Mon. Good.

Brit. A very tilting stocke for yong practisers to break their jests on.

Mon. Enough.

Hoy. Good and enough; doe you call this good enough to abuse one another thus?

Mon. Yes, this is backsword Complement: this wipes off the false praise which the first thrust on: you must bee seene in both, or you are no true garbist else.[63]

There can be no necessity for illustrating at greater length Brome's original contribution to the study of the manners of his day. We may grant that the genuine world of fashion attracts him hardly more than it had attracted Middleton. But in the portrayal of the reactions of citizen life to the fashions set by polite society, Brome easily outstrips the earlier dramatist; indeed, on this subject he is an unsurpassed authority. In those many scenes in his comedies where his discipleship to Jonson remains more a matter of technique than of spirit, we may turn with confidence to Brome for a full commentary on the social discontent of the citizen class in the London of his era. Brome's citizens have a sudden and dazzled perception of the desirability of a more modish habit of life. As they try to effect their admission into the fashionable leisure class, they have a consuming ambition, unknown to Middleton's citizens, for acquiring the artificial culture of that class. With infinite relish Brome observes and records the continuous spectacle of their clumsy masquerading as courtiers — a spectacle which never ceases to appear grotesque.

Brome's dramatic program definitely points the way to the more famous comedy of James Shirley. To our dramatic critics

[63] *Ibid.,* IV, 10, pp. 196–197.

Shirley has proved the most interesting figure of his period. As "the last of the Elizabethans" he has received full and faithful tribute. He has also been described as "the prophet of the Restoration." [64] Apparently, not a few of his critics have believed that he "carried forward the movement" [65] which culminated in Congreve. Why this last contention has never provoked explanation and illustration it is difficult to understand. The subject of Shirley's Elizabethan inheritance has been literally exhausted. We undertake a new problem, however, in attempting to determine his relationship to the Restoration comic dramatists.

Shirley's critics have, of course, been justified in insisting that much of his work shows a distinct Elizabethan emphasis. Over and over again the ghosts of Jonsonian humours reappear, often indulged at the expense of a more original dramatic impulse. *The Ball* (1632),[66] for example, is a play which might have had a particularly impressive social significance, were it not for the fact that its unity is completely vitiated by the leisurely exposition of humours. A "May lord," a cynic, a braggart, a foppish French dancing master, and a pretended traveller are forever crowding the more legitimate personages of the comedy off the stage. In the construction of Shirley's plots Fletcher's influence is conspicuous; [67] this influence dominates in Shirley's complications of love intrigue, in his pursuit of dramatic surprises, and in his character contrasts. In Shirley's dialogue "the traditions of a stronger and more masculine style of comedy are still perceptible." [68] There are no traces of a conversational brilliancy like Congreve's. Shirley's moral conservatism, too, — witness the numerous conversions of his young reprobates — is fully as often illustrated as that

---

[64] A. H. Nason, *James Shirley, Dramatist*, p. 1.
[65] C. M. Gayley, *Representative English Comedies*, III, p. xcii.
[66] Cf. Robert S. Forsythe, *The Relations of Shirley's Plays to the Elizabethan Drama*. Forsythe's chronological table, pp. 41–46, is followed for the dates of Shirley's plays.
[67] *Ibid.*: see especially pp. 48–115.   [68] Ward, *op. cit.*, III, p. 125.

of Fletcher, Middleton, or Brome, and is usually more convincing. It is clear that the Elizabethan influence is fundamental in Shirley's comedy.

How, then, does Shirley become "the prophet of the Restoration"? It cannot be denied that he has one interest which he did not derive from the dramatists to whom he owed so much. As a gentleman well received and at home in court circles, Shirley regarded attentively the fashionable society of his day and perceived with sympathetic understanding the refinement which characterized it at its best. Perhaps because he was so closely linked with the Elizabethan past, he attempted in only two of his plays an extended portrayal of this society. At any rate, in *Hyde Park* (1632) and *The Lady of Pleasure* (1635) fashionable manners are described with a charm of appreciation and a freshness of enthusiasm which bring Shirley nearer than any of the other great writers of the Elizabethan school to the standards and the spirit of Restoration comedy.

Hyde Park depicts citizen life with just one lord thrown in. But the citizens are no longer tradespeople, grotesquely aping the manners of the nobility. They are not conspicuous as citizens at all, but are people of leisure, who enact the fashions of the day with an accurate perception of social values. Carol and Julietta are quite a match for Lord Bonville. In *The Lady of Pleasure* a higher social level is illustrated, with the nobility in control of the action. Citizen life, as such, has no place in the social scheme. Celestina, the widow of a lord, is a confirmed, though attractive snob. Shirley rationalizes her taste for fashionable gaieties. She explains sensibly:

> It takes not from the freedom of our mirth,
> But seems to advance it when we can possess
> Our pleasures with security of our honour;
> And that preserv'd, I welcome all the joys
> My fancy can let in.[69]

---

[69] *The Lady of Pleasure* (*Works*, ed. Dyce, IV), II, 2, p. 32.

Lord Bornwell, Shirley's ideal noble gentleman, is by no means puritanical in his attitudes. He esteems a life of social pleasure, temperately pursued. In both plays the poise and good temper of society's privileged members present an agreeable spectacle.

From the point of view of the gentleman of fashion, Shirley portrays with approval the polite society of which Brome, from the point of view of the shrewd outsider, gives merely a caricature. It is a society obviously more sophisticated than the fashionable world of Fletcher's plays. Manners have become crystallized into a formal system. With thorough self-consciousness Shirley's characters adopt a social pose. They play a social game in which every gesture is observed and every move counts.

In this social comedy, as in all true comedy of manners, two types of comic situation become contrasted. To be well played the social game calls for an intellectual equipment in which certain characters are manifestly deficient. These characters are intruders in the brilliant scene. They attempt to imitate, without being able to interpret, certain conspicuous social mannerisms. The self-restraint so fundamental in the conduct of all intelligently well-bred persons, they mistake for license. They lose their heads and overact the social rôle. A marked contrast to such personages is presented by the fully initiated members of the social group, who comply intelligently with its unwritten laws. In the case of such individuals, also, comic effect is still possible. Really intelligent persons cannot completely adjust their conduct to an artificial social pattern without paying a price. A conflict ensues between their natural selves and the selves which society prescribes for them. They may sacrifice the former even willingly, but the dramatist knows and the audience knows that the social compensation, however gracious, is transitory and inadequate. In contrasting social pretenders with these accomplished people of fashion, the dramatist asserts a double comic standard, upon which he relies for enlarging the scope of his comedy.

It is true that in *Hyde Park* and *The Lady of Pleasure* Shirley gives only a partial interpretation of this society. The Bonavent intrigue in *Hyde Park* is developed in accordance with familiar conventions regulating that type of Elizabethan disguise plot.[70] The conversions of Lord Bonville in *Hyde Park* and of Lady Bornwell, Lord A., and Kickshaw in *The Lady of Pleasure* support a popular Elizabethan program for the reformation of wayward persons, a program which Shirley seems to have found peculiarly suited to his tastes. The crew of foppish gallants and their university pupil in *The Lady of Pleasure* exist mainly in the interests of Lady Bornwell's reformation, and their social mannerisms are only faintly indulged. In this play, too, Lord Bornwell's passion for moralizing frequently gets the better of his social urbanity, and the acid sarcasms of his wife's steward strengthen the conversion program at the expense of social portraiture. On the other hand, Shirley's deliberate elaboration of a limited number of social portraits is well worth our consideration. The relations of Carol and Fairfield, to which *Hyde Park* owes all its piquant animation and merriment, are developed completely within the new social mode just reviewed. Lady Bornwell as a social imposter and Celestina as a brilliant young woman of fashion are definitely contrasted, although the contrast is not always enforced as emphatically as Etherege or Congreve would have enforced it. We may fittingly devote some attention to these three conspicuous studies in social affectation.

An amusing situation occurs early in the second act of *The Lady of Pleasure*, when Frederick, fresh from the university, first appears in the presence of his aunt, Lady Bornwell, and her gallants, Kickshaw and Littleworth:

[70] Cf. Forsythe, *op. cit.*, p. 350.

Fred. My most loved aunt!

Lady B. Support me, I shall faint.

Little. What ails your ladyship?

Lady B. Is that Frederick,
In black?

    Kick. Yes, madam; but the doublet's satin.

    Lady B. The boy's undone! [71]

Lady Bornwell is not in any real danger of fainting, but the circumstances, she thinks, demand that she should appear so. All her subsequent relations with Frederick are determined by the same social pose. Unfortunately, Lady Bornwell judges wholly by external appearances. She plays an affected rôle with no clarity of vision. Frederick at last horrifies her, when he emerges from her tutelage and that of her gallants a social monstrosity, the inevitable product of her pernicious school of manners. To be sure, Lady Bornwell remains a trifle pale as a "lady of pleasure" through Shirley's strong insistence, in the majority of the scenes in which she figures, on the moral implications of her conduct. In this insistence on morals he resolutely supports the old Elizabethan tradition. He withdraws emphasis from the ridicule of Lady Bornwell's extravagance and silliness, in order to pursue with gravity a program for her soul's salvation. Shirley portrays manners most successfully when moral considerations do not obtrude themselves, to demand his primary consideration.

The fashions which beguile Lady Bornwell, Celestina comprehends perfectly. The latter, also, has numerous affectations, all of which, however, are related to an intelligently adopted social pose. Celestina's first speech, as she appears in conference with her steward, is:

Fie! what an air this room has! [72]

She proceeds to take the poor man roundly to task because he

[71] *The Lady of Pleasure* (*Works*, IV), II, 1, p. 25.
[72] *Ibid.*, I, 2, p. 17.

provides her with cheap perfumes, because her hangings are not rich enough, because her coach is coarsely lined and its nails not double gilt. From the energy that goes into these upbraidings one would suppose her completely preoccupied with frivolous matters. Yet a little later she gravely explains and justifies her behavior in a confidential talk with some friends. Nearly every one misunderstands her because of the reckless gaiety of her assumed mood. She adopts a code of conduct whereof

> 'Tis the chief principle to keep your heart
> Under your own obedience; jest, but love not.[73]

She is disposed to employ a polite language of compliment toward the most contemptible of her suitors, at whom, in private, she cannot laugh half enough. Even Lord A., adroit courtier as he is, utterly misinterprets her compliant manner.

But it is Carol in *Hyde Park* who is Shirley's finest study in social affectation. Of course, in some respects she and her lover are fairly conventional figures. She accepts Fairfield through "pure intention to preserve his life," [74] as Beatrice had taken Benedick in *Much Ado about Nothing* [75] and Isabella through "pure pity" [76] had taken Francisco in *Wit without Money*. And Fairfield, in giving her tit for tat, behaves as Benedick with Beatrice, Mirabel with Oriana,[77] and Valentine with his widow [78] had behaved before him. Yet Carol appears in a new light

---

[73] *Ibid.*, II, 2, p. 30.
[74] *Hyde Park* (*Works*, IV), V, 1, p. 526.
[75] *Much Ado about Nothing* (ed. Furness), V, 4, p. 194.
[76] *Wit without Money* (*Works*, IV), V, 4, p. 194.
[77] *The Wild-Goose Chase* (*Works*, VIII), V, 6, p. 205.
[78] *Wit without Money* (*Works*, IV), V, 4, p. 193. Valentine observes:
  Take me quickly, while I am in this vein; away with me;
  For if I have but two hours to consider,
  All the widows in the world cannot recover me.
Compare with this *Hyde Park* (*Works*, II), V, 1, p. 535:
  Car. I know you love me still; do not refuse me.
If I go once more back you ne'er recover me.
  Fair. I am as ticklish.

through the emphasis on her social attitudinizing. She has always aimed to be absorbed in social pleasures. One recalls her pert warning to Fairfield against infringement of her liberties:

> I will not be confin'd to make me ready
> At ten, and pray till dinner; I will play
> At gleek as often as I please, and see
> Plays when I have a mind to't, and the races.

And again,

>   I'll not be
> Bound from Spring-garden, and the 'Sparagus.[79]

The fact that she falls in love must not interfere with the contradictory social rôle that she has to play and that she plays brilliantly to the end. Her assumed gaiety becomes actually contagious, as she runs about in the Park, excitedly observes and bets (silk stockings) on the races, drinks healths, flirts with her cast-off suitors, and jests with a lord's pretty page. Once she retires to the coach to give way to her overwrought feelings, but in a moment she is back again in the gay throng and in answer to Mistress Bonavent's

> You look as you had wept,

is ready with the cavalier rejoinder:

> I weep! For what?
> Come toward the lodge, and drink a syllabub.[80]

She knows just how closely she is being observed, and she makes no false moves.

> Am I not a witch? [81]

she asks Fairfield teasingly. Fairfield himself acknowledges her power, admitting:

> I love thee better
> For thy vagaries.[81]

Carol's "vagaries" are, in large part, her social poses.

[79] *Hyde Park* (*Works*, II), II, 4, p. 490.
[80] *Ibid.*, IV, 3, p. 512.   [81] *Ibid.*, III, 2, p. 503.

It is significant that in two of his comedies, at least, Shirley gathers up and brings to a focus whatever tendencies in Elizabethan drama may be said to point most surely toward Restoration comedy of manners. The world of fashion, the increasing authority of which Middleton and especially Brome had suggested, in *Hyde Park* and *The Lady of Pleasure* stands out in splendid isolation from the world at large; its fastidious members constitute a supreme commonwealth in their own conceit, supporting no laws, save in matters of moral estimates, beyond those of their own ingenious making. Shirley has not studied this group with completeness of detail. In over-refinements of speech he has little interest. He does not break away from the Elizabethan tradition sufficiently to recognize a socially revised moral code for his people of fashion. He attempts only a few full studies in social affectation. Yet he successfully illustrates the two pronounced types of comic effect which were never to be obscured in the work of the Restoration dramatists. With amusement Shirley observes Lady Bornwell, incompetent and fantastic in her posing. With amusement of another sort he observes Carol, graceful in every gesture but masking her humanity in the cause of wit.

CHAPTER III

COURT INFLUENCES ON SERIOUS DRAMA IN THE REIGN OF CHARLES I

THE period of the reign of Charles I boasts no great names, by right of peculiar possession, on the honor-roll of its dramatists. Shirley and Brome were Elizabethan survivals. Suckling, with all his talent, wrote eccentric and wayward plays. D'Avenant was unsuited to the work assigned him. But, to a marked degree, the court had social distinction, and its influence was to be unusually far-reaching. Never before had an English court exerted a more powerful influence on contemporary manners and through that channel on contemporary literature. The French queen, Henrietta Maria, had the hardihood to impose on her followers a highly specialized system of formal etiquette, destined to have lasting effects, not only on court literature in her own day, but also on court literature in the reign of her son, Charles II. The *précieuse* fashions authorized by the queen had a particularly significant influence on court drama, providing it with a social mode which vastly increased its resources for the study of manners and from which, through gradual stages, the social mode of Restoration comedy developed.

When Henrietta Maria came to England in 1625 as the bride of Charles I, she brought with her social prejudices which, through her effective encouragement, were to take root and flourish in English soil. Henrietta's girlhood had witnessed the rise of the salon of the Marquise de Rambouillet, where the most brilliant and cultivated French society of the day assembled. The salon was chiefly distinguished for its encouragement of a

new system of etiquette, known as *préciosité*, which was intended
to effect both "the purification of the language and of the relations between the sexes."¹ Outside this salon and others, the
cult also acquired widespread literary recognition through its
"code-book," Honoré d'Urfé's popular pastoral romance *Astrée*
(Part I pr. 1607, II, 1610, III, 1619, IV and V, 1627²). Although not herself a frequenter of Madame de Rambouillet's
famous "chambre bleue," Henrietta could hardly have escaped
a social influence so diffusive. Not immediately upon her arrival
in England, however, did the young queen attempt to impose
this foreign culture on the English court. Only after a period of
homesickness, of difficult adjustment to what seemed a hostile
new environment, did she find it worth while to exert the influence of her French taste on court activities.

The initial triumph of French *préciosité* in English society
took the form of a court craze over "Platonic love." On June 3,
1634, James Howell, in a letter written to a friend at Paris, made
the interesting observation:

> The Court affords little News at present, but there is a Love call'd
> Platonic Love, which much sways there of late; it is a Love abstracted from
> all corporeal gross Impressions and sensual Appetite, but consists in Con-
> templations and Ideas of the Mind, not in any carnal Fruition. This Love
> sets the Wits of the Town on work; and they say there will be a Mask
> shortly of it, whereof Her Majesty and her Maids of Honour will be part.³

The mask proved to be William D'Avenant's *The Temple of Love*,
presented on Shrove-Tuesday (February 18), 1635. The author
of the mask celebrates the court Platonic fashion as lately
adopted, and admits:

> Certain young Lords at first disliked the philosophy
> As most uncomfortable, sad, and new;
> But soon inclined to a superior vote,
> And are grown as good Platonical lovers

---

¹ J. B. Fletcher, *The Religion of Beauty in Woman*, p. 172.
² Part V was composed by Balthazar Baro, after D'Urfé's death.
³ James Howell, *Familiar Letters*, I, pp. 317–318.

> 'As are to be found in an hermitage, where he
> That was born last reckons above fourscore.[4]

In the prologue to *The Platonic Lovers* (licensed November, 1635), D'Avenant again emphasizes the newness of the doctrine, and in the play itself comments on the word "Platonical" as

> A new court epithet scarce understood.[5]

Once established, from 1635 to 1640, the Platonic mode surely maintained a court supremacy, if we may judge by its literary manifestations. A few critics have discussed briefly its influence on non-dramatic literature of the time [6] and have reviewed more briefly its influence on the drama.[7] They have not, as it happens, been interested in observing how completely the English court became absorbed in Platonic gallantry, what the development of the fashion meant in England, as compared with its development in France, and to what extent its principles became permanently incorporated in literary tradition.

To Queen Henrietta, as to her French contemporaries, the cult of "Platonic love" meant quite simply the social fashion interpreted with such elaborate fullness in D'Urfé's *Astrée*.[8] Of course, D'Urfé's Platonism represented no new phenomenon in literary history. It had its sources in the sonnets of Petrarch, the sixteenth century Italian pastorals, Spanish romance, French Renaissance poetry and prose,[9] in fact, in such literature as also inspired the Elizabethan sonnet sequences and pastoral romances.

[4] *The Temple of Love* (*Works*, I), pp. 293–294.
[5] *The Platonic Lovers* (*Works*, II), I, p. 17.
[6] Cf. especially Fletcher, *op. cit.*, pp. 166–205, and J. S. Harrison, *Platonism in English Poetry*, pp. 155–166.
[7] The fullest treatment of the subject is to be found in A. H. Upham, *The French Influence in English Literature*, pp. 321–344.
[8] For a review of the influence of *Astrée* on contemporary French society, see Victor Du Bled, *La Société française du XVIᵉ siècle, Iʳᵉ Série, XVIᵉ et XVIIᵉ siècles*, pp. 141–145.
[9] For a discussion of D'Urfé's sources see Bernard Germa, *L'Astrée d'Honoré d'Urfé*, pp. 100–147.

And the sources of D'Urfé's sources might even carry us as far back as the days of medieval chivalry and the medieval courts of love. But the Platonic cult which D'Urfé described and which the members of the Hôtel de Rambouillet practised, in its original purity, for nearly half a century, acquired, in its period of dominance, an influence genuinely distinct from the earlier influences of similar systems of gallantry. D'Urfé's genius for detail made it possible for him to blend the most important elements of Platonic tradition in a social system as complete as the chivalric system of the Middle Ages and yet thoroughly suited to the more tranquil tastes and more philosophic temper of modern society. The shepherds and shepherdesses of *Astrée*, absorbed in graceful love-making in their Arcadian setting, illustrate a rule of life so perfect in all its adjustments that it was capable of regulating even the most trivial aspects of polite conduct in the salon assemblies of Madame de Rambouillet and her successors. The conversation of D'Urfé's shepherds became in itself a fine art, in which the conceits of Renaissance love compliment were developed with precision in a quaint pattern of formal argument.

Platonic love, as defined by D'Urfé's model lover Sylvandre, is an ideal love, divine in its essence, forever freed from the limitations of mere physical passion. To the inconstant Hylas, Sylvandre declares that "le bien dont amour recompense les fidelles Amants, est celuy-là mesme qu'il peut donner aux Dieux, & à ces hommes qui s'esleuans par dessus la nature des hommes, se rendent presque Dieux." [10] The lover's passion is completely unselfish in its emphasis. On a certain occasion Sylvandre remarks to Hylas: "Scauez-vous bien que c'est qu'aimer? c'est mourir en soy, pour reuiure en autruy, c'est ne se point aimer que d'autant que l'on est agréable à la chose aimée: & bref c'est une volonté de se transformer, s'il se peut, entierement

10 *L'Astrée de Messire Honoré d'Urfé*, vol. II, bk. ix, p. 676.

en elle." [11] The spiritual nature of the lover's experience Sylvandre makes still clearer in explaining that "ce n'est pas le corps qui aime, mais l'ame, & ainsi ce n'est que l'ame qui se transforme en la chose aymée, & non pas le corps." [12] This love is perfect without possession. [13] It may be even more perfect in the lover's absence from the lady loved than in her presence, although Sylvandre admits ruefully that he cannot yet bring himself to leave Diane in order to meditate more deeply upon her beauty, inasmuch as "l'imperfection de l'humanité ne peut estre ostée tout à coup." [14]

The gods themselves ordain and direct the loves of men. Céladon asserts with conviction: "Le Ciel l'a voulu, car c'est par destin que je l'aime." [15] The worthy lover feels that he was born to love a certain lady, endowed by heaven with the beauty that attracts him. Others may have the misfortune to love him, but once he has met his destined lady, he can only politely remind the rest that fate has already disposed of his affections and trust to their good judgment to convince them that, by heaven's decree, "un coeur n'est capable que d'un vray Amour." [16] D'Urfé's nymphs and shepherdesses are nearly always generous, prompt to recognize, to their disadvantage, all honest claims of love prior to their own. Oracles and omens, too, are on the side of destined lovers. Indeed, other remedies failing, heaven boldly intervenes in tempest and altar smoke to insure a happy outcome for the faithful loves of Céladon and Astrée, Sylvandre and Diane.

The laws of courtship are largely prescribed by the lover's mistress. Astrée asserts her authority over Céladon in announcing to him that "il faut que mes volotez soient des destinées, mes opinions des raisons, et mes comandemens des lois inuiolables." [17]

---

[11] *Ibid.*, vol. I, bk. viii, p. 505.
[12] *Ibid.*, vol. II, bk. vi, p. 454.
[13] *Ibid.*, vol. II, bk. ix, p. 670.
[14] *Ibid.*, vol. II, bk. iii, p. 201.
[15] *Ibid.*, vol. II, bk. viii, p. 550.
[16] *Ibid.*, vol. I, bk. xii, p. 835.
[17] *Ibid.*, vol. I, bk. iii, p. 105.

The lover's first duty as his mistress' "vassal" is to have perfect faith in her sovereignty. He is not to declare his affection until he has first obliged her to some degree of good will; otherwise,
she will rightly make him feel that even his voluntary death
would be a feeble recompense for such a presumptuous suit.
After she has recognized his love, he must keep the affair secret
under penalty of her lasting displeasure. Also, he must never be
jealous of his rivals, for all jealousy implies distrust in her
integrity and is likely to result in his complete loss of her favor.
The lover's duty further involves his perfect service to his lady.
He must ever burn, sigh, and languish in his courtship. When
absent from her, he must never cease to contemplate her beauty.
He must humbly serve her in every possible way, never expecting
from her any reward beyond the inestimable privilege of his
continued service. The lady, on the other hand, has certain
obligations to her lover. She may suffer many lovers, but may
encourage but one. Where she loves she must in some way reward faithful service. Although large concessions do not become
her in the early stages of a courtship, small favors will be sufficient to raise the lover to the seventh heaven of bliss. When
Diane bids Sylvandre kiss her hand and replaces upon his head
the flower hat which he had thrown at her feet in his love pleading, directing him, besides, to wear the hat always, renewing the
flowers as they fade,[18] her graciousness has been all that could
have been dreamed of, and his gratitude properly knows no
bounds.

The lover's distinction as one of Love's servants is assured,
finally, by his skill in argument on the numerous problems connected with the science of love. Courtship scenes almost always
become elaborate debates, in which lovers' passions fade into
formal controversy between the two opponents. The arguments
are not necessarily between lovers, but the procedure is in all

[18] *Ibid.*, vol. III, bk. ix, p. 893.

cases the same. Again and again, the shepherds and shepherdesses debate, in thoroughly conventional style, on the nature of
love, on its "temperature," on the significance of fruition in love,
on the value of absence from the person loved, on the function
of jealousy, on the merits of constancy. At times, similitudes
are exchanged. When Hylas, the outstanding rebel in this
Arcadia of devout Platonics, argues in behalf of inconstancy
against the shepherd Thamyre, he presents along series of similitudes in support of variety as the law by which nature rules and
men live, and Thamyre in his response attacks each comparison
in chronological order.[19] More often a single image is played
with, turn and turn about, until its meaning is quite exhausted.
A characteristic debate on jealousy between Sylvandre, seconded
by Diane, and Phylis may be cited by way of illustration.
Sylvandre raises the issue: Can love and jealousy exist in the
same heart? He proceeds with abundant Platonic enthusiasm
to assail jealousy:

L'Amour n'est-ce pas un desir, & tout desir n'est-il pas de feu, & la
ialousie n'est-ce pas une crainte, & toute crainte n'est-elle pas de glace &
comment voulez-vous que cét enfant gelé soit né d'un pere si ardent? Des
cailloux, respondit Phylis, qui sont froids, on en void bien sortir des etincelles
qui sont chaudes. Il est vray, repliqua Syluandre, mais iamais du feu ne
proceda le froid. Et toutesfois, reprint Phylis, du feu mesme procede bien
la cendre qui est froide. Ouy, adjousta le Berger, mais quand la cendre est
froide, le feu n'y est plus. A cette replique Phylis demeura troublée, & plus
encores quand Diane prenant la parole. De mesme, dit-elle, quand la froide
ialousie naist, il faut que l'Amour meure. Ma maistresse, repliqua Phylis, ie
ne doute point que mon ennemy n'ait la victoire, ayant un si bon second
que vous estes.[20]

In such contests these lovers pass their days, abjuring the reality
of passion for its cold and artificial analysis in endless *précieuse*
discourse.

In various types of contemporary French literature, D'Urfé's
Platonism received prompt reënforcement. The writers of

---

[19] *Ibid.*, vol. IV, bk. v, pp. 383–392.
[20] *Ibid.*, vol. II, bk. iii, pp. 155–156.

fashionable love letters early acknowledged the graces of the language of love compliment in *Astrée*. Balzac, between 1620 and 1635, wrote a series of polite letters [21] in the best Platonic vein. To one mistress, whose conversation has been "a schoole of austeritie" [22] to him, he owes, he admits, a debt which he "can never pay." [23] Her influence directs his every act. Indeed, he insists: "I have no longer any power of my selfe, but what you leave me; and in all your Empire, which is neither meane, nor consists of meane subjects; I can assure you, that you possesse nothing with more soveraigntie, than my will." [24] Voiture, writing from 1633 to 1644 to Mademoiselle de Rambouillet and to other ladies of her mother's salon, adopts a tone of more delicate badinagè, outwardly serious, however, in its Platonic emphasis.[25] Théophile de Viau [26] in his love letters to Caliste acquiesces, if somewhat reluctantly, in his lady's Platonic sovereignty. He writes submissively: "Je m'accorde donc, ô mon bel ange! à la rigoureuse facon de vivre que me prescript vostre vertu, d'autant plus volontiers que cette parfaite soubmission de mes volontez aux vostres vous sera sans doute une asseurance extraordinaire de la perfection de mon amour, qui ne s'est point encore proposé de fin plus proche ou plus glorieuse que l'acquisition de vos bonnes graces, ny de contentement plus solide ou plus accomply que leur durée." [27] Cyrano de Bergerac,[28] wearing his Platonic fetters with greater ease and gaiety, draws for his mistress amusing pictures of his desperate state, declaring himself so feverish that "la moindre étincelle qui me

---

[21] Cf. *Letters of Mounsieur de Balzac*, translated by Sir Richard Baker (1654), I, III, pp. 89–96; III, I, pp. 28–38, 40–51, 54–57; IV, I, pp. 16–17, 43–44.   [22] *Ibid.*, III, 1, p. 31.
[23] *Ibid.*, III, 1, p. 33.   [24] *Ibid.*, III, I, p. 37.
[25] Cf. *Oeuvres de Voiture*, ed. M. A. Ubicini, 2 vols.
[26] Cf. *Oeuvres. complètes de Théophile*, ed. M. Alleaume, II, pp. 341–343, 364–368, 373–374.   [27] *Ibid.*, p. 364.
[28] Cf. *Oeuvres comiques, galantes et littéraires de Cyrano de Bergerac*, ed. P. L. Jacob, "Lettres amoureuses," pp. 203–233.

touchera, c'est fait de moi," [29] or again so inflamed with passion that he has become "un Amant salamandre." [30]

The same philosophy, embellished with elaborate conceits, is conspicuously illustrated in the French love poetry of the period. In a characteristic rondeau Voiture demands severest punishment for the jealous lover; [31] in another he rapidly outlines the lover's creed of service.[32] Théophile de Viau describes with fanciful *précieuse* imagery the beauty of Corine's fingers [33] and the softness of Cloris' breath [34] and sketches Sylvie fishing, with the fish fighting to lose their lives in her honor and night fearing to approach while her beauty enflames the waves.[35] He affirms that he is the incense burning before his mistress' altar[36] and again, wonders why her heart of ice holds out against his fire.[37] Saint-Amant pleads to have the "rubis animez" of his lady's lips mention his name, while embracing each other, so that in some sort he may be admitted among those kisses.[38] Yet in the same moment he cries for death, for he recalls that he has committed the sin of declaring to Amarante his passion, —

O faute sans example! [39]

In French dramatic pastoral and tragi-comedy, especially between the dates of 1625 and 1635, D'Urfé's influence remained dominant to an extraordinary degree. Faithful but uninspired reworking of episodes in *Astrée* is evident in such plays as Mairet's *Sylvie* (pr. 1628) and *Chriséide et Arimant* (pr. 1630); Auvray's *Madonte* (pr. 1631) and *Dorinde* (pr. 1631); Rayssiguier's *Tragicomédie Pastorale* (pr. 1630), *Palinice, Circeine et Florice* (pr. 1634), and *Célidée* (pr. 1635); Du Ryer's *Rosiléon* (pr. c.

[29] *Ibid.*, p. 227.   [30] *Ibid.*, p. 213.
[31] Voiture, *Works*, II, p. 325.   [32] *Ibid.*, p. 328.
[33] Théophile de Viau, *Works*, I, p. 179.
[34] *Ibid.*, I, p. 209.   [35] *Ibid.*, II, pp. 196–204.
[36] *Ibid.*, I, p. 208.   [37] *Ibid.*, I, p. 203.
[38] *Oeuvres complètes de Saint-Amant*, ed. Ch. L. Livet, I, p. 254.
[39] *Ibid.*, p. 252.

1634); and Scudéry's *Ligdamon et Lidias* (pr. 1631) and *Eudoxe* (pr. 1634).[40] These adapters confined themselves to the more serious love histories in the romance. With none of D'Urfé's occasional humor and with none of his interest in sustained analysis of emotions, these dramatists turned out play after play extravagant in intrigue and ludicrously pompous in diction, productions which could hardly have won a merely ephemeral success, had it not been for the astonishing vogue of the Platonic cult.

The earliest English translation of *Astrée*, the work of a certain John Piper, was printed in 1620.[41] By 1627 the Platonic theories popularized by D'Urfé appeared in an English narrative, *The Private Memoirs of Sir Kenelm Digby*,[42] written by one of the most distinguished gentlemen at Charles' court. With considerable detail, using fictitious names, Digby describes in this record his own courtship, which was, in the main, a Platonic affair. Save in moments of weakness, the author's conduct has been directed by a high ideal of Platonic service. Love, he maintains, is "a free gift of the will of the lover to the person beloved, making her the mistress, and giving her absolute power of it; and the will having command and sovereignty over all other faculties and parts of a man, it carrieth them along with it; so that his will being drowned and converting itself into hers, the like doth all the rest, and thus they become one, by the transmutation of the lover into the person loved." [43] In this autobiography Digby seems to have anticipated by several years the court enthusiasm regarding Platonic fashions. By 1636, at last, if we may accept the testimony of Shakerley Marmion's comedy *The Antiquary* (1636), court Platonism had assumed full sway. According to

[40] For a discussion of D'Urfé's influence on these dramatists see O. C. Reure, *La Vie et les oeuvres de Honoré d'Urfé,* pp. 289–301.
[41] *Ibid.*, p. 222.
[42] The work was circulated in MS. among the author's friends.
[43] *Private Memoirs of Sir Kenelm Digby*, pp. 76–77.

Marmion, the fashionable gallant of this date likes nothing better than to "lie a-bed, and expound Astraea, and digest him into compliments; and when he is up, accost his mistress with what he had read in the morning." [44]

Sir John Suckling's love letters to "Aglaura" must have been written between 1632 and 1641. From these it has been rightly claimed that "one may draw up . . . almost a code-book of Platonic love." [45] Surely Suckling here availed himself of French models. The abrupt beginnings of the letters, the antithetical precision of the phrases, the graceful Platonic compliments seem particularly reminiscent of Balzac.[46] At the same time, the English cavalier writes with a gay tenderness of emotion not apparent in Balzac or, indeed, in the other French letter-writers. Suckling's Platonic philosophy is conventional. He is aware "how good the stars were to me" [47] in Aglaura's love. However, he means to keep his bliss from "profane eyes," for privacy in love is "the best part of devotion." [48] The beauty of others will but remind him of her supreme beauty. So great is his devotion that he declares: "I am not myself, but when I am yours wholly." [49] At Aglaura's request, without knowing her reason, he will give up his favorite diversion of gaming, yet she must assign him a new sin in place of this.[50] Since she wills it so, he will not entertain Desire, although to the lover Desire is "like too much sail in a storm," [49] most difficult to control at will. Nor may the wages of his unselfish devotion be high, for his heart "hath been brought up under Platonics, and knows no other way of being paid for service than by being commanded more." [51]

---

[44] *The Antiquary*, II, 1, p. 246.   [45] Fletcher, *op. cit.*, p. 186.
[46] Various translations of Balzac's letter appeared in England between 1634 and 1638. Cf. Upham, *op. cit.*, pp. 437–438.
[47] *The Poems, Plays and Other Remains of Sir John Suckling,* ed. W. Carew Hazlitt, II, p. 195.
[48] *Ibid.*, p. 198.   [49] *Ibid.*, p. 197.
[50] *Ibid.*, pp. 182–183.   [51] *Ibid.*, p. 180.

English Platonic love poems became even more numerous than the French. William Habington, the most devout of the English Platonics, was the first English poet to define with exactness of detail the Platonic system described in *Astrée*. In the poems of his love-sequence *Castara* (1634), Habington makes it clear that he is chronicling "no dull Sublunary flame." [52] He assures Castara:

> And though we be of severall kind
>   Fit for offence:
> Yet are we so by Love refin'd,
> From impure drosse we are all mind.
> Death could not more have conquer'd sence.[53]

Conceits abound, all of Platonic emphasis. The same philosophy is set forth in three poems on *Platonic Love* and a number of other poems by Lord Herbert of Cherbury, as ardent a Platonic as Habington but inspired by a less prolific muse.

Waller's lyrics to Sacharissa, written before the latter's marriage in 1639, illustrate a very pretty Platonic wooing. The poet

> vows this endless love
> Springs from no hope of what she can confer,
> But from those gifts which heav'n has heap'd on her.[54]

Waller also tries his hand at Platonic debate, devising affirmative arguments against his friend Suckling's negative ones on the subject of fruition in love.[55] In 1642 Sir Francis Kynaston published his *Amorous Sonnets* to Cynthia. This lady is all flint and steel, yet manages to burn "the tenement" [56] of his heart where the poet has welcomed her. His Platonic wages are "quarterly a kiss." [57] In like fashion, Lovelace celebrates Ellinda, and Carew his Celia. Carew in *Four Songs, by way of Chorus to a Play at an Entertainment of the King and Queen* describes at length the essen-

---

[52] *Castara*, ed. Edward Arber, p. 92.   [53] *Ibid.*, p. 52.
[54] *The Works of Edmund Waller, Esq., in Verse and Prose*, ed. [Elijah] Fenton, p. 43.
[55] *Ibid.*, pp. 97–100.
[56] *Minor Poets of the Caroline Period*, ed. George Saintsbury, II, p. 158.
[57] *Ibid.*, p. 161.

tial tenets of the Platonic faith.[58] The queen he hails as "great commandress"[59] of the "law" of love which he tries to follow. Happily, Carew did not live to see the queen in a less commanding rôle.

Among these court poets Suckling occupies a distinguished place. No lines in the work of Waller, Lovelace, or Carew are quite so charming as certain stanzas in the *Ballad upon a Wedding* (1641), in which the similitudes descriptive of the bride[60] display a colloquial ease of expression markedly opposed to the customary stiffness and formality of a *précieuse* style. Perhaps the similitudes in the song *When, dearest, I but think of thee*,[61] though of a more conventional sort, are only less charming. Suckling's genius was essentially imitative. From Shakespeare he was an eager borrower of lines and rhythms. From Lyly he may have derived, to some extent, his taste for strings of odd comparisons. To Donne he certainly owed some of his most ingenious figures. By the manner of such poems by Donne as *Loves Growth* and *Confined Love*[62] Suckling was probably also influenced in his own numerous verse arguments on the theory of love. But Suckling's heart had been "brought up under Platonics" in a strictness of discipline unknown to the earlier writers whom he imitated. The significance of the Platonic influence on his work becomes duly apparent in the numerous poems where that influence overbalances all others. The poet has a Platonic mistress whose "Love's philosophy"[63] he endeavors to accept. Love's flame, he promises, shall purge him of "the dross — desire."[64] In two poems entitled *Against Fruition*[65] and in a similar poem *Against Absence*[66] he repeats, with many similitudes, familiar

[58] *The Poems of Thomas Carew*, ed. Arthur Vincent, pp. 83–87.
[59] *Ibid.*, p. 125.   [60] Suckling, *Works*, I, pp. 36–37.
[61] *Ibid.*, pp. 74–75.
[62] *The Poems of John Donne*, ed. H. J. C. Grierson, I, pp. 33–34 and 36.
[63] Suckling, *Works*, I, p. 58.   [64] *Ibid.*, p. 73.
[65] *Ibid.*, pp. 18–19 and 33–34.   [66] *Ibid.*, pp. 26–27.

Platonic arguments of *Astrée*. In *To His Rival* he reminds his companion in the lady's service that

> no debt shall be
> From service or fidelity;
> For she shall ever pay that score,
> By only bidding us do more.[67]

The height of this Platonic devotion is reached when he generously arranges with the friendly rival that whichever one of them dies first shall bequeath his share of love to the survivor:

> For no one stock can ever serve
> To love so much as she'll deserve.[68]

In his light and buoyant verses Suckling succeeds in giving a more memorable account of Platonic fashions than any of the other court poets with whom he joined in popularizing the queen's French tastes.

In England the dramatic literature connected with the Platonic cult, in contrast to the French Platonic drama, soon surpassed other literary forms in effective interpretation of the new mode. It has been suggested that as early as 1629 Platonic doctrines are evident in Jonson's *The New Inn*.[69] However, the play was a notorious failure. At this date court interest in Platonism could not have been very keen. Besides, Jonson was peculiarly disqualified, not only by age and weariness but also by temperament, for the rôle of an interpreter of Platonic theory. Probable references to Platonic customs have been noted in two of Shirley's comedies, *The Ball* and *The Lady of Pleasure*.[70] But Shirley gives no evidence of serious interest in the cult. When the English court became really absorbed in Platonism, the strength of the Elizabethan tradition was exhausted.

[67] *Ibid.*, p. 74.
[68] *Ibid.*, p. 40.
[69] Fletcher, *op. cit.*, p. 179.
[70] Cf. H. T. Parlin, *A Study in Shirley's Comedies of London Life, Bulletin of the University of Texas*, no. 371, p. 64.

We may suppose that in 1634, as James Howell assures us,[71] Platonic gallantry first became conspicuously practiced at the English court.   Yet we have sure proof that as early as 1632, royal instruction in the new art had commenced.   Through the late autumn months of 1632,[72] the queen and her ladies were rehearsing their parts for a Platonic pastoral drama, *The Shepheard's Paradise*.   The author of the play was Walter Montague, a gentleman who had been much in France and whom the queen highly esteemed.   The queen herself was pleased to become "the prime actress" [73] in the comedy, "as well for her recreation as for the exercise of her English." [72]   In January, 1633, this play was acted at court, the performance consuming "seven or eight hours." [74]

In *The Shepheard's Paradise* the Platonic doctrines of *Astrée* are stiffly moulded into dramatic form.   Such typical Platonic themes as the value of "possession" and the merits of "second love" are debated from every angle by literal-minded disciples of D'Urfé's Platonism.   The rules of Platonic discipline are illustrated with painful fullness of detail.   Moramente learns that his renunciation of his mistress, who is pledged to a rival, will afford him "a diviner happinesse then can be due by any acquisition" although "a hard happinesse, which is not at the first so easily understood." [75]   Later on, he confesses to Martiro his new passion for Bellesa, the queen, and is at once reproved for his offense "in so essentiall a point as secrecie." [76]   For every trace of earthly frailty Moramente must suffer.   Having surreptitiously kissed the hand of the queen, he begs punishment for his body and receives from her the just rebuke: "'Tis a new insolence, this punishment that you aske, that I should descend so low as but

---

[71] Cf. p. 44, n. 3, of this volume.
[72] Quoted from court correspondence by Thomas Birch, *The Court and Times of Charles the First*, II, p. 176.
[73] *Ibid.*, p. 187.   [74] *Ibid.*, p. 216.
[75] *The Shepheard's Paradise*, I, pp. 5–6.   [76] *Ibid.*, III, p. 66.

think upon your body." [77]   Martiro, the strictest Platonic in this Arcadia, announces quaintly:

> My love's not that materiall flame,
> That's let but by attraction from the same.
> It is a lightning in my soule, which is
> Kindled by an Antiperistasis.[78]

Such a way of loving the queen commends to the more worldly Moramente. At last, Bellesa agrees to marry her sufficiently humbled lover, and from the dizzy pinnacle of his own severe Platonism Martiro descends to concede that her "divine example" proves the virtue of wedded love.

Montague wrote no more plays, — perhaps because he became occupied in foreign diplomatic service, perhaps because he found the new cult too difficult to interpret.[79]   But his labored pastoral prepared the way for a considerable group of Platonic plays by other authors. In the dramatic exposition of the new cult, William D'Avenant was apparently constrained by Henrietta, somewhat against his will, to assume leadership. D'Avenant observes in the prologue to *The Platonic Lovers* (1635):

> 'Tis worth my smiles to think what enforc'd ways
> And shifts, each poet hath to help his Plays.
> Ours now believes the Title needs must cause,
> From the indulgent Court a kind applause,
> Since there he learnt it first, and had command
> T'interpret what he scarce doth understand.[80]

---

[77] *Ibid.*, V, p. 114.   [78] *Ibid.*, IV, p. 94.
[79] In Suckling's *A Session of the Poets* (*Works*, I, pp. 9–10), the following stanzas occur:

> Wat Montague now stood forth to his trial,
> And did not so much as suspect a denial;
> But witty Apollo asked him first of all,
> If he understood his own pastoral.
>
> For, if he could do it, 'twould plainly appear,
> He understood more than any man there,
> And did merit the bays above all the rest,
> But the Monsieur was modest, and silence confessed.

[80] *The Platonic Lovers* (*Works*, II), p. 6.

It may be doubted whether D'Avenant had much actual sympathy with Platonic tastes. The subtleties of Platonic dialogue seem to have been quite beyond him; at any rate he did not attempt them. Nevertheless, he tried hard to execute the royal commission. Between 1634 and the closing of the theatres he wrote, besides the mask of *The Temple of Love*, four Platonic tragi-comedies, *Love and Honour* (1634), *The Platonic Lovers*, *The Fair Favourite* (1638), and *The Distresses* (1639), and one Platonic tragedy, *The Unfortunate Lovers* (1638).

In all of these plays there is rather monotonous repetition of the rules of love philosophy which had been so graciously phrased in *Astrée*. Like D'Urfé, D'Avenant strongly urges the Platonic love principle that human love, when worthy of its divine origin, is an intellectual experience. The most admirable of D'Avenant's Platonic lovers, the Queen in *The Fair Favourite*, affirms:

> . . . Peculiar and distinct
> Affections are but small derived parts
> Of what we call the universal love;
> And universal love, undoubtedly,
> Must be the best, since 'tis ascribed to heaven.[81]

This divinity of love becomes most apparent when love is purged of all gross corporeal passions. D'Avenant's ideal lovers are forever sprouting wings and assuring each other that their converse is like that of angels. The cult allows unusual liberties. Theander in *The Platonic Lovers* and the King in *The Fair Favourite* prefer to visit their ladies in the night watches, a time consecrated to the exchange of elegant compliments. In the latter play, the King's love for Eumena, rather than for the Queen, his bride, is quaintly excused by one of the courtiers on the basis:

> Could he be wrought to wed a Princess for
> Dull human ends, when's love was formerly
> Engag'd? Where are the old Arcadian lovers? [82]

---

[81] *The Fair Favourite* (*Works*, IV), IV, p. 255.
[82] *Ibid.*, I, p. 214.

The model lover can talk soberly about "the severe discretion of my heart"[83] and becomes capable of worshiping virtue in his mistress, rather than his mistress, who is virtuous. The impersonality of love may even become so accentuated that it is possible for a lady to exchange an accepted lover for his rival, at parental bidding, without the slightest qualm. Such is the case with Evandra, who, at the close of *Love and Honour*, turns sweetly to Leonell, whom her father has preferred to Alvaro, with the words:

> Alvaro's virtues, Sir, and yours, have both
> An equal claim. Persons I ne'er admired
> So much to make a difference in my choice.[84]

D'Avenant frequently emphasizes the Platonic doctrine that the lover's passion is heaven-ordained and heaven-directed. For the lover to set his own will against divine arrangements is futile if not impious. Duke Altophil in *The Unfortunate Lovers* regrets that he cannot reward with love Amaranta's services to him. He laments:

> What strange malicious courtesy, you stars!
> Was this? to make the first election of
> My love so excellent, and with Arthiopa
> So fill my breast, that there was no room left
> To entertain the lady's [85] true affection
> Till it came too late.[86]

The King's infidelity to the Queen in *The Fair Favourite* is accepted quite philosophically by that poor lady, on the ground that heaven has decreed his prior regard for Eumena.[87] In *The Distresses*, again, a lover voluntarily resigns his mistress, reverencing his brother's "elder claim" and explaining to the lady that —

---

[83] *Love and Honour* (*Works*, III), V, p. 173.
[84] *Ibid.*, V, p. 184.
[85] That is, Amaranta's.
[86] *The Unfortunate Lovers* (*Works*, III), III, p. 57.
[87] *The Fair Favourite* (*Works*, IV), III, p. 240.

                         fate did not decree your virtue and
                Your beauty mine.[88]

The main rules of Platonic courtship D'Avenant describes in
the conventional fashion, although not with D'Urfé's delicacy of
perception. A lady must accept a lover's service as her due,
must give him a patient hearing, and must reward him as she
sees fit. A jealous lover, however, no longer merits her regard.
Beyond failure to acknowledge love's summons, the great offense
against love is jealousy. When Alvaro in *Love and Honour* is
informed by his two rivals of their state of mind, he at once soars
into a Platonic rapture, assures them of his "prompt and warm
delight" in their rivalship, and bids them seal with him an invio-
late friendship.[89] Similarly, when the Duke in *The Unfortunate
Lovers* learns of the Prince's love for his own mistress, Arthiopa,
he cherishes no resentment and no jealousy. He simply philoso-
phizes:

> Ah me! Where is a lover's wealth? what joy
> Is there of beauty, when once conceal'd more than
> Of jewels in the dark? but when reveal'd,
> We stand to th' hazard of another's claim.[90]

The Platonic lady's standard of a love free from jealousy on her
own part is equally high. The Queen in *The Fair Favourite*
clearly states that standard in one of her conversations with the
King.

> *King.* Are you not weary of your virtue yet?
> *Queen.* Nor of your love unto my rival, Sir.
> If it were low and sinful love, I should
> Not think it worth my envy or my fear;
> If pure and noble, as my strictest faith
> Believes, it is too great a treasure to
> Be made particular and own'd by me
> Alone, since what is good doth still encrease
> In merit of that name by being most
> Communative.

---

[88] *The Distresses* (*Works*, IV), V, p. 363.
[89] *Love and Honour* (*Works*, III), IV, p. 169.
[90] *The Unfortunate Lovers* (*Works*, III), II, p. 34.

King. This doctrine, Madam, will
Be new, and much unwelcome to your sex.
        Queen. True love admits no jealousy. . . .[91]

D'Avenant gives hints, now and again, of his lively sense
of the limitations of the new faith. Yet he seems to have had
honest esteem for the Platonic ideal at its best, at least as exemplified in Queen Henrietta Maria. Partly, perhaps, through personal attractiveness,[92] partly through the real integrity of her
character, Henrietta was evidently able to inspire her courtiers,
in certain moods, with something of her own romantic enthusiasm for the new religion. In D'Avenant's mask *Salmacida Spolia,* performed by personages of the royal court in 1640, so shortly
before all court gaieties were to be concluded, he fancies the
queen's soul ever looking through her eyes, and adds:

> And with its beams, she doth survey
> Our growth in virtue, or decay;
> Still lighting us in honour's way!
>   All that are good she did inspire!
> Lovers are chaste, because they know
> It is her will they should be so;
>   The valiant take from her their fire! [93]

The lines have a fine ring, and express, one must believe, a noble
loyalty. They suggest the power of high seriousness in the
queen's nature which could encourage, within the limits of a
fashion so artificial and so dangerous as that of Platonic love, the
not infrequent illustration of genuine idealism and the habitual
expression of gracious courtesy.

A more unwavering defender of the Platonic love fashion than
D'Avenant was the popular courtier Lodowick Carlell. Carlell
was the author of eight dramas, seven tragi-comedies and one

---

[91] *The Fair Favourite* (*Works,* IV), IV, pp. 264–265.
[92] Howell, *op. cit.,* I, p. 238, in a letter relating the queen's arrival in
London, comments upon her beauty, noting that "she hath Eyes that
Sparkle like Stars; and for her Physiognomy she may be said to be a
Mirror of Perfection."
[93] *Salmacida Spolia* (*Works,* II), p. 324.

tragedy. If we may place faith in the title-page announcements of the quarto editions, these plays were greeted "with great applause." They were acted, if Langbaine's testimony is correct, even after the closing of the theatres, "notwithstanding the prohibition of the Stage in those days." [94] Modern critics have taken little interest in Carlell's "degenerate" [95] art. It has even been asserted: "The value of Carlell's works is simply negative; they show what rubbish was palatable to Charles and Henrietta." [96]

To the student of the court literature of the period, and perhaps to him alone, Carlell's "rubbish" is of interest. For Carlell devoted himself, with an almost fanatic zeal, to the service of Platonic drama. He concentrates all his powers, such as they are, upon two great problems in the new love ethics: (1) What constitutes the perfect lover? and (2) What constitutes the perfect friend? In his elaborate portrayal and analysis of lovers' conduct he supports the Platonic creed of D'Avenant, with a more sober faith than D'Avenant's and a more audacious psychology.

Like all the Platonics, Carlell places marked emphasis upon the chastity of love. Clarimant in *The Passionate Lovers* (c. 1636) is satisfied to experience "a love without a possibility of satisfaction." [97] His lady is so exalted above poor mundane matters that, in refusing to allow her suitor to kiss her hand, she chides him:

> . . . the mind being the noblest part,
> Is't not enough if that be happy? [98]

In *The Deserving Favourite* (1629) Lysander, going to his execution, has a cheering crumb of Platonic comfort to offer his Clarinda in the assurance:

> Weep not Clarinda, you may live happily.
> You and the Princesse may together make
> A kind of Marriage, each one strongly

---

[94] Gerard Langbaine, *An Account of the English Dramatic Poets*, p. 46.
[95] Schelling, *op. cit.*, II, p. 356.   [96] Fleay, *op. cit.*, I, p. 48.
[97] *The Passionate Lovers*, Part II; I, p. 97.   [98] *Ibid.*, Part I; I, p. 16.

> Flattering themselves, the other is Lysander;
> For each of you's Lysander's better part. . . .[99]

That these earthly loves are heaven-ordained Carlell, like D'Avenant, maintains. When Clarinda tells Lysander that she is heartily resolved against wedding his friend the Duke, Lysander, who has been so woefully torn betwixt love and friendship, concedes in a tone of relief:

> . . . I perceive the fates
> Had fore-ordain'd we should enjoy each other.[100]

With special emphasis, also, Carlell denounces the crime of jealousy, "the canker of true love." [101]

Carlell illustrates in much greater detail than D'Avenant the code of behavior for Platonic lovers. The necessity for excessive humility on the lover's part he reiterates again and again. Clorinda in *The Passionate Lovers* reminds Clarimant that his mistress has no less power over him "then that of Kings over their subjects." [102] Clarimant himself, an almost perfect lover, rebukes Agenor for referring to the former's "unequal'd merit":

> Merit! dear brother, it is impossible:
> Since what I have done, or shall ever do,
> Grows from her influence upon me.[97]

Extravagant gratitude for the slightest favors is equally incumbent upon the worthy lover. When Clorinda dresses Clarimant's wounds and they bleed afresh, he exclaims joyously:

> Know dear Clorinda, it was a thankful heart
> That sent these few drops forth to kiss your hand
> For so great favours.[103]

Nor are Carlell's ladies a whit behind their lovers in sensitiveness to love's obligations. The charity, it must be confessed, often assumes eccentric forms. Clorinda goes so far as to beg her lover

---

[99] *The Deserving Favourite*, reprint by Gray, p. 147.
[100] *Ibid.*, p. 102.   [101] *Ibid.*, p. 129.
[102] *The Passionate Lovers*, Part I; V, p. 83.
[103] *Ibid.*, Part II; III, p. 119.

to kill her, since she can think of no other way in which to reward his devotion. She announces:

> Those servants are esteem'd the truest,
> That do the last and greatest offices of duty.
> Having no love to pay your vows of service,
> My gratitude proposed this as your recompense.[104]

For once the lover demurs, although he displays some anxiety in not fulfilling his lady's will.

As might be expected, William Habington's one play, *The Queen of Arragon* (1640), is rich in Platonic love philosophy. The noble Queen receives due Platonic tribute from her suitors, who are quick to feel exhibited in her beauty —

> that care
> Heaven had to keep part of itself on earth
> Unruin'd.[105]

The humble devotion of the Queen's servant Florentio is at length rewarded, though even a king has to yield to Florentio's "priority of service." [106] In the fall of 1668 Pepys witnessed a revival of this play which happened to delight his capricious taste, evoking his comment: "an old Blackfriars play, but an admirable one, so good that I am astonished at it, and wonder where it hath lain asleep all this while that I have never heard of it before." [107]

The tragi-comedies of Henry Glapthorne, Sir William Berkeley, Jasper Mayne, and Thomas Killigrew all present similar material. In Glapthorne's *Argalus and Parthenia* (c. 1638) the heroine's beauty becomes disfigured by leprosy, but the hero consoles her with the assurance that this small loss of "fleshly glory" [108] is no impediment to their love. Lysicles in Berkeley's *The Lost Lady*

---

[104] *Ibid.*, Part II; I, p. 102.
[105] *The Queen of Arragon* (Hazlitt's Dodsley, XIII), II, p. 358.
[106] *Ibid.*, IV, p. 393.
[107] Pepys, *Diary*, ed. Henry B. Wheatley, VIII, p. 118.
[108] *Argalus and Parthenia* (*Works*, I), II, 2, p. 30.

(pr. 1639) is a model Platonic, though his noble sacrifices in behalf of love and friendship are, of course, sadly misunderstood by those for whom he makes them.   In Mayne's *The Amorous Warre* (1639) there is plenty of Platonic sentiment and compliment, exhibited in some ingenious wooing scenes, in which certain court ladies, disguised as Amazons, test the fidelity of their own husbands.   To the period before the civil war belong three of Killigrew's Platonic tragi-comedies: *The Prisoners* (before 1637), *Claracilla* (*c.* 1636), and *The Princesse* (before 1640).   In *The Princesse* occurs the conventional renunciation of a mistress by an unselfish lover, in deference to a brother's claim.   Very gallantly Lucius hands over the lady to Facertes, exclaiming:

> Here Facertes from Fate receive this Jewel, 'tis a Wealth I cannot hope to possess, but by being unworthy of it; and it shall be Lucius his glory to say To keep his Fame, he gave that away.[109]

Pepys saw a representation of *The Princesse* in 1661 which, he declared, was the first "since before the troubles." [110]

William Cartwright was regarded by his own generation as a particularly promising young dramatist.   In his brief career he managed to win by his plays great popularity and an especial share of the royal favor.   In his tragi-comedies, *The Lady Errant* (1635), *The Royall Slave* (1636), and *The Siedge, or Love's Convert* (*c.* 1637), he effectively emphasized the admired Platonic doctrines.   No contemporary dramatist knew better how to drive home each article of the Platonic creed.   On an occasion when jealousy, for example, must be anathematized, the jealous Charistus is forced to have a duel with his best friend.   The fighting over, after much blood has been lost on both sides, the two opponents stand weakly leaning against opposite trees, conversing while breath shall last.   Presently a new light dawns upon Charistus, and he assures his friend:

[109] *The Princesse, or Love at First Sight*, V, 8, p. 67.
[110] Pepys, *Diary*, II, p. 137.

> . . . we shall go
> Down equall to the Shades both, two waies equall,
> As Dead, as Friends. And when Lucasia shall
> Come down unto us (which Heavens forbid
> Should be as yet) I'l not be Jealous there.[111]

The ultimate recovery of the contestants could hardly detract, in the opinion of a Caroline audience, from the glory of such a scene.

But Cartwright's dialogue marks his real distinction in the new genre. It is much more elaborately organized than the dialogue of D'Avenant, Carlell, and the other dramatists just discussed. Its systematization is in full accordance with *précieuse* taste and indicates Cartwright's definite interest in a mannered style. Even the raillery appears to have been studiously prepared and conned by the speakers beforehand, as notably in the extended encounters of wit between three gay court ladies and three courtiers in *The Lady Errant*.[112] At times, the dialogue acquires the precision of formal argument.

In a formal debate on love Lucasia is won by her lover, a better debater.[113] By a similar method Attosa convinces King Arsamnes, her husband, of her loyalty to him. Attosa's argument, displaying her *préciosité*, deserves citation. The queen urges that her Platonic regard for Cratander is honorable both to herself and to her husband. Conducted on a quite impersonal basis, the debate proceeds as follows:

> *Ato.* Doth not the Sun (the Sun, which yet you worship)
> Send beams to others than your self? yet those
> Which dwell on you lose neither light, nor heat,
> Comming not thence lesse vigorous, or lesse chast.
> Would you seal up a Fountain? or confine
> The Air unto your walk? would you enjoyn
> The Flower to cast no smell, but as you passe?
> Love is as free as Fountain, Air, or Flower:
> For't stands not in a point; 'tis large, and may,

---

[111] *The Lady Errant*, V, 2, p. 72.   [112] *Ibid.*, esp. I, 1 and 2, and II, 2.
[113] *Ibid.*, IV, 6, pp. 61–62.

Like streames give verdure to this Plant, that Tree,
Nay that whole field of Flow'rs, and yet still run
In a most faithfull course toward the bosome
Of the lov'd Ocean.

    Arsam. But when you divert
And break the Stream into small Rivulets,
You make it run more weak than when it kept
United in one Channell.[114]

    Atos. If it branch
Into a smaller twining here, and there,
The water is not lost, nor doth it quit
The former Name; this is not to destroy
But to enlarge the stream: did it dry up,
And leave the Fountain destitute, indeed
You'd reason to be angry.

    Arsa. But what should make you
Present him with a gift? you might have smother'd
A good opinion of him in your Breast,
(As some digressing streams flow under ground)
And so have rested; but you shew it now,
And make the world partaker.

    Atos. Who would stifle
An honest Fire? that flame's to be suspected
That hides it self. When that a man of valour
Graceth his Country with a good attempt,
You give a Sword, an Horse, a Mannour, nay
Sometimes a whole Province for reward. We have
A sense of Vertue too, as well as you:
And shall we be deny'd the Liberty
To shew we have that sense? A Favour is
The Almes of Love; I do not pass away
My heart in Charity. Vertuous Cratander
Shews forth so full a Transcript of your life
In all but his misfortunes, that me thinks,
You may admire your self in him, as in
Your shade. But yet let chast Atossa rather
Not be at all, than not be wholly yours.

    Arsam. Thou art still vertuous my Atossa, still
Transparent as thy Crystall, but more spotless.

---

[114] Cf. Lyly's *Love's Metamorphosis* (*Works*, III), III, 1, pp. 312–313.
Silvestris pleads with his lady, who wishes to entertain more than one lover:
    Sweet *Niobe*, a ryuer running into diuers brookes becommeth shallow,
and a mind diuided into sundrie affections, in the end will haue none.

Fooles that we are, to think the Eye of Love
Must always look on us. The Vine that climbes
By conjugall embracements 'bout the Elme,
May with a ring or two perhaps encircle
    Some neighbouring bough, and yet this twining prove
    Not the Offence, but Charity of Love.[115]

Here is demonstrated with a vengeance, surely, the *précieuse* "horreur du mot propre." Like many of the debaters in *Astrée*, the queen vindicates her position not by explanation of her own conduct but, curiously enough, by a skilful use of similitudes, which the king inspects and criticizes and the force of which he is ultimately obliged to acknowledge.

The promises of Cartwright's best scenes are fulfilled in the far more important plays of Suckling. Modern critics are likely to forget the fame of Suckling in his own age. His contemporaries seem to have esteemed his plays, which are rarely read nowadays, no less highly than his poetry. Pepys witnessed revivals of *Brennoralt* (1639) in 1661,[116] 1667,[117] and 1668.[118] He observes that *Aglaura* (c. 1637), revived in 1662 [119] and 1668,[120] is a play "which hath been always mightily cried up." [120] Langbaine, writing near the close of the century, makes a similar comment on *Aglaura:* "This Play is much priz'd at this Day." [121] The modern critic who declares that all Suckling's plays [122] "are not worth his handful of incomparable lyrics" [123] is probably correct in his judgment. Yet the plays repeat and enlarge the philosophy of the poems. With all their dramatic weaknesses they reveal, besides, the true pattern of Platonic dialogue, as the court must have known it, gracefully recorded, at last, by the most accomplished and most gifted courtier of the time.

[115] *The Royall Slave*, III, 5, pp. 124–126.
[116] Pepys, *Diary*, II, p. 64. [117] *Ibid.*, VII, pp. 62 and 147.
[118] *Ibid.*, VII, p. 328. [119] *Ibid.*, II, p. 323.
[120] *Ibid.*, VII, p. 258. [121] Langbaine, *op. cit.*, p. 497.
[122] Suckling's one comedy, *The Goblins*, is discussed in the following chapter.
[123] Ronald Bayne, "Lesser Jacobean and Caroline Dramatists," in *Cambridge History of English Literature*, VI, p. 240.

The chief characters in the tragi-comedy of *Aglaura* are Platonics and anti-Platonics. All the ladies belong to the former group, and as they have the sovereignty, their arguments are the most authoritative. Aglaura herself upholds the new code in its more difficult aspects. When Orithie tells her, hesitatingly, that she, too, loves Thersames, Aglaura's husband, the princess graciously observes:

> Blush not, Orithie, 'tis a sin to blush
> For loving him, though none at all to love him.
> I can admit of rivalship without
> A jealousy, nay, shall be glad of it.[124]

Orithie's own Platonic idealism is impeccable. At the close of the (revised) fifth act of *Aglaura*, the princess turns to Orithie with the apology:

> Orithie,
> How for thy sake now could I wish love were
> No mathematic point, but would admit
> Division, that Thersames might, though at
> My charge, pay thee the debt he owes thee.

With dignity Orithie rejoins:

> Madam, I loved the prince, not myself.
> Since his virtues have their full rewards,
> I have my full desires.[125]

The hero of the tragedy *Brennoralt* boasts of his lady's other servants:

> She does triumph when she does but appear:
> I have as many rivals as beholders.[126]

In the same play the jealous lover Almerin receives from his mistress the severe rebuke:

> jealousy's
> No better sign of love, my lord, than fevers are
> Of life; they show there is a being, though

---

[124] *Aglaura* (*Works*, I), IV, p. 136.
[125] *Ibid.*, V [2], p. 179.
[126] *Brennoralt* (*Works*, II), II, p. 98.

Impair'd and perishing: and that, affection,
But sick and in disorder.[127]

In his unfinished tragedy *The Sad One* (*c.* 1640) Suckling supports the Platonic tenet of secrecy in love intrigue.   When Florelio discovers his wife's intimacy with Bellamino, the latter makes him swear not to disclose the secret but reflects, after allowing Florelio to depart, that further precaution must be taken in defense of the lady's honor.   Bellamino soliloquizes:

> One of us two must die:
> And charity tells me, better he than I.
> But how? it is not for my honour
> To kill him basely; nor is it   [*Studies*
> For hers to kill him otherwise;
> Th' whole court will guess the quarrel,
> If it be a duel.   [*Studies again*
> It is decreed; no matter which way, so he fall:
> Mine, in respect of hers, are no respects at all.[128]

Thus in his plays, as in his poems and letters, Suckling's polite allegiance to the new philosophy is amply demonstrated.

Only in his plays could Suckling do justice to Platonic dialogue.   He seized the opportunity with eagerness.   *Aglaura* is little more than a tissue of ingenious arguments.   Of course, the new social mode offered the logical stimulus to such discourse; its fashions were beautifully precise, and its methods of reasoning had been carefully formulated.   By Lyly's similitude contests Suckling may well have been influenced.   But he owed the formal symmetry of his dialogue, so opposed to Lyly's whimsical twists and turns of fancy, to the discipline of Platonic conventions.

[127] *Ibid.*, IV, p. 119.   See the close parallel phrasing in the following passage from Sedley's *The Mulberry Garden* (1668), III, 1, p. 66:

> So fevers are of life sure proofs we know,
> And yet our lives they often overthrow:
> Diseases, though well cur'd, our bodies mar,
> And fears, although remov'd, our loves impair:
> True love, like health, should no disorder know.

[128] *The Sad One* (*Works*, II), IV, p. 158.

In Suckling's plays there are fixed rules for conversation; and conversation, whether of love philosophy or of other matters, is always calmly judicial and finely discriminating. However startling the vicissitudes of fate which descend upon the speakers of the drama, their splendid reasoning faculties remain unimpaired. The power of conversing well is always the noblest and most reliable equipment of gentlemen, no matter what pressing demands for heroic action in mazes of exotic adventure Suckling's luxuriant imagination may foist upon them. While holding a secret interview, Thersames and his bride, Aglaura, are interrupted. Although an ominous noise is heard outside the room and the lovers perceive impending danger, Thersames finds the occasion an appropriate one for sharpening his wit.

> *Agl.* . . .
> Hide, hide yourself; for love's sake, hide yourself!
> *Ther.* As soon the sun may hide himself as I.
> The Prince of Persia hide himself!
> *Agl.* O, talk not, sir; the sun does hide himself,
> When night and blackness comes.
> *Ther.* Never, sweet ignorance, he shines in th' other world then;
> And so shall I, if I set here in glory.[129]

It is as if Thersames had vowed to die, if die he must, with a similitude on his lips. When a friend tries to convince Thersames of the wisdom of a special procedure, he trades similitudes with him. The action, it must be confessed, is decidedly delayed, but Thersames' judgment is slowly but surely won over by the friend's conceits.[130] In *Brennoralt* Almerin and Brennoralt declare a truce in a mortal combat, in order to kiss their dead ladies and indulge in appropriate comparisons.

> *Alm.* . . .
> Hold! pr'ythee, give me leave
> To satisfy a curiosity —
> I never kissed my Iphigene as woman.

---

[129] *Aglaura* (*Works*, I), III, pp. 122–123.
[130] *Ibid.*, I, pp. 106–107.

Bren. Thou motion'st well, nor have I taken leave.
It keeps a sweetness yet, as 'stills from roses,
When the flowers are gone.   [*Rises*
   Alm. Even so have two faint pilgrims, scorch'd with heat,
Unto some neighbor fountain stepp'd aside.
Kneel'd first, then laid their warm lips to the nymph,
And from her coldness took fresh life again,
As we do now.
   Bren. Let's on our journey, if thou art refresh'd.[131]

The situation has been exploited for conversational purposes, apt comment has been suitably given, and Almerin is now free to die with a clear conscience.

The longer conversations illustrate distinct types of dialogue. Sometimes a contention is formulated and then supported by appropriate similitudes, presented by each speaker in turn. Orsames pauses in the pursuit of a runaway horse to discuss with his friends the similarity between the life of the huntsman and that of the courtier. When he has noted the general resemblance and offered the first comparison, it becomes the duty of the other wits to meet him and, if possible, outstrip him on his own ground.[132]   In like manner, Brennoralt and his friend Doran prove by alternate similitudes that court life breeds corruption.[133]   The argument may take the form of a debate, in which two opponents contend, aided sometimes by sympathetic comrades. When Thersames and Aglaura hold their first interview, they engage in a discussion for and against fruition in love.[134]   The discussion at other times becomes a contest in raillery, in which each participant strives to surpass his fellows in the satirical emphasis of his thrusts. To this type of dialogue belongs the conversation in which Orsames, Philan, and two other courtiers vie with one another in decrying Platonic love

---

[131] *Brennoralt* (*Works*, II), V, p. 131.
[132] *Aglaura* (*Works*, I), I, pp. 99–100.
[133] *Brennoralt* (*Works*, II), I, p. 77.
[134] *Aglaura* (*Works*, I), I, p. 100.

notions.[135]   What?ver the pattern of the dialogue, the exchange of similitudes remains essential.

The importance of fruition in love, surely one of Suckling's favorite themes, is debated at some length by Semanthe and Orsames, the former seconded by Orithie, the latter by Philan. The two ladies maintain a Platonic, the two gentlemen an anti-Platonic emphasis. Semanthe opens the discussion:

> *Sem.* Think you it is not then
> The little jealousies, my lord, and fears:
> Joy mix'd with doubt, and doubt reviv'd with hope,
> That crowns all love with pleasure? these are lost,
> When once we come to full fruition:
> Like waking in the morning, when all night
> Our fancy has been fed with some new strange delight.[136]
>
> *Ors.* I grant you, madam, that the fears and joys
> Hopes and desires, mix'd with despairs and doubts,
> Do make the sport in love; and that they are
> The very dogs by which we hunt the hare;
> But as the dogs would stop, and straight give o'er
> Were it not for the little thing before;
> So would our passions; both alike must be
> Flesh'd in the chase.
>
> *Ori.* Will you, then, place the happiness but there,
> Where the dull ploughman and the ploughman's horse
> Can find it out?   Shall souls refin'd not know
> How to preserve alive a noble flame,
> But let it die — burn out to appetite?
>
> *Sem.* Love's a chameleon, and would live on air,
> Physic for agues; starving is his food.[137]
>
> *Ors.* Why, there it is now! a greater epicure
> Lives not on earth.   My lord and I have been
> In 's privy kitchen, seen his bills of fare.
>
> *Sem.* And how, and how, my lord?
>
> *Ors.* A mighty prince, and full of curiosity!
> Hearts newly slain serv'd up entire,
> And stuck with little arrows instead of cloves.

---

[135] *Ibid.*, II, pp. 111–112.

[136] This speech repeats, with a few changes, certain lines in one of Suckling's poems, *Against Fruition*, I, pp. 33–34.

[137] Cf. Lyly's *Endimion* (*Works*, III), III, 4, p. 50. Geron observes:
Loue is a Camelion, which draweth nothing into the mouth but ayre, and nourisheth nothing in the bodie but lunges.

Phi. Sometimes a cheek plump'd up
With broth, with cream and claret mingled
For sauce, and round about the dish
Pomegranate kernels, strew'd on leaves of lilies!

Ors. Then will he have black eyes, for those of late
He feeds on much, and for variety the grey.

Phi. You forget his cover'd dishes
Of jenestrays, and marmalade of lips,
Perfum'd by breath sweet as the bean's first blossoms.

Sem. Rare!
And what's the drink to all this meat, my lord?

Ors. Nothing but pearl dissolv'd, tears still fresh fetch'd
From lovers' eyes, which, if they come to be
Warm in the carriage, are straight cool'd with sighs.

Sem. And all this rich proportion perchance
We would allow him:

Ors. True! but therefore this is but his common diet:
Only serves when his chief cooks,
Liking and Opportunity, are out of the way.[138]

In such fluent and fanciful argument, Suckling elaborates the pattern of D'Urfé's dialogue.

The most ambitious debate in Suckling's drama occurs in a courtship scene where Iolas pleads for Semanthe's favor and she scorns his suit.

Sem. . . . if I do shun you, 'tis
As bashful debtors shun their creditors.
I cannot pay you in the self-same coin,
And am asham'd to offer any other.

Iol. It is ill done, Semanthe, to plead bankrupt,
When with such ease you may be out of debt.
In love's dominions native commodity
Is current payment; change is all the trade,
And heart for heart the richest merchandise.

Sem. 'Twould here be mean, my lord, since mine would prove
In your hands but a counterfeit, and yours in mine
Worth nothing. Sympathy, not greatness,
Makes those jewels rise in value.

Iol. Sympathy? O, teach but yours to love then,
And two so rich no mortal ever knew.

[138] *Aglaura* (*Works*, I), I, pp. 102–103.

76 Restoration Comedy

Sem. That heart would love but ill that must be taught;
Such fires as these still kindle of themselves.

Iol. In such a cold and frozen place as is
Thy breast, how should they kindle of themselves,
Semanthe?

Sem. Ask how the flint can carry fire within!
'Tis the least miracle that love can do.[139]

Iol. Thou art thyself the greatest miracle,
For thou art fair to all perfection,
And yet dost want the greatest part of beauty —
Kindness. Thy cruelty (next to thyself)
Above all things on earth takes up my wonder.

Sem. Call not that cruelty, which is our fate.
Believe me, Iolas, the honest swain,
That from the brow of some steep cliff far off,
Beholds a ship labouring in vain against
The boisterous and unruly elements, ne'er had
Less power or more desire to help than I . . .

Iol. So perishing sailors pray to storms,
And so they hear again. So men,
With death about them, look on physicians, that
Have given them o'er, and so they turn away:
Two fixed stars, that keep a constant distance,
And by laws made by themselves must know
No motion eccentric, may meet as soon as we:
The anger that the foolish sea does show,
When it does brave it out, and roar against
A stubborn rock that still denies it passage,
Is not so vain and fruitless as my prayers.
Ye mighty powers of love and fate, where is
Your justice here? . . . [140]

With great exactness these debaters fulfill the complicated rules
of the conversational game. It is hard to conceive of anything
in the way of dialogue more symmetrical or more artificial.
In a few scenes in *Aglaura,* in the occasional gossiping of

[139] Cf. *Astrée,* vol. I, bk. iii, p. 160:
. . . A la verité, respondit Ligdamon, me faire brûler & geler en mesme
temps n'est pas une des moindres merueilles qui procedent de vous: mais
celle-cy est bien plus grande, que c'est de vostre glace qui procede ma
chaleur, & de ma chaleur vostre glace.
[140] *Aglaura* (*Works,* I), IV, pp. 139–140.

groups of courtiers, Suckling allows his dialogue, though still crowdéd with similitudes, to become fairly informal and familiar. At such times conversation assumes the ease which must have marked Suckling's own speech on those occasions when, according to his friend D'Avenant, "he was the bull that was bayted," [141] and many gallants stood by, admiring his repartee. In one scene of this sort, a number of courtiers are commenting on Thersames' brave encounter with the guards and the subsequent confusion at court.

1 Court. By this light, a brave prince!
He made no more of the guard, than they
Would of a tailor on a masque night, that has refused
Trusting before.

2 Court. He's as active as he is valiant too!
Didst mark him how he stood like all the points
O' th' compass, and, as good pictures,
Had his eyes towards every man?

3 Court. And his sword too.
All th' other side walk up and down the court now,
As if they had lost their way, and stare,
Like greyhounds, when the hare has taken the furze.

1 Court. Right.
And have more troubles about them
Than a serving-man that has forgot his message
When he's come upon the place.

2 Court. Yonder's the king within chasing and swearing,
Like an old falconer upon the first flight
Of a young hawk, when some clown
Has taken away the quarry from her;
And all the lords stand round about him,
As if he were to be baited, with much more fear
And at much more distance,
Than a country gentlewoman sees the lions the first time.[142]

After a prolonged inspection of these similitude contests, we are disposed to beg of Suckling, in the language of Congreve's Millamant, "truce with your similitudes." [143] Yet Millamant

---

[141] Suckling, *Works*, I, Preface, p. xxii.
[142] *Aglaura* (*Works*, I), IV, pp. 125–126.
[143] *The Way of the World*, II, 2, p. 345.

herself was a notable offender in that way. She was also an admirer of Suckling. On one memorable occasion, walking about in her room, she diverts her leisure by quoting from two of Suckling's poems and apostrophizes: "Natural, easy Suckling!" Sir Wilfull enters in time to overhear this piece of commendation, and attempts to turn it gracefully to his own account, with the reminder: "Suckling! no such suckling, neither, cousin, nor stripling: I thank Heaven, I'm no minor." Whereupon Millamant checks him with asperity: "Ah, rustic, ruder than Gothic!"[144]

We may infer that Congreve's own regard for Suckling was not a merely casual esteem. Anyone who preserves the memory — as who does not? — of the brilliant scene in which Millamant makes her first appearance in *The Way of the World*[145] cannot fail to be impressed by the way in which the dialogue of this scene is related to Suckling's dialogue. Here Congreve presents a contest in raillery, more flexibly managed than the dialogue of the earlier dramatist but, none the less, depending for its effectiveness on a very similar interplay of similitudes. It will be recalled, likewise, that in the only two interviews of any importance between Cynthia and Mellefont in *The Double-Dealer*[146] the lovers engage in ingenious discussions of the nature of marriage, supporting their conclusions by illustrative similitudes, in the style of the wit encounters of Suckling's Platonic lovers. It is a striking fact that the triumph of Congreve, the greatest artist of Restoration comedy, must be explained partly in terms of his renewal and perfection of a dialogue pattern already well established in the drama of Suckling.

It is perhaps difficult to realize the closeness of the relationship, in general, between the serious Platonic drama of Suckling's time and the comedy of the Restoration period. Platonic drama,

[144] *Ibid.*, IV, 1, p. 376. [145] *Ibid.*, II, 2, pp. 344–347.
[146] *The Double-Dealer*, II, 1, pp. 122–123, and IV, 1, pp. 150–151.

with its solemn philosophy and its tedious rhetoric, seems far enough removed from the cynical gaiety and rapid flow of wit of Restoration comedy. Yet Suckling and Etherege have pronounced social sympathies which neither shares with Shirley. Platonic drama and Restoration comedy both depict small aristocratic social groups, in which morals as well as manners have become regulated by an exacting social code. In Restoration comedy, polite gallantry, although less ceremonious than it had been a few decades earlier and interpreted in a new spirit, is still the chief business of life, an engrossing game with many rules. With other dramatists besides Congreve, old habits of wit survive to a surprising degree. Comic dialogue acquires a new vigor and variety but continues to enforce, in the fashion of Platonic drama, the artificial temper of the social game.

CHAPTER IV

COURT INFLUENCES ON COMEDY IN THE
REIGN OF CHARLES I

WE ARE not forced to bridge by a mere act of the imagination the gap between formal Platonic drama and Restoration comedy. Platonic tragi-comedy triumphed but a few brief
years, while its popularity was insured by the queen's gracious
influence. Before the Platonic fashion had a chance to become
self-destructive through its own excesses, court authority became
suddenly annulled. With the loss of that royal enthusiasm
which had been its purest stimulus, the cult rapidly declined.
Only its outward ceremonies survived the gray chill of the first
months of civil war. During the last years of the court vogue
of Platonism, its artificial emphasis was already being satirized
in comedy. The comedies of this period are very limited in
number and certainly not rich in dramatic interest. They usher
in, however, with a rather naïve gesture, the dramatic program
of Restoration comedy.

It is not strange that the chivalric creed which Henrietta
Maria sought to impose on the English court was accepted by
the sophisticated and worldly members of that court with some
reservations. As soon as there were Platonics, there were inevitably anti-Platonics. At the English court anti-Platonic fires
were at first partially smothered, although the air was full of the
smoke. In France they already burned brightly in D'Urfé's
Astrée, the code-book of the entire Platonic system. Interesting
from many points of view, *Astrée* is of unique interest in its
early anticipation of the Restoration comic spirit.

Even while gravely enforcing Platonic ceremonies, D'Urfé was too keen a student of human nature to be blinded to their comic possibilities. The love-making of his devout Platonics never becomes really tedious, for it is constantly assailed, in its most solemn moments, by the cynical wit of the inconstant shepherd Hylas. A superb comic figure, Hylas is the one notorious rebel against the beguilements of love among the Platonizing shepherds of *Astrée*. He is the flesh and blood embodiment of D'Urfé's own laughter at the unreality of the Platonic pageant.

Gay, confident, irresponsible, Hylas jests his way through D'Urfé's romance, arguing his sceptical creed, singing derisive love songs, and playing mad pranks to irritate sober lovers. All who tend their flocks along the shore of the Lignon know, from his own lips, the story of his passing loves for Carlis, Stilliane, Cloris, Florice, Chryseide, Phylis, Laonice, and a host of others. Of course, the Arcadians perceive that, single-handed, Hylas can never overthrow the faith which they honor; consequently they feel safe in humoring him, like a spoiled child. When he engagingly exploits the Platonic sanctities, a group of pretty shepherdesses is always at hand to smile indulgently and to admire his gleeful caprice. Sylvandre alone takes Hylas seriously. The two shepherds oppose each other in page after page of heated debate, in which Hylas, by his light and graceful fencing, regularly foils his opponent's soundest contentions. Sylvandre may uphold with glowing rhetoric the spiritual excellence of Platonic love, but Hylas is ready with the merry rejoinder: "Mais . . . i'aime le corps aussi bien que l'ame," [1] and can support his point of view with all the ingenious devices of the Platonic habit of argument.

Hylas usually finds it expedient to employ for his own ends the weapons of his associates. He demonstrates to the horrified Sylvandre the neatness with which anti-Platonic heresies can be proved valid by Platonic methods of reasoning. Moreover, the

[1] *Astrée*, vol. II, bk. vi, p. 454.

inconstant shepherd wins each of his successive mistresses by
Platonic compliments as gracious as Sylvandre himself could have
devised. The joke about Hylas is that he plays so often the
fashionable social game, although he does not believe, for an
instant, in the philosophical principles which have sanctioned it.
His posing frequently brings upon him predicaments similar to
those in which like-minded heroes of Restoration comedy were
destined to become involved. Sooner or later, Hylas' beguiled
mistresses learn his duplicity, and all his wiles hardly avail to
stem the tide of their jealous fury.

On one occasion, Florice, Palinice, and Cyrcéne announce
their grievances against Hylas, unaware of his presence. Im-
petuously he reveals himself, and the three assail him in unison.
The ensuing scene is thus sketched by D'Urfé:

. . . Hylas feignant d'auoir interrompu à dessein Florice, s'en courut l'em-
brasser, & puis saluä les àutres deux; & enfin retournant vers elle: Et bien
belle discoureuse, dit-il, ne cesserez-vous iamais de renouueller mes playes?
I'auois opinion, dit-elle, de chanter vos louanges: & depuis quand les
estimez-vous autres? I'ay de tout temps, dit-il, accoustumé d'appeller
chaque chose par son nom: & n'est-ce pas reblesser que de remettre le fer
dans les vielles cicatrices? Et y-a-t'il un fer plus trenchant que la veuë
de vos beautez, & le souuenir de mes premiers amours? O! dit Florice,
l'offense n'est pas grande si ie ne vous fay que cette playe, & vous ne deuez
pas auoir peur d'en mourir, puis que vous en sçauez de si bons remedes.
Cela seroit bon, respondit Hylas, si toutes les blssurees se guerissoient par
des remedes semblables: mais n'entrons point si tost en ce discours, & me
dites quel bon dessein vous conduit en ce lieu? Ce n'est pas, respondit
Florice, celuy de vous y voir. Si vous estiez, adjousta Hylas, aussi cour-
toise que vous m'estes obligée, cette consideration auroit bien assez de force,
pour vous y conduire, vous ayant assez fait de seruices à toutes pour vous
laisser la volonté de me reuoir: mais ie voy bien que i'ay semé une terre
ingrate, & qui ne rend pas la peine qu'on y prend. Quelquesfois, respondit
Cyrcéne, pource que le laboureur est mauuais, & la graine mal-choisie &
mise hors de saison, le bon terroir rapporte des ronces au lieu de bled:
prenez garde que quelqu'une de ces choses ne soit cause de l'infertilité dont
vous nous blasmez.

Ie sçay bien, dit-il, Cyrcéne, que comme vous auez tousiours eu beau-
coup de beauté pour vous faire aimer, de mesme vous n'auez iamais eu faute
de desdain pour mespriser ceux qui vous ont adorée. Et moy, dit Palinice,
ie sçay encore mieux, que comme vous auez toujours esté tres-fertile en
nouueaux desirs, & nouuelles affections, de mesme vous n'auez iamais eu

faute de paroles pour accuser autruy de vostre faute. Alors Hylas se recu-
lant deux ou trois pas: C'est trop, dit-il, d'auoir à combatre contre trois, les
plus vaillans mesmes ne le veulent entreprendre contre deux. . . . [2]

This scene has much in common with a scene in Etherege's *The
Man of Mode*, where Dorimant is attacked, at a critical moment,
by the united malice of Loveit and Belinda and, after attempting
a few suave phrases, has to withdraw.[3] Hylas is used to the
sensation of being "le plus confus homme du monde,"[4] but
rallies surprisingly after each fresh embarrassment. When
Florice's letter, summoning him to an assignation in her husband's absence, has been intercepted by a rival mistress and the
enlightened husband has taken Florice out of town, Hylas,
awaiting her return, falls in love with the still more charming
Chryseide and is promptly restored to the best of spirits.[5] To
Hylas, as to the typical hero of Restoration comedy, such perilous gallantry is the very breath of life.

In Stelle Hylas finally meets a mistress who is his match.
When he boasts of his fickleness, she boasts of hers. Each falls
in love with the other's humor. Deciding upon a unique partnership, the two draw up, in the presence of witnesses, a "proviso" contract insuring their mutual rights of inconstancy. The
contract includes the following twelve items:

Que l'un n'usurpera point sur l'autre cette souueraine authorité, que
nous disons estre Tyrannie.

Que chacun de nous sera en mesme temps, & l'Amant & l'aymé, &
l'aymee & l'Amante.

Que nostre amitié sera eternellement sans contrainte.

Que nous aymerons tant qu'il nous plaira.

Que celuy qui voudra cesser d'aymer, le pourra faire sans reproche
d'aucune infidelité.

Que quand nous voudrons, sans nous separer d'amitié, nous pourrons
aimer qui bon nous semblera, & tant qu'il nous plaira continuer cette
amitié, ou la quitter sans congé.

---

[2] *Ibid.*, vol. II, bk. iii, pp. 200–202.
[3] *The Man of Mode*, V, 1, pp. 352–354.
[4] *Astrée*, vol. II, bk. iv, p. 268.   [5] *Ibid.*, pp. 290–295.

Que la ialousie, les plaintes, & la tristesse seront bannies d'entre nous comme incompatibles auec nostre parfaite amitié.

Qu'en nostre conuersation nous serons libres, & sans nous contraindre, chacun fera & dira ce qu'il luy plaira, sans nous incommoder l'un pour l'autre.

Que pour n'estre point menteurs, ny esclaues en effet, ny en parole, tous ces mots de fidelité, de seruitude & d'eternelle affection ne seront iamais meslez parmi nos discours.

Que nous pourrons tous deux ou l'un sans l'autre continuer ou cesser de nous entre-aymer.

Que si cette amitié cesse de l'un des costez, ou de tous les deux, nous pourrons la renouueller quand bon nous semblera.

Que pour ne nous abstraindre à une longue amour ou à une longue haine, nous serons obligez d'oublier & les faueurs & les outrages.[6]

At the suggestion of Sylvandre, who acts as secretary, one more article is added in conclusion:

Que toutesfois nous Stelle & Hylas sommes si soigneux de nostre liberté, & tant ennemis de toutes sortes de contrainte, qu'il nous sera permis quand bon nous semblera, de n'obseruer une seule de toutes les conditions cy-dessus escrites & accordées.[7]

There are "proviso" scenes in late Elizabethan comedy in which the mistress makes conditions favoring her sovereignty in love.[8] But here for the first time two lovers frame an argument, item by item, in which the freedom of each is liberally safeguarded with legal precision. The contract anticipates the famous bargain scene between Mirabell and Millamant in Congreve's *The Way of the World*.[9] Unfortunately, no amount of gay jesting can disguise the fact that Hylas is at last in love. He is in love, too, with a coquette, who will not give him the satisfying assurance of her love for him. At the end of the narrative, Hylas is

[6] *Ibid.*, vol. III, bk. ix, pp. 838–839.

[7] *Ibid.*, p. 844.

[8] Cf. Massinger's *The City Madam* (II, 2, pp. 431–432); Fletcher's *Rule a Wife and Have a Wife* (II, 3, pp. 416–418); Shirley's *Hyde Park* (II, 4, p. 490); and Brome's *A Mad Couple well Match'd* (III, 1, pp. 58–60). For a discussion of "proviso" scenes, see my article, "D'Urfé's *Astrée* and the 'Proviso' Scenes in Dryden's Comedy," in *Philological Quarterly* (October, 1925), IV, pp. 302–308.

[9] *The Way of the World*, IV, 1, pp. 378–381.

obliged, by a perverse fate, to kneel at the Fountain of Love as humbly as the most loyal Platonic and to rejoice at seeing mirrored in its enchanted waters Stelle's face, the symbol, strange as it may seem, of a constant love.

The anti-Platonic point of view successfully invaded French *précieuse* poetry. Voiture expresses it in the lines:

> J'approuve un cœur enflammé
> Qui se glorifie
> D'aimer sans qu'il soit aimé
> Et son plaisir sacrifie:
> Je le fais bien quelquefois;
> Mais quand cela passe trois mois,
> Ma foi, je m'en ennuie.[10]

Théophile de Viau habitually wavers between love longing and a desire for freedom. Frequently the latter impulse triumphs. In a moment of relief he boasts:

> Le Ciel en soit loué! Cloris, je suis guery.[11]

He takes pleasure in prophesying that his fickle mistress will become the most degraded of courtesans, scorned on every hand.[12] Perhaps he will give her one more chance; then, if she still spurns him, let her hold him "pour un infame"[13] if ever he thinks of her again. Saint-Amant refreshes himself from the fatigue of Platonic compliments with riotous drinking songs. In his Bacchic revels he, too, is an inconstant, affirming:

> Je n'ay pas si-tost dit que j'ayme,
> Que je sens que je n'ayme plus.[14]

Such raillery emphasizes a perfectly normal reaction against the excessive refinements of Platonic gallantry.

In French drama, on the other hand, anti-Platonic sentiment won few victories. Among the pastoral plays inspired by

---

[10] Voiture, *Works*, II, pp. 342–343.
[11] Théophile de Viau, *Works*, II, p. 48.
[12] *Ibid.*, I, p. 266.   [13] *Ibid.*, II, p. 89.
[14] Saint-Amant, *Works*, I, p. 131.

Astrée, Antoine Mareschal's *L'Inconstance d'Hylas* (pr. 1635) stands quite alone in stressing the comic possibilities of inconstant love. Although the play was most successful,[15] for some reason it failed to stimulate other dramatic ventures in the same field. It has been claimed that Pierre Corneille's early plays mark the significant transformation of pastoral drama into "comédie galante." [16] A few anti-Platonic characters oppose the prevailing Platonism of these comedies. Tircis in *Mélite* (1629) and Alcidor in *La Place Royale* (1635) are inconstant lovers. Tircis explains that his love hyperboles mean nothing, for —

> La mode nous oblige à cette complaisance.[17]

Mélite, Hippolyte in *La Galerie du Palais* (1633), and Phylis in *La Place Royale* all exhibit something of the coquetry of Stelle. Mélite observes:

> Je ne reçois d'amour et n'en donne à personne.
> Les moyens de donner ce que je n'eus jamais? [18]

But throughout these plays, such comic emphasis is relatively unimportant. Conspicuous Platonic absurdities are satirized in a few plays of the period, such as *Les Visionnaires* (pr. 1637) by Jean Desmarets de Saint Sorlin and *Le Berger Extravagant* (pr. 1653), adapted by Thomas Corneille from Charles Sorel's romance of that title. Once, in Thomas Corneille's *L'Amour à la Mode* (pr. 1651), Hylas lives again in the guise of a Parisian gallant. With a dexterity befitting the successor of Hylas, Oronte courts at the same time Dorotée, her maid Lisette, and Lucie. His predicaments in love-making are numerous, but he carries through each affair with a flourish. When he has mistaken mistress for maid, he assures the former that he had really known her identity all the while. When Dorotée and Lucie

---

[15] Cf. Reure, *op. cit.*, p. 293.
[16] Cf. *La Galerie du Palais*, ed. Thomas B. Rudmose-Brown, p. xviii.
[17] *Mélite* (*Oeuvres*, ed. Marty-Laveux, I), I, 1, p. 146.
[18] *Ibid.*, I, 2, p. 151.

unite in reproaching him, he politely remarks that he cannot imagine what they are talking about. Dorotée's final conquest of Oronte may well justify her delight, as she exclaims:

> Vous reduire à l'hymen! qui l'auroit pû prevoir! [19]

Why this attractive type of gallantry occupies so small a place in French drama, during the height of D'Urfé's popularity, it is difficult to understand. In English comedy the case is altered.

In English *précieuse* poetry "the cavalier spirit" became illustrated by anti-Platonic enthusiasms quite as fully as by those graceful and delicate love compliments which admirers of the cavalier poets so justly acclaim. Waller assures his Phyllis that he will be content with her present love; he does not pledge his constancy, nor does he require hers.[20] Because Celia has been inconstant, he vows to assail every Fair. Lovers,

> like good falc'ners, take delight,
> Not in the quarry, but the flight.[21]

In a dialogue by Waller entitled *Chloris and Hylas*, D'Urfé's inconstant shepherd appears in his own person and, according to his custom, presents his perverse love theories.[22] The cavalier poet Lovelace insists that a constant love is a "fond impossibility" and demands of his mistress:

> Have I not lov'd thee much and long,
>   A tedious twelve moneths space?
> I should all other beauties wrong,
>   And rob thee of a new embrace;
>   Should I still dote upon thy face.[23]

Carew, for his part, on more than one occasion unblushingly boasts his defiance of the "goblin Honour." [24]

The raillery of Suckling exhibits many gradations of tone. From the pretty mockery of *Out upon it, I have loved* [25] to the

---

[19] *L'Amour à la Mode (Oeuvres,* I), V, 10, p. 361.
[20] Waller, *Works*, p. 62.   [21] *Ibid.*, p. 72.   [22] *Ibid.*, pp. 96–97.
[23] *Lucasta*, ed. W. Carew Hazlitt, p. 89.   [24] Carew, *Works*, p. 75.
[25] Suckling, *Works*, I, p. 48.

captious rage of *I will not love one minute more, I swear,*[26] Suckling depicts an amazing variety of lover's moods. The inade-
quacy of his Platonic faith he frankly discloses. He praises his
Platonic mistress, to be sure, because she has advanced so far in
"Love's philosophy" that she can picture to herself "a love without desire."[27] For himself, however, he declares:

> But I must needs confess, I do not find
>   The motions of my mind
> So purified as yet. . . .[28]

Frequently Suckling's license of expression does not admit of
quotation. His more impudent verses were not intended, of
course, for the ears of Her Majesty the Queen.

Even in serious Platonic drama occasional anti-Platonic sentiments intruded. In most cases, as in the tragi-comedies of Cartwright,[29] such satire was limited to a few sly jests on the part of
the scornful. At times, however, a bolder stand was taken. In
D'Avenant's *The Platonic Lovers* the spiritual courtship of Theander and Eurithea is ridiculed in a rather daring fashion.
Eurithea's maid complains:

> I've newly dress'd her like a shepherdess;
> And he, i' th' old Arcadian habit, meets
> Her straight, to whine and kiss. That's all they do.[30]

The moral pointed by the play as a whole is decidedly rationalis-
tic. At the close of the last act, Theander himself is almost con-
verted to the side of the anti-Platonics and asserts that to this
philosophy he will "incline in time."[31] It may be guessed that
D'Avenant's own convictions are nowhere more tersely expressed
than in the retort of the philosopher Buonateste to a certain
young man's declaration that he is Platonically in love. In great
contempt Buonateste exclaims:

---

[26] *Ibid.*, pp. 49–50.   [27] *Ibid.*, p. 58.   [28] *Ibid.*, p. 59.
[29] *The Lady Errant*, IV, 2, p. 53, and *The Royall Slave*, II, 5, p. 109.
[30] *The Platonic Lovers* (*Works*, II), III, p. 52.   [31] *Ibid.*, V, p. 104.

Fie! fie! profess a friendship, and presume
To gull me with a lady's paradox.[32]

Yet D'Avenant, like Cartwright, was essentially cautious in his anti-Platonic confessions. Among romantic dramatists, Suckling alone indulged in a really spirited arraignment of the new religion. Suckling's raillery is striking in view of the decided romantic bias of all but a few pages of his dramatic work. In *Aglaura* the group of sceptical gallants hold their own quite successfully against the opposing party. In one scene Orsames, Philan, and a couple of courtiers actually assail the popular mode in a raillery contest.

Ors. . . . I'll tell you, gallants; 'tis now, since first I
Found myself a little hot and quivering 'bout the heart,
Some ten days since; a tedious ague, sirs:
But what of that?
The gracious glance and little whisper pass'd,
Approaches made from th' hand unto the lip,
I came to visit her, and, as you know we use
Breathing a sigh or two by way of prologue,
Told her that in love's physic 'twas a rule,
Where the disease had birth, to seek a cure.
I had no sooner nam'd love to her, but she
Began to talk of flames, and flames
Neither devouring nor devour'd, of air
And of chameleons.

1 Court. O the Platonics!

2 Court. Those of the new religion in love! your lordship's merry,
Troth, how do you like the humour on't?

Ors. . . .
A mere trick to enhance the price of kisses.

Phi. Surely, these silly women, when they feed
Our expectation so high, do but like
Ignorant conjurors, that raise a spirit,
Which handsomely they cannot lay again.[33]

---

[32] *Ibid.*, IV, p. 65.
[33] Cf. Jonson's *The New Inn* (*Works*, V), III, 2, pp. 371–372. Prudence, presiding officer of the Court of Love, warns Lady Frampul, who begins to encourage her eloquent Platonic suitor:

Beware you do not conjure up a spirit
You cannot lay.

Ors. True, 'tis like some that nourish up
Young lions, till they grow so great they are afraid of
Themselves: they dare not grant at last,
For fear they should not satisfy.
    Phi. Who's for the town? I must take up again.
    Ors. This villanous love's as changeable as the
philosopher's stone, and thy mistress as hard to compass too!
    Phi. The Platonic is ever so; they are as tedious,
Before they come to the point, as an old man
Fall'n into the stories of his youth.
    2 Court. Or a widow into the praises of her first husband.[34]

A more serious attack on Platonic notions would not have been feasible in a drama designed for court performance.

Suckling wrote a single comedy, *The Goblins* (1638). The play is memorable, despite its lack of dramatic merit, for its pronounced emphasis on anti-Platonic views. Suckling was quite aware of the sources of comic effect inherent in the artificial attitudes of the new religion. Although, as a favored courtier, he could never indulge his comic muse with real freedom, in *The Goblins*, under cover of a thin comic intrigue, he ventured to laugh more heartily and more indiscreetly than in his other plays. In *The Goblins* the Platonic pageant is no longer insured at its face value; its agreeable illusions are perceived as such.

The young prince Orsabrin, an important character in this comedy, becomes an adept in Platonic courtship as soon as he falls in love. His original sympathies, however, are of the opposite sort. Early in the play, Orsabrin avails himself of a servant's mistake as to his identity to rush into the apartment of an unknown lady, where, hardly daring to speak and uncertain how to proceed, he takes a chance at kissing the lady. Sabrina, mistaking him for her expected lover, indignantly chides him:

> What saucy heat hath stol'n into thy blood,
> And height'nd thee to this? I fear you are
> Not well.

---

[34] *Aglaura* (*Works*, I), II, pp. 111–112.

And the chagrined young adventurer exclaims in a dismayed aside:

> Sfoot! 'tis a Platonic:
> Now cannot I so much as talk that way neither.[35]

Sabrina and her lover Samorat are rigid Platonics. Yet Suckling does not permit their love ceremonies to remain unchallenged. Samorat's companions, the saucy cavaliers Nassurat and Pellegrin, seize every opportunity to poke fun at the Platonic madness of their friend. Their amusement is at its height when, in the course of a dangerous journey, they discover Samorat absorbed in a love trance, meditating, as the faithful Platonic should, on the charms of the absent Sabrina.

> *Nassurat.* Look, four fathom and a half O O S
> In contemplation of his mistress.
> There's a feast! you and I are out now, Pellegrin.
> 'Tis a pretty trick, this enjoying in absence!
> What a rare invention 'twould be,
> If a man could find out a way to make it real!
>   *Pellegrin.* Dost think there's nothing in't, as 'tis?
>   *Nassurat.* Nothing, nothing.
>   *Pellegrin.* Didst never hear of a dead Alexander
> Rais'd to talk with a man?
> Love is a learned conjuror, and with
> The glass of fancy will do as strange things!
> You thrust out a hand; your mistress
> Thrusts out another. You shake that hand:
> That shakes you again: you put out a lip:
> She puts out hers. Talk to her; she shall
> Answer you. Marry! when you come
> To grasp all this, it is but air.[36]

The cynical cavaliers have a distinct advantage over their victim, for they are on the side of common sense.

Nassurat and Pellegrin are responsible for most of the merriment in *The Goblins*. They are cavaliers on a holiday, revelling in their liberty. In former times, they confess, they were such

---

[35] *The Goblins* (*Works*, II), II, p. 19.
[36] *Ibid.*, IV, p. 40.

"dull fools" [37] as to besiege a face three months for the trifle of a kiss. But from such Platonic bondage they are temporarily released. Light-hearted flirtations become their most serious activities. Drinking songs and wit contests fill in the remaining hours. A sojourn in prison, under sentence of death, has no sobering effect upon the joyous pair. Nassurat merely regrets that he must pass his mistress' window on his way to execution and Pellegrin that he must break an appointment with a merchant's wife.[38] In their general outlook on life Nassurat and Pellegrin resemble the gay young heroes of Restoration comedy. On the other hand, the two cavaliers are but minor characters, and their career has no vestige of dignity. Suckling does not deprive them of natural sagacity, but he cannot safely permit them to set an anti-Platonic standard for his romantic comedy. In their more frivolous pastimes, Suckling frequently degrades these rebel gallants to about the status of Restoration false wits.

The favorite sport of Nassurat and Pellegrin is the exchange of similitudes. Each prides himself upon his ingenuity in devising unique comparisons or in matching those of his comrade, and each compliments the other upon his rare conceits. In one amusing scene they sharpen their wits at the expense of a gaoler whom they have gagged.

> *Nassurat.* . . .
> How d' you, Sir?   [*To the Gaoler gagg'd*
> You gape, as if you were sleepy. Good faith,
> He looks like an *O yes*!
>
> *Pellegrin.* Or as if he had overstrain'd himself
> At a deep note in a ballad.
>
> *Nassurat.* What think you of an oyster at a low ebb? [39]

This last masterly similitude, it is interesting to note, was achieved, at a later date, by the coxcomb Brisk in Congreve's *The Double-Dealer*. In a conversation in which Lord Froth and Brisk are trying to outdo each other in malicious gossip about the so-

---

[37] *Ibid.*, IV, p. 47.   [38] *Ibid.*, V, p. 60.   [39] *Ibid.*, III, p. 29.

ciety people of their acquaintance, Brisk remarks triumphantly that the aspect of Lady Toothless' mouth, when she laughs, is "Like an oyster at low ebb, egad — Ha! ha! ha!" [40] Sometimes the similitudes are not produced with ease. Nassurat, striving for one more figure with which to distinguish the gaoler mentioned above, observes:

> . . . You are —
> Pox on him, what is he, Pellegrin? [39]

Again, Pellegrin, attempting to picture Nassurat disguised as a fiddler, exclaims, impatient at the failure of his invention:

> Pox on thee, thou look'st like, I cannot tell what.[41]

In the same fashion, the similitude-loving Dapperwit in Wycherley's *Love in a Wood* toils after trivial comparisons. Struggling to characterize a wit who is without vanity, Dapperwit falters dejectedly: "He is like — I think I am a sot to-night, let me perish." [42] It can hardly be by accident that the false wits of Wycherley and Congreve revive the conversational habits of Suckling's cavaliers.

The most elaborate similitude contest of Nassurat and Pellegrin occurs after a country dance, when the two wits rival each other in descriptions of some of the dancers:

> *Nassurat.* 'Tis a rare wench, she i' th' blue stockings:
> What a complexion she had, when she was warm!
> 'Tis a hard question of these country wenches,
> Which are simpler, their beauties or themselves.
> There's as much difference betwixt
> A town lady and one of these,
> As there is betwixt a wild pheasant and a tame.
>   *Pellegrin.* Right:
> There goes such essencing, washing, perfuming,
> And daubing to th' other, that they are
> The least part of themselves. Indeed,
> There's so much sauce a man cannot taste the meat.

---

[40] *The Double-Dealer*, III, 3, p. 147.
[41] *The Goblins (Works,* II), IV, p. 42.
[42] *Love in a Wood*, V, 1, p. 104.

> *Nassurat.* Let me kiss thee for that.[43]
> By this light, I hate a woman drest up to her height,
> Worse than I do sugar with muscadine.
>
> .   .   .   .
>
> Sirrah, didst mark the lass i' th' green upon yellow,
> How she bridled in her head,
> And danc'd — a stroke in and a stroke out,
> Like a young fillet, training to a pace?
>   *Pellegrin.* And how she kiss'd!
> As if she had been sealing and delivering herself
> Up to the use of him that came last:
> Parted with her sweetheart's lips still
> As unwillingly and untowardly
> As soft wax from a dry seal.[44]

The dialogue suggests the methods of argument of the companion fops, Witwoud and Petulant, in Congreve's *The Way of the World*. Indeed, the main conventions governing the display of Restoration false wit are already well outlined in Suckling's comedy.

It is not surprising that the influences of contemporary *préciosité* manifested themselves but slightly in the realistic comedies composed during the reign of Charles I. Any sustained satire of the new vogue would have been foolhardy enough, at a time when its chivalric passions were fanned by Majesty itself. Such plays as D'Avenant's *The Wits* (1634) and *News from Plymouth* (1635), Cartwright's *The Ordinary* (1635), and Mayne's *The City Match* (1639) are typical representatives of contemporary. comedy, showing how persistently the fashions of Jonson, Fletcher, and Shirley still dominated this field of dramatic production and how rarely new court fashions found expression there.

At times, comedies written mainly in the Elizabethan style afford a few hints of *précieuse* influence. Such is the case with Shakerley Marmion's three comedies, *Holland's Leaguer* (1632),

[43] Cf. Congreve's *The Way of the World*, IV, 1, p. 383. Witwoud commends Petulant:

> Thou dost bite, my dear mustard-seed; kiss me for that.

[44] *The Goblins* (*Works*, II), IV, pp. 46–47.

A Fine Companion (1633), and *The Antiquary* (1636). For the most part, these plays are "rather thin imitations of Jonson." [45] Yet Marmion has a new interest in grotesquely affected gallantry, the natural consequence of the exaggerated *préciosité* of the day. At a time when the behavior of the most accomplished cavaliers of the court reached the farthest verge of decorous affectation, there were naturally a thousand comic possibilities for ludicrous conduct on the part of the foppishly inclined. In each of his plays Marmion gives at least one full-length portrait of a ridiculous gallant. Spruse in *A Fine Companion* is probably the best of the type. He makes his initial appearance with an untied garter, apropos of which he delivers to his friend Careless the woeful announcement:

> I met with a disaster coming up. Something has ravisht the tassel of my garter, and discompos'd the whole fabric, 'twill cost me an hour's patience to reform it; I had rather have seen the Commonwealth out of order.[46]

Under his arm he bears a black box full of elegant love letters, any one of which can be directed and sent off at a moment's notice to the next fair mistress who shall attract his fancy. He is past master of the art "to counterfeit a passion and dissemble." [47] The sensible Valeria, to whom he confidently presents his suit, regrets that "the time's disease" of "compliment" [48] has so prevailed upon him. Of course, another lover gets ahead of him and carries off Valeria. But Spruse is still able to reflect cheerfully: "I have more mistresses than I can tell what to do with." [49] The career of Spruse indicates how amply the abuse of Platonic mannerisms could enlarge the rôle of the successors of Jonson's Fastidious Brisk.

In *The Varietie* (c. 1638) [50] by William Cavendish, Duke of Newcastle, anti-Platonic sympathies are to some extent illus-

---

[45] Bayne, *op. cit.*, p. 239.
[47] *Ibid.*, II, 1, p. 125.
[49] *Ibid.*, V, 2, p. 195.
[46] *A Fine Companion*, I, 5, p. 118.
[48] *Ibid.*, p. 128.
[50] Schelling, *op. cit.*, II, p. 284.

trated in the portrayal of the young hero Newman.　Through a love prognostication Newman has been warned that in a melancholy humor he will do something to endanger his life.　He scoffs at such fortune-telling and retires with his friends to a tavern, where he drinks sack and rails against love through most of the scenes in which he appears.　His songs are quite in the tone which Suckling adopts when he turns rebel to *précieuse* affectation. In a certain song which has, we are assured, "the pure spirit of Sack in't," [51] Newman jubilantly proclaims the cavalier program:

> For foure lines in passion I can dye
> As is the lovers guise,
> And dabble too in Poetry
> Whilst love-possesst, then wise
> As greatest States-men, or as those
> That know love best, yet live in Prose.[52]

Three realistic comedies written before the closing of the theatres in 1642 are thoroughly in the *précieuse* tradition.　These comedies are *The Country Captaine* (*c.* 1639), also by the Duke of Newcastle,[53] *The Guardian* (1641) by Abraham Cowley, and *The Parson's Wedding* (composed by 1642)[54] by Thomas Killigrew. All three authors, although devoted royalists, were very mediocre dramatists, and the plays have received very little attention from critics.　Each of the plays, however, brings valuable evidence to

[51] *The Varietie*, IV, p. 63.　　　　　[52] *Ibid.*, IV, pp. 62–63.
[53] It is frequently claimed that in *The Country Captaine* Shirley collaborated with the Duke of Newcastle (cf. Forsythe, *op. cit.*, p. 424).　It will be observed that the Platonic courtship scenes, which are the most important in the play, are quite foreign to Shirley's tastes.
[54] According to its title-page in the 1664 folio edition, *The Parson's Wedding* was written at Basel.　Fleay, *op. cit.*, II, p. 25, believes that the date of composition was *c.* 1635 and that the play was acted *c.* 1640 at Blackfriars, during a time when the plague was subsiding.　He notes a reference to the decline of the plague in III, 1, p. 109 (folio edition).　Montague Summers, *Restoration Comedies*, Introduction, p. xxix, argues that the play was not performed until 1663, when it was entered in Sir Henry Herbert's Office Book with the licensing fee for a new play.　At the same time, this critic concedes that very likely "Killigrew had his script ready and perhaps even in the actors' hands during the summer of 1642."

bear upon the ways in which Platonic customs acquired a new emphasis, as the court mode waned, and began to enforce new interests in realistic comedy. The romantic seriousness which Suckling never wholly excluded from his drama no longer dignifies these plays. Platonic gallantry is still admired, but the wise have ceased to believe its protestations. Those who still read its signs with solemn literalness have become the best possible victims of the Comic Muse.

The Country Captaine records an interesting Platonic courtship in Sir Francis' wooing of Lady Huntlove. "Noble Sir Francis," [55] as the Lady's husband terms him, is by no means a second edition of crude Kickshaw in *The Lady of Pleasure*. He is a polished courtier, well trained in the elegant ceremonies of the day, but enacting them in an anti-Platonic spirit. The Lady herself is unmistakably a *précieuse*. In wooing her, her "servant," Sir Francis, takes cognizance of that fact, and gracefully and ingeniously exploits the principles of the new religion to serve his ends. The first wooing scene deserves quotation.

Fran. Will you consider, Madam, yet, how much a wounded heart may suffer?

Lad. Still the old buisnesse; indeede you make me blush, but, I forgive you, if you will promise to solicite this unwelcome cause no more.

Fran. Tis my desire; I take no pleasure in A pilgrimage. If you instruct A nearer way: 'tis in your selfe to save your eares, the trouble of my pleadinge, Madame, if with one softe breath you say I am intertained, but for one smile, that speakes consent; you make my life your servant.

Lad. My husband, Sir.

Fran. Deserves not such a treasure to him self, and starve a nobler servant.

Lad. You but plead for vanitie, for if I could, forgetting my honour and my modestie, allow your wild desires, it were impossible that wee should meete more then in thought and shaddow.

Fran. If those shaddowes be but dark enough, I shall account it happinesse to meete you, but refer that to opportunity which our kinde Starrs, in pittie will soone offer to both our joyes.

---

[55] *The Country Captaine*, V, p. 92.

Lad. But hee is very Jealous.

Fran. That word assures my victory, I never heard any wife accuse her husband of cold neglect or Jealousie, but she had a confirm'd thought to trick his forehead. *Asid.* It is but Justice, Madam, to reward him for his suspicious thoughts.

Lad. Doe you think it fitt, to punish his suspition, yet perswayd to act the sinn he feares?

Fran. Custome and nature make it less offence in women . . . then men to doubt their charities,[56] this flowing from poysoned natures, that excused by fraylties, yet I have hearde the way to cure the feare has bin the deede, at truth the scruples vanish. I speake not Madame, with A thought to suffer A fowle breath, whisper Your white name, for hee that dares tradduce you, must beleeve me dead, for my fame twisted with your honnor, must not have pitty on the accusers blood.[57]

The Platonic aspects of this wooing, it will be observed, are: the lover's promise of constancy, his conviction that worthy love must not be denied, his assurance that this love is heaven-directed, his denunciation of jealousy, and his pledge of secrecy at all costs. The Lady is so overcome by his charming discourse that she cannot reply to his final burst of eloquence.

Throughout the play this courtship proceeds with the same outward show of Platonic fervor. Sir Francis' ecstatic soliloquies are all couched in elegant rhetoric. Only once does his love service fail in courtesy, upon which occasion he chides himself, in the usual fashion of Platonic lovers, with the rebuke:

. . . How shall I looke upon her face, whose love and bold adventure I have thus rewarded? but passion will not cure my wounde which must bleede till I see her, and then either ceasse blessed by her pardon; or dismisse a life though just, too poore a sacrifice to her Anger.[58]

For her yielding to Sir Francis' solicitation, the Lady has a novel excuse to offer, an excuse which had not been possible in the case of Shirley's Lady Bornwell. Her lover's eloquence, Lady Hunt-

[56] Cf. Suckling, *Works*, I, p. 37:

> I hate a fool that starves her love
> Only to feed her pride.

[57] *The Country Captaine*, I, pp. 17–18.
[58] *Ibid.*, IV, p. 70.

love maintains, has beguiled her. When he reforms,[59] at the close of the play, she can assert:

> There is a blessing falne upon my bloud: your only thoughts charme had power to make my thoughts wicked, and your conversion disenchants me. . . . [60]

The play ends with a stout moral emphasis, Sir Francis' tardy conviction: " Preserve your Marriage faith — " [60] Yet it is evident that Lady Huntlove's intrigue has not been viewed, even by the dramatist, as an altogether ugly affair, and that her weakness he has at least partially condoned. The verdict called for seems to be such a one as Suckling, in a certain letter to a friend, shrewdly bestowed upon the conduct of a group of Platonic ladies at court: "and if there be any have suffered themselves to be gained by their servants, their ignorance of what they granted may well excuse them from the shame of what they did." [61] Without knowing it, Lady Huntlove has been playing with fire. Her perfect faith in Platonic formulas is naïve and amusing. Because of her lack of astuteness, Sir Francis is able to traduce in practice, with dangerous. success, the courtly idealism of the Platonic creed.

Cowley's *The Guardian* is a play which is chiefly remembered for one ludicrous character. It is a rather crude and boisterous comedy, written by the author while he was still at Cambridge. Never quite satisfied with this youthful effort, Cowley rewrote the play in the Commonwealth period as *The Cutter of Coleman-Street*. Charles Lamb regarded *The Cutter of Coleman-Street* as "a link between the Comedy of Fletcher and of Congreve." [62] The

---

[59] Sir Francis plans to feign an accident in order to obtain a secret meeting with Lady Huntlove. The accident actually occurs, and both repent. Cf. Fletcher's *Rule a Wife and Have a Wife* (*Works*, IX), V, 3, pp. 464–467, where an intriguing lover feigns a wounded state in order to interview his lady; the husband learns the trick, and the guilty pair repent.

[60] *Ibid.*, V, p. 92.   [61] Suckling, *Works*, II, "Letters," p. 210.

[62] *The Works of Charles and Mary Lamb*, ed. E. V. Lucas, IV; "Dramatic Specimens and the Garrick Plays," p. 432.

character of Puny especially attracted Lamb's attention and appeared to him "the prototype of the half-witted Wits, the Brisks and Dapper Wits" [62] of Congreve. This admirable, although apparently forgotten, criticism is also applicable to *The Guardian.* The first Puny is somewhat hurriedly sketched, but he "pretends to wit" in the same manner as the more delightful Puny of a later date. In the false wit of this affected gallant the extravagances of *précieuse* speech are plainly satirized.

In addition to Puny, *The Guardian* features two other grotesque cavaliers, Cutter, a "sharking" soldier, and Dogrel, a "sharking" poetaster. The three gallants frequently appear together. Cutter and Dogrel have some taste for matching similitudes, and are loudly praised by Puny for their occasional achievements in this line. But in the main the field of similitude invention is Puny's own. To his amazing comparisons, turned out in brisk succession, the others listen, half in amusement, half in scorn. Although a minor actor in the drama, in his own estimation Puny is a very important person. He has immense confidence in his power to conduct an intrigue. Adopting his first disguise, he assures Dogrel: "I warrant you I'll whisper like wet wood in a Justice's chimney at Christmas." [63] As a matter of fact, he bungles affairs absurdly and is a notorious coward. His similitudes justify his existence. They grace his first speech and almost his last. Whenever he appears, quaint figures and preposterous epithets form the fabric of his conversation. Puny himself osberves: "I shall ne'er abstain from these fine things, hyperboles and similitudes." [64] Captain Blade reproves him:

. . . Yet you forsooth, because you see some Gentlemen and Poets of late, a little extravagant sometimes in their similitudes; because they make a pretty kind of sound to those that mark 'um not; make that your way of

---

[63] *The Guardian* (ed. Waller), III, 4, p. 193.
[64] *Ibid.*, III, 4, p. 194.

wit, and never speak without comparisons. But never were comparisons so odious as thine are . . . [65]

Whereupon Puny retaliates: " The Captains raging mad like a Baker when his oven is over heated." [65] The similitudes of Puny are much like those of Suckling's Nassurat and Pellegrin. But Suckling's cavaliers are shrewd enough in their way, while Puny is nine-tenths pure foppishness, like Brisk or Witwoud. Cowley was the first among seventeenth century dramatists to deride false wit in the spirit of Congreve.

Killigrew's *The Parson's Wedding* is not greatly superior as a comedy to *The Country Captaine* and *The Guardian*. With considerable monotony of effect Killigrew revives in this play the well-worn stock incidents of Elizabethan comedy.[66] He indulges so immoderately in licentious humor that Pepys' verdict, "a bawdy loose play," [67] is perhaps not too severe. The play is also carelessly organized and most tediously discursive. Nevertheless, as an historical document, *The Parson's Wedding* is much more important than either of the two plays just reviewed. It furnishes our only available record, and an apparently authentic one, of the decline of the Platonic cult and of the social readjustment that followed.

With curious exactness *The Parson's Wedding* defines the cavalier spirit in England on the eve of civil warfare. Clearly, the old order is passing. Pleasant reminds the widow:

I, I, and they were happy dayes, Wench, when the Captain was a lean, poor, humble thing, and the Souldier tame, and durst not come within the City, for fear of a Constable and a Whipping-post; they know the penal Statutes give no Quarter; then Buff was out of countenance, and sculk'd from Ale-house to Ale-house, and the City had no Militia but the Sheriffs-

---

[65] *Ibid.*, IV, 3, p. 207.
[66] Summers, *op. cit.*, pp. xxi–xxvii, discusses at some length the sources and analogues of *The Parson's Wedding*.
[67] Pepys, *Diary*, IV, p. 247. Pepys refers to the 1664 performance. Modern criticism has mainly echoed Pepys' opinion. Cf. Ward, *op. cit.*, III, p. 166, and Schelling, *op. cit.*, II, p. 302.

CARL A. RUDISILL LIBRARY
LENOIR RHYNE COLLEGE

men: in those merry days a Bailiff trode the streets with terror, when all the Chains in the City were rusty, but Mr. Sheriffs, when the people knew no evil but the Constable and his Watch; Now every Committee has as much power, and as little manners and examines with as much ignorance, impertinence and authority, as a Constable in the Kings key.[68]

The social gallantries of the régime of Charles I are darkly shadowed. The "divine Lovers"[69] still dwell at court, but the once famous Platonic fashions are sadly in decline. Regarding the scarcity of Platonic servants, the Widow assures Pleasant:

> Faith, Niece, this Parliament has so destroy'd 'em, and the Platonic Humour, that 'tis uncertain whether we shall get one or no; your leading Members in the lower House have so cow'd the Ladies, that they have no leisure to breed any of late; Their whole endeavors are spent now in feasting, and winning close Committee-men, a rugged kind of sullen Fellows, with implacable stomachs and hard hearts, that make the gay things court and observe them, as much as the foolish Lovers use to do.[70]

Among the Widow's acquaintances there is only one Platonic lady of renown, "smitten in years o' th' wrong side of forty," who still graces "this lean Age for Courtiers."[70] Meditating on the former charms of this elderly Penthesilea, Pleasant reflects ruefully:

> And that Tongue, I warrant you, which now grows hoarse with flattering the great Law-breakers, once gave Law to Princes: was it not so, Aunt? Lord, shall I die without begetting one story?[70]

It is plain that Pleasant and the Widow have romantic leanings in the direction of this now old religion in love.

The young cavaliers of the play have no such sentimental regrets at the passing of that "spiritual Non-sence the age calls Platonick Love."[71] They gaily exploit its conventions. Jolly and the Captain gracefully extract Lady Love-all's jewels from her possession by masquerading as her Platonic suitors. This amorous old woman, precursor of one of the most familiar types in Restoration comedy, blandly assures the world that "there's none that sacrifices more to friendship-love then I."[72] Careless

[68] *The Parson's Wedding*, I, 2, pp. 79–80.   [69] *Ibid.*, II, 7, p. 105.
[70] *Ibid.*, V, 2, p. 140.   [71] *Ibid.*, I, 3, p. 86.   [72] *Ibid.*, II, 2, p. 90.

well knows her for what she is, "a right broken Gamester, who, though she lacks wherwithall to play, yet loves to be looking on." [73] The Platonic hypocrisies of the unlovely old coquette have become fitting material for purely comic treatment.

The Platonic inclinations of the two heroines, on the other hand, are more genuine and require more artful consideration on the part of their cavalier lovers. The cavaliers take revenge in characteristic fashion. Careless and Wild confidentially discuss with each other an amusing twofold program which they intend to employ in all future courtship of ladies.

Care. I am resolv'd to put on their own silence and modesty, . . . sigh when 'tis proper, and with forc'd studies betray the enemy, who seeing my eye fix'd on her, her vanity thinks I am lost in admiration, calls and shakes me e'er I wake out of my design, and being collected, answer out of purpose. Love, divinest? yes, who is it that is mortal and do's not? or which amongst all the Senate of the Gods, can gaze upon those eyes, and carry thence the power he brought? this will start her.

Wild. Yes, and make her think thee mad.

Care. Why that's my design; for then I start too, and rub my eyes as if I wak'd, then sigh and strangle a yawn, 'till I have wrung it into tears, with which I rise, as if o'ercome with grief; then kiss her hands, and let fall those witnesses of faith and love, brib'd for my design. This takes; for who would suspect such a Devil as Craft and Youth to live together? . . .

Wild. This is the way; and be sure to dislike all but her you design for, be scarce civil to any of the sex besides.

Care. That's my meaning, But to her I mean my prey, all her slave; she shall be my Deity, and her opinion my religion.

Wild. And while you sad it thus to one, I'll talk freer than a privileg'd fool, and swear as unreasonably as losing Gamesters, and abuse thee for thinking to reclaim a woman by thy love; call them all bowls thrown that will run where they will, and Lovers like fools run after them, . . . I believe none fair, none handsome, none honest but the kind. [74]

Thus the chivalric ceremonies of court Platonism have degenerated into a meaningless ritual, lightly and cynically garbled and openly scoffed at by its own votaries.

[73] *Ibid.*, IV, 8, p. 121. Cf. Wycherley's *Love in a Wood*, IV, 3, p. 88. Dapperwit uses the figure, "as a bankrupt gamester loves to look on, though he has no advantage by the play."

[74] *Ibid.*, II, 5, pp. 94–95.

The new ethics is still hotly debated, however. *The Parson's Wedding* is provided with one especially long *précieuse* debate on the subject of lovers' conduct. At a very formal dinner party, the Widow and Pleasant, supported by their servants Sadd and Constant, combat the arguments in defense of inconstancy in love presented by Careless, Jolly, the Captain, and Wild. The ladies hope that the mild Sadd and Constant will be able to return "hit for hit," but, as a matter of fact, the opposed party wins a conspicuous triumph. A brief portion of the dialogue may be submitted, to indicate the temper of the whole.

Capt. I am but a poor Souldier, and yet never reach'd to the Honour of being a Lover; yet from my own observations, master Sadd, take a Truth; 'tis a folly to believe any Woman loves a Man for being constant to another; they dissemble their hearts only, and hate a man in love worse than a Wencher.

Jolly. And they have Reason; for if they have the grace to be kind, he that loves the Sex may be theirs.

Care. When your constant Lover, if a Woman have a mind to him, and be blest with so much grace to discover it; He, out of the noble mistake of Honour, hates her for it, and tells it perchance, and preaches Reason to her Passion, and cryes, miserable beauty, to be so unfortunate as to inhabit so much frailty!

Capt. This counsel makes her hate him more than she lov'd before; These are troubles, those that love are subject to; while we look on and laugh, to see both thus slav'd while we are free.

Care. My prayers still shall be, Lord deliver me from Love.

Capt. 'Tis Plague, Pestilence, Famine, Sword, and sometimes sudden death.

Sadd. Yet I love, I must love, I will love, and I do love.

Capt. In the present tense.

Wid. No more of this argument, for Loves sake.

Capt. By any means, Madam, give him leave to love; and you are resolv'd to walk tied up in your own Armes, with your Love as visible in your face, as your Mistresses colours in your hat; that any Porter at Charing-Cross may take you like a Letter at the Carriers, and having read the superscription deliver Master Sadd to the fair hands of Mistress or my Lady such a one, lying at the sign of the hard heart.

Pleas. And she, if she has wit (as I believe she hath) will scarce pay the Post for the Pacquet.

Wid. Treason! how now, Niece, joyn with the Enemy?
(*They give the Captain wine.*
Capt. A health, Ned, what shall I call it?
Care. To Master Sadd, he needs it that avowes himself a Lover.[75]

No other conversation in the play is managed with such elaborate formality. Yet all the actors are of an argumentative turn of mind. Even Wanton, the courtesan, prefers an argument with her maid Baud on the subject of the qualities desirable in a husband, to any less earnest form of discourse.[76] Wit is most frequently exercised through the medium of raillery. In one notable scene a group of gallants "comb their heads, and talk," [77] debating the pleasures of the town versus those of the country and kindred themes.

The ambitious dialogues in *The Parson's Wedding* are by no means succinct and finished specimens of their kind. Nevertheless, "the Noble Science of Wit" [78] is duly esteemed, and its mastery is regarded as the first requisite of fine conduct. Pleasant desires for a husband "a gentleman that has wit and honour, though he has nothing but a sword by his side." [79] And the Captain excuses the doubtful propriety of the bride-stealing engaged in by Careless and Wild on the basis that if the ladies "have wit" [80] they will forgive the adventure. When morality suffered through the priority of regard accorded to wit, it was doubtless more often in appearance than in reality. When Careless impudently courts Wanton in the presence of his bride, Wild explains to the troubled Widow:

. . . Aunt, take my word for your husband, that have had more experience of him then all these; . . . and you must not wonder, nor quarrel at what he says in his humor, but Judge him by his Actions. . . . [81]

Here, for a moment, the social mask has been lifted, as Shirley lifted it in the case of his heroine Carol. But now graver issues

[75] *Ibid.*, II, 7, p. 102.
[77] *Ibid.*, I, 3, p. 80.
[79] *Ibid.*, I, 2, p. 78.
[81] *Ibid.*, V, 4, p. 151.

[76] *Ibid.*, II, 3, pp. 92–93.
[78] *Ibid.*, II, 7, p. 100.
[80] *Ibid.*, IV, 7, p. 134.

are involved, for social attitudinizing is no longer innocent of ethical compromise.

As perceived in comedy, the *précieuse* game assumes a new significance. No longer, as in D'Avenant's drama, do mere good faith and a fluent mastery of courtly phrases promise successful gallantry. Those who read aright the signs of the times scoff at Platonic ideals, although they still illustrate with ready zeal Platonic mannerisms. A sober Platonic like Lady Huntlove is the dupe of a clever lover. An old coquette like Lady Love-all, who through vanity accepts in earnest Platonic compliments, is easily beguiled by sagacious cavaliers. The stage is already set for Etherege's Lady Cockwood and Congreve's Lady Wishfort. In like manner, the aping of wit by such a dullard as Puny is to true gentlemen a reasonable source of mirth. As in Restoration comedy, facile abuse of similitudes is unmistakable evidence of false wit.

The Parson's Wedding makes clear what the social game means to those who can play it adroitly. No longer believing in the Platonic cult, people of fashion still regard its artifices of conduct as attractive and its *préciosité* of speech, when not muddled by fools, a brave habit. It is true that the popular mode restricts within its rigid limits the vitality of all participants in the social game and effectively curbs genuine self-expression. Judged by an implied rational standard, the posing of the most skilful gamesters is comic, just as, judged by the social standard, the cruder posing of their victims is also comic. From the social standard there is no authorized appeal. Discerning gallants perceive its artificiality, even rail at it sometimes, but its graciousness still charms them, as it was to charm, a few years later, the fashionable world of *The Man of Mode*.

CHAPTER V

THE PRÉCIEUSE TRADITION, 1642–1664

BETWEEN the closing of the theaters in 1642 and the performance of Etherege's first comedy in 1664, the dramatic critic, however sedulous his investigation, finds little progress to record in any form of English drama. The popular assumption, however, that the drama was actually without life during this period, or at least during the interregnum, has no foundation of truth. Under the Commonwealth régime old plays were still acted, at great hazards, and earlier dramatic traditions were not allowed to fade into oblivion. It is of little consequence that few new plays were written. The *précieuse* impulse, which had directed court tastes in the reign of Charles I, denied a favorable expression in dramatic literature, was diffused through other channels. At the Restoration in 1660 familiar dramatic conventions were revived. A few years of transitional experiment were, of course, inevitable. Yet even before 1664 the dominance of the *précieuse* mode was already pledged in both heroic drama and comedy. Only by examining this obscure historical background can we perceive what *The Comical Revenge* really signified to Etherege's contemporaries.

Our knowledge of dramatic performances during the interregnum will perhaps never be as extensive as we might well desire to have it. We are just beginning to realize that plays were acted much more frequently in the Commonwealth period than the meagre evidence ordinarily presented would lead us to suppose. For a good many years critics were obliged to rely heavily, for their guarded assertions, on the brief account of stage conditions during these years furnished by James Wright in his

107

Historia Histrionica (1699). Wright testifies that at the close of the civil war, in which most of the actors had served the king "like good men and true," there were some attempts at surreptitious stage performances. The actors still alive formed one company "and in the winter before the king's murder, 1648, they ventured to act some plays, with as much caution and privacy as could be, at the Cockpit." [1] While presenting *The Bloody Brother* these actors were arrested by a party of footsoldiers, conveyed to prison, and plundered of their clothes before being released. In Oliver's time, Wright continues, there was some private acting, especially at noblemen's houses; and annually at Christmas and Bartholomew Fair performances were given for a few days at the Red Bull, subject to raids by the soldiers.

The sparseness of Wright's record has recently been made apparent by the discoveries of Hyder E. Rollins, who has written "the first coherent story of the Commonwealth Drama." [2] From Commonwealth documents, especially from news-books, Rollins has collected a fairly large number of items regarding the activity of certain theaters between 1642 and 1660. He has shown conclusively that plays were acted at the Fortune in 1643 and 1647, that they were given from time to time, at any rate, at the Cockpit and at Salisbury Court, and that the Red Bull "managed to present plays with some regularity throughout the entire interregnum." [3] In 1647, when the war was considered ended, plays were acted with little or no attempt at concealment, at the Fortune, Cockpit, and Salisbury Court. Nor did the ordinance of July 17, which was to enforce the suppression of plays until the following January, effectively check these unlawful diversions. On February 9, 1648, a much stricter ordinance was passed, requiring the punishment of actors, the demolishing of theatrical

[1] James Wright, *Historia Histrionica*, in Hazlitt's Dodsley, XV, p. 409.
[2] Hyder E. Rollins, "A Contribution to the History of English Commonwealth Drama," in *Studies in Philology* (July, 1921), XVIII, p. 268.
[3] *Ibid.*, p. 271.

equipment, and the fining of all spectators of plays. By the next September, however, the actors had recovered composure, and the House of Commons was informed "that Stage-playes were daily acted, either at the Bull or Fortune, or at the private House at Salisbury Court." [4] Theaters were frequently raided, to be sure, and the actors experienced many hardships. Rope-dancing, drolls, and amateur theatricals fared considerably better than the regular drama.

By dint of much tactful negotiation with government officials, Sir William D'Avenant managed to produce in May, 1656, his "operatic venture," [5] *The First Day's Entertainment at Rutland House.* The fact that D'Avenant had a very definite ulterior purpose beyond the tedious debates of this composition is revealed in the challenge of the closing lines of the epilogue:

> Perhaps, some were so cozen'd as to come,
> To see us weave in the dramatic loom:
> To trace the winding scenes, like subtle spies
> Bred in the Muses' camp, safe from surprise:
> Where you by art learn joy, and when to mourn;
> To watch the plot's swift change and counterturn:
> When Time moves swifter than by nature taught,
> And by a *Chorus* miracles are wrought,
> Making an infant instantly a man:
> These were your plays, but get them if you can.[6]

This entertainment was followed by D'Avenant's opera of *The Siege of Rhodes* (Part I), given at Rutland House in August, 1656, and at the Cockpit in 1659, and two more operas, *The Cruelty of the Spaniards in Peru* (1658) and *The History of Sir Francis Drake* (1659), both presented at the Cockpit. D'Avenant no doubt "trusted through this new medium of dramatic expression to lead gradually to the abolition of laws against the stage." [7] In December, 1658, Richard Cromwell and the Council of State

---

[4] Rollins, *op. cit.*, p. 291 (a quotation from *Perfect Occurrences*, September 1–8, p. 434). [5] *Ibid.*, p. 324.
[6] *The First Day's Entertainment at Rutland House* (*Works*, IV), pp. 229–230. [7] Rollins, *op. cit.*, p. 325.

appointed a committee to examine D'Avenant and the actors of *The Cruelty of the Spaniards in Peru*,[8] but nothing came of the investigation, and apparently "operas" remained unprohibited. With the Restoration D'Avenant's anxieties came to an end. In August, 1660, dramatic companies were established under the direction of D'Avenant and Killigrew, and the authority of the Restoration stage was assured.

The Commonwealth government was naturally hostile to the printing and acting of new plays. The new plays actually published or performed in defiance of Puritan sentiment were largely written by men of very indifferent talents and were decidedly ephemeral in their nature. Most of them took the form of satirical attacks on the present régime. John Tatham's *The Scots Figgaries* (pr. 1652) is probably the most outstanding play of the group. Among less ambitious efforts, most of them playlets rather than plays, may be mentioned *The Committee-Man Curried* (pr. 1647)[9] by Samuel Sheppard, *The Cuckows Nest at Westminster* (pr. 1648)[10] *Craftie Cromwell* (pr. 1648),[11] *The Tragedie of King Charles I* (pr. 1649, and surreptitiously acted),[12] *The Tragi-Comedy called New-Market-Fayre* (pr. 1649),[13] and *The Disease of the House* (pr. 1649)[14] by John Capon. The scope of these plays is indicated by their titles.[15]

Fortunately, the theaters still open continued to make use of the more popular masterpieces of the older drama. Even the

---

[8] *Ibid.*, p. 329.   [9] Cited by Rollins, *op. cit.*, p. 294.
[10] *Ibid.*, p. 297.   [11] Cited by Nettleton, *op. cit.*, p. 19.
[12] Cited by Rollins, "The Commonwealth Drama: Miscellaneous Notes," in *Studies in Philology* (January, 1923), XX, pp. 56–57.
[13] Rollins, *Studies in Philology*, XVIII, p. 298.
[14] *Ibid.*, pp. 306–307.
[15] Two pastoral dramas published during this period were *Astraea, or True Love's Myrrour* (pr. 1650) by Leonard Willan, a dramatic version of certain episodes in D'Urfé's *Astrée*, and *The Enchanted Lovers* (pr. 1658) by Sir William Lower. Cf. Homer Smith, "Pastoral Influence in the English Drama," in *Publications of the Modern Language Association of America* (1897), V, pp. 448–456.

drolls fulfilled a recognizable service in keeping fresh in the public mind certain comic scenes, culled chiefly from Beaumont and Fletcher, and Shakespeare, although even Newcastle's *The Varietie* was represented. We possess evidence of performances of *Wit without Money* (January, 1648, and December, 1654),[16] *The Scornful Lady* (summer of 1647),[17] *A King and No King* (October, 1647),[18] and *The Bloody Brother* (winter of 1648).[19] No doubt other well-known plays were revived, for our records are obviously fragmentary. At the risk of being "tuged to peisuses at them," [20] as one contemporary commentator puts it, many people still eagerly attended these theatrical performances. At all times, moreover, those who so desired might read their favorite plays in the new editions [21] that were issued throughout the interregnum period. In "The Prologue to the Gentry" of *The Tragedie of King Charles I* the audience is reminded:

> Though Johnson, Shakespeare, Goffe, and Davenant,
> Brave Sucklin, Beaumont, Fletcher, Shurley want
> The Life of action, and their learned lines
> Are loathed by the Monsters of the times;
> Yet your refined Soules can penetrate
> Their depth of merit.[22]

When the theaters were officially re-opened, Restoration dramatists needed only to quicken and invigorate dramatic sympathies and prejudices which had never really grown cold.

As long as the interregnum lasted, the leading royalist writers worked, at best, under depressing conditions. D'Avenant was an exile in France and subsequently a prisoner in England until 1654. Cowley and Thomas Killigrew were exiles until the

---

[16] Rollins, *Studies in Philology*, XVIII, p. 316, and Adams, *Shakespearean Playhouses*, p. 304.

[17] Rollins, *Studies in Philology*, XVIII, p. 280.

[18] *Ibid.*, p. 283.

[19] Cf. p. 108, n. 1, of this volume.

[20] Rollins, *Studies in Philology*, XX, p. 63 (quoted from *Memoirs of the Verney Family*).

[21] Cf. Rollins, *Studies in Philology*, XVIII, p. 302.

[22] Rollins, *Studies in Philology*, XX, p. 57.

Restoration.   Nevertheless, such men quietly went on writing, hoping for better days.   As dramatists they could not expect any immediate triumphs, but they had other ways of reaching the public ear.   Royalist poets and prose writers did much to preserve throughout this gloomy period the more gracious spirit of the court which they had loved and championed.

To cavalier poetry after 1642 Cowley's *The Mistress* (1647) seems to have been the most conspicuous contribution.   *The Mistress* is a collection of Platonic love poems in the style favored by Suckling and Carew a few years earlier.   In *My Diet* [23] Cowley reveals himself the perfect Platonic lover, asking his lady for no wages but the recognition of his service.   In *Coldness* [24] he discusses the temperature of love with all the frigid ingenuity of a Sylvandre.   He attempts an argument *Against Fruition* [25] in which he dutifully repeats Suckling's former conclusions.   His anti-Platonic moods are recorded with the same conventionality in such poems as *Honour* [26] and *The Inconstant.* [27]   The latter poem at once recalls Suckling's *The Guiltless Inconstant.*   Cowley boasts that he now loves all "Women-kind," detecting a different charm in every mistress and revelling in the fact that his own heart is mere tinder which "by every Spark is set on Fire." [28]   Cowley was an extremely popular poet in the seventeenth century, and his influence counts for a good deal in the continuance of the *précieuse* tradition.

A number of minor poets whose verses were published during this interval deserve some notice.   John Hall's *Poems* (1646)

---

[23] Abraham Cowley, *Poems*, ed. A. R. Waller, p. 89.
[24] *Ibid.*, pp. 113–114.   [25] *Ibid.*, pp. 98–99.
[26] *Ibid.*, pp. 144–145.   [27] *Ibid.*, pp. 133–134.
[28] See the opening lines of *The Guiltless Inconstant*, Suckling, *Works*, I, p. 54:

> My first love, whom all beauties did adorn,
> Firing my heart, suppress'd it with her scorn;
> Since like the tinder in my breast it lies,
> By every sparkle made a sacrifice.

include several interesting Platonic pieces. In *Platonick Love* [29] and *The Lure* [30] this poet praises a love freed from all taint of "earthliness." *A Sea Dialogue* [31] and *The Antipathy* [32] are fanciful debates, in which the speakers exchange similitudes in support of opposing points of view. Patrick Carey was the author of *Trivial Poems and Triolets* (1651), a small volume of gay cavalier lyrics. He resembles Suckling in the light-hearted celebration of his inconstancy. His heart, like Suckling's, is a "looking-glass," [33] which reflects the beauties of many mistresses. He also repeats Suckling's favorite rhymes. A serious Platonic emphasis is renewed in the *Poems, Elegies, Paradoxes and Sonnets* (1657) of Henry King. It is pleasant to remember that King's Platonic muse inspired the really lovely poem, *Tell me no more how fair she is.* Here the lover, having affirmed his endless but hopeless passion, voices the modest plea:

> I ask no pity, Love, from thee,
>   Nor will thy justice blame,
> So that thou wilt not envy me
>   The glory of my flame:
> Which crowns my heart whene'er it dies,
>   In that it falls her sacrifice.[34]

The most interesting of these minor poets is Mrs. Katherine Philips, "the Matchless Orinda." She was an ardent admirer of "the mighty Cowley" [35] and also of that "Prince of Fancy," [36] William Cartwright, whose "restored Poetry" [36] was enlightening a dull age. In her own eccentric fashion Mrs. Philips vigorously enforced the Platonic faith of both authors. In 1651 she founded her "Society of Friendship," a Platonic circle in which various persons, particularly women, under assumed poetic names illustrated as "friends" the ritual formerly associated in the

[29] *Minor Poets of the Caroline Period*, ed. George Saintsbury, II, p. 196.
[30] *Ibid.*, pp. 194–195.   [31] *Ibid.*, p. 191.   [32] *Ibid.*, p. 202.
[33] *Ibid.*, p. 456. See Suckling's elaborate use of this figure in *The Guiltless Inconstant.*
[34] *Ibid.*, III, p. 173.   [35] *Ibid.*, I, p. 577.   [36] *Ibid.*, p. 549.

Platonic system with lovers. The laws which regulated this unique fellowship are eloquently described in a group of poems written by Mrs. Philips herself between 1651 and 1664. As the director of the society Mrs. Philips appears to have had frequent difficulties with the recalcitrant Rosania, Regina, and others, who sometimes neglected for mere carnal pleasures their severe Platonic mission. However, Mrs. Philips had such a faith as martyrs die for and an optimistic disposition, and she wielded persistently her all too fluent pen. Her verses are important documents merely because of their ample exposition of revised Platonic doctrines. Love, even as Céladon and Sylvandre understood it, Mrs. Philips suspects of impurity. She transfers all the old habits of Platonic love to the "science" of Friendship, which is "Love refin'd and purg'd from all its dross." [37] Even by "friends" of opposite sexes thoughts of marriage may not be entertained. In such poems as *Friendship*,[38] *A Friend*,[39] and *Friendship in Emblem, or the Seal* [40] Orinda defines, with abundance of similitudes, each important step in the progress of a perfect friendship. Like the Platonic lovers of *Astrée*, Orinda and her Lucasia boast the angelic innocence of their affection, its divine sanction, its secrecy, and welcome the challenge of absence, when their souls may "hold intelligence" [41] in a sublime communion denied to common mortals.

Among Mrs. Philips' poems several Platonic dialogues are to be found. The best of these is *A Dialogue of Friendship Multiplied*. Musidorus and Orinda here debate as to whether a person should have more than one intimate friend. The argument is as follows:

Musidorus
Will you unto one single sense
Confine a starry Influence;
Or when you do the rays combine,

---

[37] *Ibid.*, p. 561.   [38] *Ibid.*, pp. 552–553.   [39] *Ibid.*, pp. 561–563.
[40] *Ibid.*, p. 529.   [41] *Ibid.*, p. 522.

To themselves only make them shine?
Love that's engross'd by one alone
Is envy, not affection.

Orinda
No, Musidorus, this would be
But Friendship's prodigality;
Union in rays does not confine,
But doubles lustre when they shine,
And souls united live above
Envy, as much as scatter'd Love.
    Friendship (like rivers) as it multiplies
    In many streams, grows weaker still and dies.

Musidorus
Rivers indeed may lose their force
When they divide or break their course;
For they may want some hidden Spring,
Which to their streams recruits may bring:
But Friendship's made of purest fire,
Which burns and keeps its stock entire.
    Love, like the Sun, may shed his beams
        on all
    And grow more great by being general.

Orinda
The purity of Friendship's flame,
Proves that from sympathy it came,
And that the hearts so close do knit,
They no third partner can admit;
Love like the Sun does all inspire,
But burns most by contracted fire.
    Then though I honour every worthy guest,
    Yet my Lucasia only rules my breast.[42]

The entire poem is reminiscent of Cartwright. Minor poet
though she was, Mrs. Philips unquestionably occupies an important position in both the social and the literary history of
Platonism in the interregnum period.

Translations of popular French romances absorbed the
energies of a number of English writers of this period. These
romances, the literary descendants of *Astrée*, were peculiarly
influential in keeping alive in France and in England the Platonic

[42] *Ibid.*, p. 588.

tastes of D'Urfé's time. The romances of La Calprenède and of Mademoiselle de Scudéry were in special favor in England from 1652 to the Restoration. The French originals were in most cases promptly translated, and new editions were frequently issued.[43] In the collection of *Letters from Dorothy Osborne to Sir William Temple* has been preserved the record of one young Englishwoman's intense delight in these romances, a delight which she undoubtedly shared with a host of her contemporaries.[44] *Artamène ou le Grand Cyrus* by Mademoiselle de Scudéry was Dorothy's favorite narrative and probably that of many other romance readers.

Artamène (translated as *Artamenes or The Grand Cyrus*) emphasizes a much more somber Platonism than D'Urfé's. The Platonic mistresses of *Artamène* are obsessed with a chilling sense of duty to parents or husbands, and their conduct is uniformly decorous. Gallants are too much frowned upon to become playful. Ligdamon and Cleonice are guilty of unusual levity in their trifling with what they term the "foolish affected Passion of Love,"[45] but even such supposedly madcap lovers are the palest possible shadows of Hylas and Stelle. Platonic ideals which are more rigorous, at times, than those of the most devout lovers in *Astrée*, are exhibited in innumerable "histories" of flawless gallantry. The Platonism of Cyrus is magnificent. He has never been jealous, his generosity to rivals knows no bounds, and in the presence of his mistress he dares "not so much as think upon his Passion, much lesse express it."[46] Intriguing women are responsible for his occasional quarrels with Mandana,

[43] For accounts of these translations see Herbert W. Hill, *La Calprenède's Romances and the Restoration Drama*, pp. 51–53, and Upham, *op. cit.*, pp. 390–398.

[44] Dorothy Osborne herself preferred the romances in their French form.

[45] *Artamenes, or The Grand Cyrus* (1653–1655 edition), vol. I, part IV, bk. 3, p. 298.

[46] *Ibid.*, vol. I, part I, bk. 2, p. 83.

merely because he is scrupulously polite to all women and never does anything "but in a gallant manner." [47] He is aware that Mandana's graciousness is excessive when she permits him to continue to love her. It is her austere conviction that "Love . . . is doubtless a Passion, which if it were possible we ought not to have." [48] Elisa and Sapho are still stricter Platonics. The latter declares: "And if I found in my heart only a base desire of marrying any one, I should blush as for a crime." [49] She persuades her Platonic servant Phaon to her point of view, although Phaon is sometimes pensive, remembering the hopelessness of his suit. The conversations of these Platonics generally take the form of debates on conventional themes of love and jealousy. The debates are quite as formal and artificial as those in *Astrée*, although similitudes are less frequently exchanged.[50] On one important occasion the issue is raised: *Which is most unfortunate, the lover whose mistress is dead, the absent lover, the lover not loved, or the jealous lover?* [51] This controversy particularly interested Dorothy Osborne, who carefully reasoned out her own verdict and begged Temple to agree with her.[52]

The other French romances differ from *Artamène* only by slight variations of emphasis. *Clélie*, also by Mademoiselle de Scudéry, has more ambitious Platonic discourses than occur elsewhere. The romances of La Calprenède, on the other hand, surpass all of Mademoiselle de Scudéry's in narrative interest. Everywhere the laws of Platonic gallantry are enforced.

Impressed by the popularity of these numerous romances,

[47] *Ibid.*, vol. II, part VI, bk. 3, p. 130.
[48] *Ibid.*, vol. I, part I, bk. 3, p. 130.
[49] *Ibid.*, vol. II, part X, bk. 2, p. 107.
[50] See, however, the elaborate similitude contest in vol. II, part IX, bk. 2, pp. 113–115, on the subject: *May a lover love the same lady twice?*
[51] *Ibid.*, vol. I, part III, bk. 1, p. 83.
[52] *Letters from Dorothy Osborne to Sir William Temple*, ed. Edward A. Parry, pp. 153–154.

Roger Boyle, Lord Broghill, later Earl of Orrery,[53] attempted to write an English romance of the same style in *Parthenissa* (1654, 1665). Dorothy Osborne began reading this romance in 1654 and was disappointed in it. While admiring the author's "handsome language," she found the book dull and insipid in comparison with *Artamène*.[54] It may be doubted whether many modern readers have had the patience to wade through Boyle's elegant and faded narrative. Of all the seventeenth century romances *Parthenissa* is the most artificial. For all the actors in the showy scene, life is reduced to a stupid business of fine speeches. Reality is avoided at every turn. One day, outside the temple at Hierapolis, the hero and his friend sit listening to a priest's Platonic "history" of his life, when a boat is seen ascending the river, and two ladies disembark who strikingly resemble the lost mistresses of the two young men. A servant is sent to make inquiries, but the priest and his listeners merely move away to a shadier spot, and the priest's story goes soberly on. Boyle never finished *Parthenissa*, and the two beautiful ladies will have to wait through all eternity for that tiresome priest to end his tale. Well might the Comic Muse of the Restoration stage find food for laughter in this *précieuse* habit of life.

Précieuse tastes are also reflected in the collections of model letters published during these years. Robert Loveday, translator of several parts of La Calprenède's *Cléopâtre*, issued in 1659 a volume of *Letters, Domestick and Forrein*. The letters are full of similitudes, which the author is anxious to have run upon as many "wheels" as possible. He proudly asserts that his thoughts "play like nimble flies in the serenity of an unclouded mind." [55] His usual style may be illustrated by a tribute of fraternal love which he pays his brother:

[53] Lord Broghill was the nobleman whose marriage Suckling had so delightfully celebrated, some years earlier, in his *Ballad upon a Wedding*.
[54] *Letters from Dorothy Osborne to Sir William Temple*, pp. 220–221.
[55] *Lovedays Letters* (1659 edition), p. 3.

. . . If Nature had not planted a mutuall affection in our greenest yeares, and taught it to swim (like a fish in its proper Element) in the Crimson sap we borrow'd from the same fruitfull stock, I think I should have bidden fair for your friendship with much industry, and, like a slip that fetch'd his Pedigree from some excellent root, set it with much diligence in my triangular Garden.[56]

No love letters are included. To meet the needs of inexperienced lovers such a practical volume as *Wits Interpreter, The English Parnassus* (1655) must have been designed. Among the attractions of *Wits Interpreter* may be mentioned a section entitled *Theatre of Courtship, Accurate Complements* and another entitled *The Perfect Inditer, Letters A la-mode.*

To what extent *préciosité* may have been cultivated at the exiled court, we have no means of discovering. Only occasional and very meager glimpses of the life of this court are afforded in contemporary journals and letters. We know that Henrietta herself was often harassed by financial worries. In the *Memoirs* of the Cardinal de Retz references are made to the queen's straitened circumstances in January, 1649, and in September, 1651.[57] In May, 1649, she wrote Denham of her "pressing wants."[58] Some of her letters, however, are really cheerful. In a letter of October, 1655, she commends the civility of the young French king and the French queen's generosity.[59] The small English court managed to preserve its identity, and Henrietta seems to have presided over it with much of her former imperious dignity. Lady Anne Fanshawe records in her *Memoirs* the queen's gracious hospitality to herself and her husband when they visited this court in 1648 and again in 1650.[60] As the period of exile drew to a close, the English court gained in authority. In the *Memoirs* of Sir John Reresby the following interesting item occurs:

[56] *Ibid.*, p. 11.
[57] *Memoirs of the Cardinal de Retz*, pp. 132 and 215–216.
[58] *Letters of Queen Henrietta Maria*, ed. Mary A. Green, p. 363.
[59] *Ibid.*, p. 378.
[60] *Memoirs of Lady Fanshawe*, pp. 78–79 and 101.

The court of France was very splendid this winter, 1660; a grand mask was danced at the Louvre, where the king and princess Henrietta of England danced to admiration: But there was now a greater resort to the palace than the French court; the good humour and wit of our queen mother, and the beauty of the princess her daughter being more inviting than any thing that appeared in the French queen, who was a Spaniard.[61]

Reresby admired the queen at all times and was impressed by "the influence she had over the king," [62] her son. Surely we are justified in assuming that such a queen could continue to direct and inspire the poets and dramatists who were still her loyal subjects.

With the official re-opening of the theaters at the Restoration, dramatic literature became once more widely popular. New plays were in great demand. For a time, however, the policies of the new theaters were unsettled and even chaotic. Dramatists experimented with a free hand.

D'Avenant himself was unfitted to direct the energies of his fellow-dramatists toward any definite goal. *The Siege of Rhodes* (Part II, 1661) [63] has significance as an opera and revives, as fully as its form permitted, D'Avenant's earlier Platonism, but it remains, after all, a poor substitute for regular drama. *The Law against Lovers* (1662) [64] and *The Rivals* (1664) [65] are effeminate alterations of Shakespearian comedies. *The Playhouse to be Let* (probably licensed 1663) [66] combines in a curious "pot pourri" [67] two of the earlier operas, a burlesque in heroic verse, and a translation in broken English of Molière's farce, *Sganarelle*. Some of D'Avenant's earlier plays were again presented.[68] In his own words, his muse had become "old, and therefore

[61] *The Memoirs and Travels of Sir John Reresby*, pp. 163–164.
[62] *Ibid.*, p. 166.   [63] Pepys, *Diary*, II, p. 58.
[64] *Ibid.*, II, p. 179.   [65] *Ibid.*, IV, p. 224.
[66] Cf. *The Dramatic Records of Sir Henry Herbert*, ed. J. Q. Adams, p. 138.
[67] Nettleton, *op. cit.*, p. 32.
[68] Pepys witnessed performances of *Love and Honour*, *The Wits*, and *The Unfortunate Lovers*. Cf. his *Diary*, II, pp. 116–117; II, pp. 77, 78, 81, VI, pp. 260, 262, VIII, p. 192; IV, p. 63, VII, pp. 103, 370, VIII, p. 161.

narrative"[69] and must find her chief solace in memories of the days "when she was young."[69]

Such plays as *The Rump* (acted about May, 1660)[70] by Tatham and *The Old Troop* (1665)[71] by John Lacy depended for their appeal on caustic satire of Puritan hypocrisy and folly. Restoration audiences must have loudly applauded the closing scene of the former play, in which all the discomfited Puritan leaders trail dejectedly across the stage, hawking various small wares, and old Mrs. Cromwell brings up the rear, crying kitchen stuff and surrounded by a saucy crew of street urchins. Elizabethan influences are still dominant in *The Cheats* (1663) and *The Projectors* (1665)[71] by John Wilson and *The Committee* (1662)[72] and *The Surprisal* (1662)[73] by Sir Robert Howard. Wilson had genuine ability, but his Jonsonian program, rigorous as it is, marks only a late venture in a tradition of which the essential spirit was dead. Other experiments were made in the style of Spanish *comedia de capa y espada*. *Elvira* (licensed 1663)[74] by George Digby, Earl of Bristol, and *The Adventures of Five Hours* (1662)[75] by Sir Samuel Tuke are sober adaptations of Spanish originals.[76] Tuke's play, written at the king's request, was extremely popular, and in Pepys' opinion its glories rendered even *Othello* "a mean thing."[77] Yet this "cloak and sword" type of comedy, both now and later, proved too decidedly nationalistic in spirit to become fused successfully with, or in any mem-

[69] *The Siege of Rhodes* (*Works*, IV), Part II, p. 365.
[70] Rollins, *Studies in Philology*, XX, p. 66.
[71] Nicoll, *op. cit.*, p. 200.
[72] John Evelyn, *Diary and Correspondence*, ed. William Bray, I, p. 393.
[73] Nicoll, *op. cit.*, p. 202.
[74] *Dramatic Records of Sir Henry Herbert*, p. 138.
[75] Evelyn, *Diary*, I, p. 394.
[76] Tuke's play was translated from Coello's *Los Empeños de Seis Horas*. Digby's was from Calderon's *No siempre lo peor es cierto*. Two other plays which Digby adapted from Calderon have been lost (cf. John Downes, *Roscius Anglicanus*, p. 26).
[77] Pepys, *Diary*, V, p. 383.

orable way to change, the current of English comedy of manners.
The really important first plays of the Restoration period are
those that continued the *précieuse* tradition. We need not lament the fact that minor dramatists wrote most of these early
plays. Minor writers often help us to feel keenly "the winds of
March when they do not blow." To Mrs. Katherine Philips the
Restoration brought no change of interests or of literary activities. From 1661 to 1664 she was composing, according to her
quaint notions of the "science" of Friendship, the Platonic
Letters from Orinda to Poliarchus. To Thomas Killigrew the
Restoration meant simply an opportunity to publish a complete
edition of his plays, including four new dramas in the style of his
former plays. Royalist writers and especially royalist dramatists welcomed the Restoration as a new challenge to greater
achievements.

Platonic tragedies and tragi-comedies, written in rhyming
couplets, proved to be one popular type of early Restoration
literature. The metrical pattern of these so-called "heroic plays"
had been experimented with in D'Avenant's *The Siege of Rhodes*.
A further familiarity with the couplet form became possible for
Restoration authors through a number of English translations of
Pierre Corneille's rhymed tragedies. Mrs. Philips translated
Corneille's *Pompée* (1663) [78] and left unfinished at her death a
translation of *Horace*, completed by Denham before 1669.[79] Another translation of *Pompée* (1663) [80] was the work of Waller,
Sackville, and other court "Persons of Honour." Carlell, in his
old age, translated *Héraclius* (1664).[81] Original heroic plays by
Dryden and the Earl of Orrery succeeded these translations.
Corneille's style continued to serve as a model for the new English plays. But his Platonism had yielded, in his tragedies, to
other interests. The marked Platonism of the English heroic

[78] Dorothea Canfield [Fisher], *Corneille and Racine in England*, p. 36.
[79] *Ibid.*, p. 46.   [80] *Ibid.*, p. 57.   [81] *Ibid.*, p. 64.

plays seems to have been derived chiefly from the still widely-read French romances and from the earlier Platonic drama of D'Avenant and his school.

The Indian Queen, a rhymed heroic tragedy by John Dryden and Sir Robert Howard, was first presented on the stage in January, 1664.[82] Dryden probably wrote the larger part of the play. A Platonic emphasis is maintained in many scenes through the heroic generosity of two rival lovers, Acacis and Montezuma. The former, in dying, even renounces all a lover's jealousy, as Charistus had done in Cartwright's *The Lady Errant*. Addressing his rival for the last time, Acacis cries:

> Dear Montezuma,
> I may be still your friend, though I must die
> Your rival in her love: Eternity
> Has room enough for both; there's no desire,
> Where to enjoy is only to admire;
> There we'll meet friends, when this short storm is past.

And Montezuma, although he is to have the lady and would seem to have everything to live for, rejoins dolefully:

> Why must I tamely wait to perish last?[83]

Dryden's second play, *The Rival-Ladies* (June, 1664),[84] develops Platonic principles in more detail. Gonsalvo is an ideal Platonic lover. Having rescued from captivity Julia, whom he loves at first sight, he explains with modesty:

> You owe me nothing, madam; if you do
> I make it void; and only ask your leave
> To love you still; for, to be loved again
> I never hope.[85]

Gonsalvo ultimately resigns Julia to his rival, at her request. This noble Platonic lover has a fluent mastery, besides, of the

[82] Pepys, *Diary*, IV, p. 23.
[83] *The Indian Queen* (*Works*, II), V, 1, p. 274.
[84] Nicoll, *op. cit.*, p. 359.
[85] *The Rival-Ladies* (*Works*, II), II, 1, p. 167.

language of Platonism. A long similitude debate, quite in the manner of Suckling, takes place, toward the close of the play, between Gonsalvo and his unrelenting mistress. The following arguments are exchanged:

> *Jul.* You have the power to make my happiness,
> By giving that, which you can ne'er possess.
> *Gons.* Give you to Rodorick? there wanted yet
> That curse, to make my miseries complete.
> *Jul.* Departing misers bear a nobler mind;
> They, when they can enjoy no more, are kind;
> You, when your love is dying in despair,
> Yet want the charity to make an heir.
> *Gons.* Though hope be dying, yet it is not dead;
> And dying people with small food are fed.
> *Jul.* The greatest kindness dying friends can have,
> Is to despatch them, when we cannot save.
> *Gons.* Those dying people, could they speak at all,
> That pity of their friends would murder call:
> For men with horror dissolution meet;
> The minutes even of painful life are sweet.
> *Jul.* But I'm by powerful inclination led;
> And streams turn seldom to their fountain-head.
> *Gons.* No; 'tis a tide which carries you away;
> And tides may turn, though they can never stay.
> *Jul.* Can you pretend to love, and see my grief
> Caused by yourself, yet give me no relief?
> *Gons.* Where's my reward?
> *Jul.* The honour of the flame.
> *Gons.* I lose the substance, then, to gain the name. . . . [86]

This debate has been termed "the first of the scenes of amatory battledore and shuttlecock on which Dryden was to waste his talents." [87] As a matter of fact, Dryden was following a popular tradition, and he probably prided himself on doing a conventional thing rather well.

Roger Boyle, Earl of Orrery, wrote a number of heroic plays, of which at least *Henry V* (August, 1664) [88] and *The General*

---

[86] *Ibid.*, IV, 1, pp. 189–191.
[87] *Ibid.*, p. 188 n. Saintsbury makes the comment.
[88] Pepys, *Diary*, IV, p. 202.

(September, 1664),[89] later published as *Altemira*, belong to the period under discussion.[90] In both plays rival Platonic lovers perform conspicuous rôles. In *Henry V* young Tudor exemplifies most unselfishly his abhorrence of jealousy, "of Love's fair tree the foulest Fruit." [91] In *Altemira* Clorimon spurs himself to the highest pitch of self-sacrifice, exulting:

> I'll save my Rival, and make her confess
> 'Tis I deserve what he does but possess.[92]

Sir Charles Sedley, Pepys tells us, scoffed heartily at this amazing speech, although Sedley himself was capable of writing with due propriety in a similar vein. Some anti-Platonic soldiers enliven one scene of *Altemira*, but the tone of the play, as a whole, is depressingly somber. Orrery's later plays-exhibit the same extravagant Platonism in the same way. Pepys was really justified in complaining that "so many plays of the same design and fancy do but dull one another" and that "this . . . is the sense of every body else." [93]

The later history of heroic drama will not concern us.[94] Occasionally a Restoration dramatist attempted to combine in one play the serious and comic aspects of the *précieuse* tradition. For the most part, the history of Restoration heroic drama remained distinct from that of Restoration comedy, although the two types of drama had had their origin in the same philosophic system.

Even in the earliest years of the Restoration period *précieuse*

[89] *Ibid.*, IV, p. 236.
[90] According to Pepys, Orrery's tragi-comedy, *The Black Prince*, was first acted in October, 1667. Plausible evidence for a 1663 performance of this play has been recently advanced by F. W. Payne in "The Question of Precedence between Dryden and the Earl of Orrery with Reference to the English Heroic Play," *The Review of English Studies* (April, 1925), I, pp. 173–181.
[91] *Henry the Fifth* (*Works*, I), IV, p. 329.
[92] *Altemira* (*Works*, II), III, p. 168.
[93] Pepys, *Diary*, VIII, p. 166.
[94] For a brief history of later heroic drama cf. Nicoll, *op. cit.*, pp. 90–167.

comedy rivalled heroic drama. It would have been strange if the
comic temper of *The Parson's Wedding* had been wholly extinguished by the civil war. We may appropriately recall the comment of the plucky maiden in the Duchess of Newcastle's *The
Sociable Companions* (pr. 1668) who, warned by a comrade that
"Wit was kill'd in the War," makes the confident retort: "You
are mistaken, it was only banished with the Cavaliers; but now it
is returned home." [95] Soon after the Restoration, comedies showing *précieuse* influence were again acted and published. Among
these comedies, Etherege's *The Comical Revenge* is by no means
the first play which deserves attention.

In December, 1661, Pepys saw a performance of Cowley's
The Cutter of Coleman-Street — "a new play," Pepys comments,
"and a very good play it is." [96] As we have noted already, the
play was a revision of *The Guardian*. The scene has become "London in the year 1658," and much pertinent satire of the Puritans
is included. Puny is still the one character of absorbing interest.
Cowley must have enjoyed this foolish gallant, for he takes pains,
in the revised comedy, to enlarge his rôle. Puny now trades
similitudes with Aurelia, who indulges him for her sport. His
companions, Worm and Cutter, encourage him to much livelier
flights of fancy than those with which he had favored Dogrel and
Cutter in the original play. Worm and Cutter themselves are
more fluent in similitudes than their predecessors, to Puny's infinite delight. When Worm suggests to Puny the comparison
"like a Dog with a blind man," the latter applauds: "Ha! ha! ha!
Sublimely fantastical. [97]

Puny habitually becomes ecstatic over similitudes which he feels
approach, but never quite equal, the ingenuity of his own. His
enthusiasms may very well have suggested to Congreve those of

[95] *The Sociable Companions* (1668 collection of plays), II, 4, p. 38.
[96] Pepys, *Diary*, II, p. 146.
[97] *The Cutter of Coleman-Street* (ed. Waller), IV, 6, p. 318.

Brisk and Witwoud. Brisk, it will be remembered, insists on praising Lady Froth's dubious conceits as "deuce take me, very à propos and surprising," [98] and Witwoud joyously commends one of Millamant's comparisons as "a hit! a hit! a palpable hit! I confess it." [99] In all of Cowley's similitude contests, Puny naturally takes the lead. He has fresh similitudes ever ready with which to interrupt and complete the remarks of his associates; and here again he predicts Witwoud.[100] Puny's habit is contagious; even the sensible Aurelia sometimes follows his example. Cowley may have been partly responsible for Congreve's own confusion of false and true wit in certain passages where similitudes color the speech of such characters as Mirabell, for example, and the charming Millamant.

In 1662 Margaret Cavendish, Duchess of Newcastle, published her first volume of plays. That these were written after her marriage to the Duke of Newcastle in 1645 is indicated in the words of one of her prefaces where, in very characteristic style, she acknowledges her gratitude for the Duke's literary assistance:

> My Lord was pleased to illustrate my Playes with some scenes of his own wit, to which I have set his name, that my readers may know which are his, as not to couzen them in thinking they are mine; also Songs, to which my Lords name is set; for I being no Lyrick Poet, my Lord supplied that defect of my Brain with the superfluity of his own Brain; thus our Wits join as in Matrimony, my Lords the Masculine, mine the Feminine Wit, which is no small glory to me, that we are married, Souls, Bodies, and Brains, which is a treble Marriage, united in one Love, which I hope is not in the power of Death to dissolve; for Souls may love, and Wit may live, though Bodies die.[101]

[98] *The Double-Dealer*, II, 1, p. 121.
[99] *The Way of the World*, II, 2, p. 345.
[100] Comparisons of a homely quaintness are affected by both Cowley and Congreve. Compare (Puny) "There shall be no more considering than in a Hasty Pudding" (II, 3, p. 285) with (Witwoud) "you may be as short as a Shrewsbury-Cake" (III, 3, p. 367); (Puny) "as an Alderman loves Lobsters" (IV, 6, p. 318) with (Witwoud) "worse than a quaker hates a parrot" (I, 2, p. 333); (Puny) "as humerous as a Bel-rope" (III, 12, p. 307) with (Millamant) "as melancholy as a watch-light" (II, 2, p. 349).
[101] *Plays Written by the Thrice Noble, Illustrious, and Excellent Princess, The Lady Marchioness of Newcastle* (1662), Preface, *To the Readers*.

None of the plays, mainly comedies, of this volume and of the volume published by the Duchess in 1668, were ever acted. But that fact did not concern the author. She complacently declared that contemporary opinions regarding her plays interested her very little, "since I regard not so much the present as future Ages, for which I intend all my Books." [102] As it happened, her own age paid her many glowing tributes. Sir George Etherege wrote of her:

> Those graces nature did till now divide,
> Your sex's glory and our sex's pride,
> Are join'd in you, and all to you submit,
> The brightest beauty and the sharpest wit.[103]

But "future Ages," alas, have remembered her only as a fantastic *précieuse* who dabbled in letters.

Of the Duchess' plays her only modern biographer has commented that they represent "closet drama so lifeless and so dull that one shrinks from it even on the printed page." [104] It is true that they have very slight dramatic value. *The Sociable Companions* is the only one of the plays which has a plot worthy of the name. In most of the plays the characters are little more than personified abstractions, who debate their way through scene after scene of elaborate argument. Exercises in declamation abound, chiefly undertaken by precocious maidens who, like the Duchess herself, explore easily and with dignity all fields of human inquiry, from matters of feminine etiquette to problems in metaphysics. Between ladies and gallants conversational games take place, such as the game of "dialogue-discourse" in *Wits Cabal*, a game in which each successive speaker contributes to the chosen theme a new line, all the lines rhyming in quatrains. But the best dialogue is to be found in the courtship scenes. In fact,

[102] *Plays Never before Printed* (1668), Preface, *To the Readers*.
[103] Etherege, *Works*, p. 394.
[104] Henry Ten Eyck Perry, *The First Duchess of Newcastle and her Husband, as Figures in Literary History*, p. 214.

the Duchess' plays are mainly interesting because of such scenes. In the debates of lovers the mannerisms of Suckling's dialogue are renewed, and the student of *préciosité* finds much to attract him.

In *The Several Wits* Monsieur Importunate and Mademoiselle Caprisia engage in a number of amorous controversies. A typical encounter occurs in a passageway, where Importunate stops his mistress and boldly presents his suit:

Imp. You shall not pass, until you have paid me a tribute.

Cap. What tribute?

Imp. A kiss.

Cap. I will pay no such tribute, for I will bring such a number of words armed with such strong reasons, as they shall make my way.

Imp. Your words will prove poor Pilgrims, which come to offer at the Altar of my lips.

Cap. Nay, rather than so, they shall come as humble Petitioners, and as it were, kneeling at your heart, shall with innocency beg for gentle civility.

Imp. I will shut the gates of my ears against them, and my lips as a bar shall force them back, being a precise factious rout.

Cap. Satire shall lead my sharp words on, break ope those gates, and anger like consuming fire shall destroy both your will and base desire.

Imp. I will try that.

Cap. But I will rather make a safe retreat, than venture, least your rude strength might overcome my words.[105]

Here will be noted the same stiff playing with similitudes, back and forth, as in Suckling's dialogue — and all on the subject of the granting of a kiss.

Before long, Importunate again meets Caprisia, greets her with alacrity, and the exchange of similitudes goes on:

Imp. My fair Shrew, are you walking alone?

Cap. My thoughts are my best companions.

Imp. Pray, let a thought of me be one of the company.

Cap. When you enter into my mind, you do appear so mean, as my nobler thoughts, scorns that thought that bears your figure.

---

[105] *The Several Wits* (1662 collection of plays), I, 2, p. 80.

Imp. Thoughts are as notes, and the tongue is the Fiddle that makes the Musick; but your words, as the cords, are out of tune.

Cap. You say so, by reason they are not set to your humour, to sound your prayse.

Imp. I say you are very handsome, nature hath given you a surpassing beauty, but pride and self-conceit, hath cast such a shadow, as it hath darkened it, as vaporous clowds doth the bright Sun.

Cap. Your opinions are clowdy, and your tongue like thunder, strikes my ears with rude, uncivil words.[106]

It would be tedious to quote further encounters between Caprisia and her lovers, or between Bon Esprit and Monsieur Satyrical in *Wits Cabal,* or between Lady Self-Conceit and Spend-all in *The Presence,* or still other conversations of the same order. The Duchess of Newcastle was a little pedantic, no doubt, in her methods of organizing and developing these elaborate conversations. Yet in such dialogue she was merely giving expression, perhaps with exceptional studiousness, to a current fashion, not a personal whim. Even if, as one suspects, the set forms of her *préciosité* were already a trifle out of style in 1662, conversational mannerisms quite as ingeniously conceived were to distinguish much of the best dialogue in Restoration comedy.

The fastidious Duchess of Newcastle gives us only the smooth surfaces of *précieuse* society. Thomas Killigrew saw the spectacle differently. In his second comedy, *Thomaso* (pr. 1664), Killigrew revives, as might be expected, the comic point of view of *The Parson's Wedding.* In *Thomaso,* as in *The Parson's Wedding,* the accepted standard of conduct is one of compliance with the age. Once more we have an opportunity to observe fairly intimately the process by which Platonic belief and unbelief were gradually effecting a readjustment of comic values.

Thomaso is a young English gallant, a traveller in Spain, who shamelessly carries on an intrigue with a famous courtesan, accepts gifts from her, and dazzles his companions with his fine clothes, fine manners, and merry wit, and yet in his more serious

[106] *Ibid.,* II, 16, p. 91. ·

moments is capable of pursuing an honest love affair to a perfectly decorous conclusion. The fashionable irregularities of Thomaso's conduct are excused by the heroine on the basis of a rather liberal Platonic charity. To one of her brother's friends she defends her lover's behavior with the announcement:

> ... And for his Mistresses, that great crime so often urg'd by my Brother and your self, I despise it, and inquire neither who, nor how many he has; I scorn to fear he can be such a fool as to give them his heart; and for his body, 'twas always the least of my thoughts, and only known as it went and came upon Loves Errands betwixt us; and she that is concern'd in her servants bestowing his body till he is hers, (were I the man) I should believe such An anger but darkly telling me she had a mind to it herself; come Johanne, let Thomaso keep his heart and mind fit for my value; let them be chaste, and for his body I shall never consider what it doth.[107]

The dramatist himself, quite aware that the standard of conduct illustrated by Thomaso is often at marked variance with a normal standard of conduct, makes an occasional deliberate effort to reconcile the two, as when Thomaso assures a friend of the real seriousness of his regard for Serulina, explaining:

> ... nor can this mist of rallery and mirth blind a friends eyes, to whom I shall say, 'tis no more my nature than my interest, though I chuse rather to put it on then give any womans pride the *Gusto*, to think, because I am poor 'twas in her power to despise me; but to my friend I shall still be free and serious.[108]

In reality the two standards can never be reconciled. The gay English cavalier, like his Restoration successors, follows the way of fashion, realizing that the agreeable, if artificial, rôle of fashionable gentleman is the only rôle of distinction in the society of which he forms a part.

A trace of the same Platonic influence in comedy is to be found in Sir William Killigrew's *Pandora*, published by the author, with two other plays, in 1664. Here a Platonic and an anti-Platonic lover are contrasted. The latter, Clearcus, declares of his friend: "Lonzartes does enough to illustrate the Platonick

[107] *Thomaso, or The Wanderer*, IV, 2, p. 356.
[108] *Ibid.*, II, 2, p. 404.

Name, and Eminently maintaine that high Seraffick flame, which
is above my reach."[109]   To tease his companions, Clearcus himself
talks a Platonic jargon in their presence, then suddenly assures
them that he is by no means so silly as to be in love, and that
his real philosophy is:

> Go whine fond Lover, go whine, I say, go whine,
> While we cheer our hearts with Wenches, and Wine,
> I say go whine.[110]

All the while, he is heartily in love with Pandora, though he cannot shame himself to tell her so, and the intervention of kind
friends is necessary to effect their marriage.

The year 1663 marks the date of John Dryden's first comedy,
The Wild Gallant.   Although in many respects an inferior play,
The Wild Gallant expresses, with exceptional distinctness, the
new social standard of which we have been tracing the history.
Elizabethan intrigue of a rather thin variety dominates the action
of this play.   The chief characters, however, illustrate by their
tastes and in their social intercourse the conventional attitudes
of Restoration comedy.

The most important feminine rôle in *The Wild Gallant* is
played by Isabelle, a lively young woman with "as much wit as
any wench in England."[111]   The fashions of the day constitute
her chief concern in life.   She is eager to prove her wit by captur-
ing a rich husband, a fool, to be sure, but a fool who will provide
her with "a glass coach and six Flanders mares."[112]   She is the
first of the clever young wards that were to become so popular in
Restoration comedy.   To her conservative, old-fashioned uncle
and to her boorish country lover, both very familiar types in
Restoration comedy, she triumphantly explains the modern
young woman's code of etiquette.   She reminds her uncle: "And
what are you but an old boy of five and fifty?"[113]   And she

---

[109] *Pandora*, II, p. 12.   [110] *Ibid.*, IV, p. 35.
[111] *The Wild Gallant* (*Works*, II), I, 2, p. 45.
[112] *Ibid.*, IV, 2, p. 96.

placates him at the time of her cousin's marriage, for which she is responsible, with the logic:

> Come, nuncle, 'tis in vain to hold out, now 'tis past remedy: It is like the last act of a play, when people must marry: and if fathers will not consent then, they should throw oranges at them from the galleries. Why should you stand off, to keep us from a dance? [114]

The courtship of her lover, Sir Timorous, she directs into a "proviso" argument, a discussion of the "trifles" which shall insure her liberty as a wife.[115] Like Congreve's Millamant, she cannot endure the idea of a mere husband who shall interfere with the choice of her own company, her own hours, and her own actions. It is possible that in recording this courtship Dryden may have been influenced solely by Elizabethan "proviso" scenes. But in her sophistication and lack of sentiment Isabelle is much more like D'Urfé's Stelle than like those Elizabethan maidens whose ingenuity had directed similar courtships.

Jack Loveby, the Wild Gallant, illustrates even more completely another Restoration comedy type. Like Mademoiselle de Scudéry's Cyrus, he lives in a world where manners count for everything. Yet Loveby lives in a very real London and not, like Cyrus, in Arcadia, and he knows nothing of Cyrus' exalted Platonic faith. Loveby has the tastes of a normal Restoration gallant and also the means of gratifying them. His sphere of action, although defined with equal exactness, is infinitely larger than that of Cyrus. He practises one rule of manners with his tavern companions and another with Constance, the young gentlewoman whom he loves. He knows to perfection the precise social gestures of both rôles. Like Etherege's Dorimant he might plead: "Good nature and good manners corrupt me." [116] In discoursing on the theme of cuckoldry, Loveby asserts his conviction: "Why all things are civil, that are made so by custom." [117]

[113] *Ibid.*, II, 1, p. 59.   [114] *Ibid.*, V, 3, p. 118.   [115] *Ibid.*, III, 1, 74–75.
[116] *The Man of Mode, or Sir Fopling Flutter*, II, 2, p. 277.
[117] *The Wild Gallant* (*Works*, II), III, 2, p. 83.

In a sense, he is a victim of fashion, as Fletcher's dashing young gallants had never been, and as heroes of Restoration comedy always are. He can never be quite candid. Most of his time has to be devoted to a vindication of his position as a fashionable young gentleman. Such vindication must often be effected through a good deal of fine acting, involving the young hero in embarrassing situations, from which he contrives to extricate himself with considerable gallantry, but not without some confusion.

On the occasion of Loveby's first visit to Constance and Isabelle, after the former had secretly sent him a generous gift of money, the following conversation ensues:

> *Const.* Mr. Loveby, welcome, welcome; Where have you been this fortnight?
>
> *Lov.* Faith, madam, out of town, to see a little thing that's fallen to me upon the death of a grandmother.
>
> *Const.* You thank death for the windfall, servant: But why are you not in mourning for her?
>
> *Lov.* Troth, madam, it came upon me so suddenly, I had not time: 'Twas a fortune utterly unexpected by me.
>
> *Isa.* Why, was your grandmother so young, you could not look for her decease?
>
> *Lov.* Not for that neither; but I had many other kindred, whom she might have left it to; only she heard I lived here in fashion and spent my money in the eye of the world.
>
> *Const.* You forge these things prettily; but I have heard you are as poor as a decimated cavalier, and had not one foot of land in all the world.
>
> *Lov.* Rivals' tales, rivals' tales, madam.[118]

As this same conversation continues, Loveby becomes more and more entangled in ingenious fabrications. Yet Constance, who is thoroughly in love with him, is simply testing his wit, and he is simply responding as a witty young lover should.

A still more embarrassing plight befalls Loveby on a later occasion, when Constance and Isabelle discover him in a tavern, surrounded by courtesans. Constance promptly demands the

[118] *Ibid.*, II, 1, pp. 56–56.

money he had promised her. Even now, with that engaging politeness which never fails him, Loveby rejoins: "Dear madam, let me wait on you to your coach; and, if I bring it not within this hour, discard me utterly." [119] The courtesans, he gracefully explains, are: "Persons of quality of my acquaintance; but I'll make your excuses to 'em." [120] But Constance insists on an introduction to the ladies, and manages to find out the truth, whereupon Loveby can only plead : "I beseech your ladyship, but hear my justification as I lead you." [121]

After all, Loveby has little reason to apprehend Constance's displeasure. As his servant suggests to him, Constance is angry only "from the teeth outwards." [122] Constance habitually evaluates the conduct of her young lover as Dryden himself evaluates it, on the basis of Loveby's successful compliance with social fashions. Like Killigrew, however, Dryden is perfectly aware of another and saner standard of judging, in the light of which all the artificial complexities of his hero's career appear absurd and grotesque. Because this other standard exists and is still tacitly recognized, the social standard, with which it is always in conflict, affords far-reaching comic possibilities.

The Wild Gallant is the last comedy in the *précieuse* manner before the date of Etherege's first play. The testimony of these comedies readily convinces us of the strength of social sympathies between court society just before the civil war and court society just after the Restoration. Various interregnum writers had made the transition an easy one. Loveby and Isabelle in *The Wild Gallant* still quote Suckling, [123] with a pleasant familiarity which suggests that Dryden's audience continued to cherish the

---

[119] *Ibid.*, IV, 1, p. 88. [120] *Ibid.*, p. 89.
[121] *Ibid.*, p. 90. [122] *Ibid.*, p. 91.
[123] Cf. *Ibid.*, V, 3, p. 117. Loveby and Isabelle, in discussing the subject of the latter's elopement, quote to each other phrases from the opening lines of Suckling's *Aglaura*. The passage is as follows:
Lov. Married!

memory of the greatest of cavalier wits. In the same play Dryden renews and amplifies with animation and charm the best features of earlier *précieuse* comedy and in so doing defines, to a considerable degree, the comic program of Etherege and of Congreve.

———

Isa. And in Diana's grove, boy.

Lov. Why, 'tis fine, by Heaven; 'tis wondrous fine, as the poet goes on sweetly.

In a footnote the editor (Saintsbury) comments: "I do not know the quotation if it be one."

CHAPTER VI

THE PERIOD OF ETHEREGE

IN THE twelve years from 1664 to 1676 Restoration comedy of manners became well established as a dramatic type. During these years Etherege and Wycherley produced their masterpieces, and a goodly number of other comic dramatists worked, with varying degrees of success, in the same tradition. Etherege's importance as the first dramatist to express the Restoration comic spirit with artistic completeness is now very generally recognized. The relation of his work and that of his immediate contemporaries to earlier English drama, and especially to *précieuse* drama, remains, however, an unsolved problem, inviting our attention.

When we consider *The Comical Revenge, or Love in a Tub* (1664),[1] the first of Etherege's comedies, we find ourselves involved in the famous controversy as to the sources of Etherege's plays. This play, prominent critics assure us, effected a revolution in English comedy. We may agree with Gosse that Molière inspired the new comic program, or with Palmer that a change in English social life produced the miracle; in any event, we must accept Restoration comedy as a revolutionary rebirth of English comedy, if we choose to support a conventional point of view in this matter.

Edmund Gosse, to whom credit is due for having rescued the memory of Sir George Etherege from an oblivion of many years' duration,[2] maintains that Etherege was greatly influenced by Molière, during those years when Molière's first comedies were

---

[1] The play was seen by Evelyn in April, 1664. Evelyn, *Diary*, I, p. 401.
[2] See the chapter on Etherege in Gosse's *Seventeenth Century Studies*, of which the first edition was published in 1883.

being produced in Paris and were restoring a sadly needed vitality to the French comic stage. These important new plays might easily have been seen by the exiled English cavalier. Gosse explains:

> ... What gave The *Comical Revenge* of Etheredge its peculiar value and novelty was that it had been written by a man who had seen and understood *L'Étourdi*, *Le Dépit Amoureux*, and *Les Précieuses Ridicules*. Etheredge loitered long enough in Paris for Molière to be revealed to him, and then he hastened back to England with a totally new idea of what comedy ought to be.[3]

And concerning the performance of the play the same critic adds:

> ... When the curtain went up on the first scene, the audience felt that a new thing was being presented to them, new types and an unfamiliar method.[3]

For the most part, modern critics have been disposed to regard with some misgivings Gosse's very definite account of the relations between Etherege and the great French master. John Palmer heads the opposing faction with the opinion: "Restoration comedy owed almost as little to France as to the English school it displaced."[4] Restoration society itself, argues this critic, was responsible for the new comic impulse. With reference to *The Comical Revenge* Palmer observes:

> ... Whether Sir George knew or not how original he was, his contemporaries realized it beyond a question. They had not yet seen a comedy upon the English stage in the least resembling *Love in a Tub*, and immediately they saw it they recognized it for an expression of themselves and their period for which they had unconsciously been waiting. Up to the production of *Love in a Tub* the London theatre was the theatre of Charles I. Its comedy was the Elizabethan comedy of Humours, pale, withered and exhausted. But Etherege changed all that. . .

Both theories appear to require modification. Etherege had every opportunity to introduce Molière to an English audience. But the question may well be raised whether Etherege's plays,

[3] Gosse, *op. cit.*, p. 267.
[4] Palmer, *The Comedy of Manners*, p. 66.
[5] *Ibid.*, p. 64.

unless in precision of style and in occasional details, betray the influence of the French dramatist. We may grant that, after the Restoration, the list of adaptations from Molière's plays is an impressive one.[6] But a large number of these adaptations were the work of second- and third-rate writers.[7] It may be doubted whether the spirit of Molière's comedy, even under the most favorable conditions, was ever fully realized in English Restoration comedy. *Précieuse* drama had already counted for a great deal more in England than in France; and while English comedies continued to be written mainly by courtiers, it was natural for a courtly mode to remain in the ascendency.

The influence of Restoration social life on the comedy of the period will, of course, be admitted. The Restoration dramatists themselves not infrequently acknowledge this influence. The refinement of the new comedy Dryden ascribes to the English court "and, in it, particularly to the king, whose example gives a law to it." [8] To that accomplished courtier, the Earl of Rochester, Dryden pays the following compliment:

... And not only I, who pretend not to this way, but the best comic writers of our age, will join with me to acknowledge, that they have copied the gallantries of courts, the delicacy of expression, and the decencies of behaviour from your Lordship, with more success, than if they had taken their models from the court of France.[9]

A minor dramatist of the age, Sir Francis Fane, seconds Dryden in praising Rochester's "most Charming and Instructive Conversation." [10]

The precise limits of the social influence in any period may

[6] See the list of Molière borrowings in Miles, *op. cit.*, pp. 223–241.

[7] In general, these adapters viewed their sources with an air of condescension. In the preface to *The Miser* (*Works*, III), p. 7, Shadwell states that he never knew "a French Comedy made use of by the worst of our Poets, that was not better'd by 'em."

[8] *The Conquest of Granada*, Part II (*Works*, IV), *Defence of the Epilogue*, p. 241.

[9] *Marriage à la Mode* (*Works*, IV), Dedication, pp. 253–254.

[10] *Love in the Dark, or The Man of Bus'ness*, Dedication.

never easily be determined. Palmer has admirably utilized the
best records available for defining the social aims and interests of
the Restoration dramatists. We have every reason to rejoice in
his splendid portrayal of Restoration society, and we may hardly
hope to enlarge the picture. We may assume that the new court
was considerably more brilliant than the last had been; certainly
it stimulated a more brilliant drama. Yet we have no right to
conclude, unless the plays of the time afford such testimony,
that, as Palmer suggests, this new drama owed little or nothing
to the drama which had preceded it. Such an assumption is clearly
not in accordance with the usual laws of growth of literary tradition. It becomes imperative, therefore, that we reconsider the
position occupied by Restoration comedy in the history of English drama.

It is significant that Dryden, the most distinguished critic of
his age, seems never to have regarded early Restoration comedy
as a new and unique phenomenon in English dramatic literature.
Dryden took pride in declaring that the comedy of his day, despite its original excellences in graceful dialogue, was the natural
outgrowth of a magnificent English tradition. In *An Essay of
Dramatic Poesy* (1668) he insists that to French dramatists he
and his contemporaries owed nothing.

... We have borrowed nothing from them; our plots are weaved in English
looms; we endeavour therein to follow the variety and greatness of characters,
which are derived to us from Shakespeare and Fletcher; the copiousness and
well-knitting of the intrigues we have from Johnson; and for the verse itself
we have English precedents of elder date than any of Corneille's plays.[11]

Was Dryden nearer the truth, we wonder, than our modern
critics have been? Surely, the plays themselves will reveal the
facts of the case.

The Comical Revenge does not, after all, materially help us in
the solution of our problem. A candid study of the play makes it

---

[11] *An Essay of Dramatic Poesy* (*Works*, XV), p. 341.

apparent that this first venture of Etherege's genius has been much overrated. Etherege's last two plays represent remarkable achievements in the genre of Restoration comedy. In *The Comical Revenge* he was merely feeling his way. We are forced to observe in this early play the predominance of conventional dramatic material, treated in a conventional manner and, in the main, without distinction.

The serious action of *The Comical Revenge*, the history of the loves of Beaufort and Graciana, Bruce and Aurelia, rather gravely set forth in heroic couplets, offers a condensed illustration of the sort of Platonically inspired love and friendship drama to which Carlell had devoted his energies. Again there is emphasis on love as heaven-ordained. Graciana excuses her inconstancy by virtue of that assumption which had sustained the Queen in D'Avenant's *The Fair Favourite*:

> We of ourselves can neither love nor hate:
> Heaven does reserve the power to guide our fate.[12]

Heroic generosity in love is displayed at every turn. Aurelia struggles against her romantic attachment for Bruce, whose affections are already pledged, as disinterestedly as Cleonarda in Carlell's *The Deserving Favourite*. Beaufort is a magnanimous and high-souled rival. Lovis is an ideal friend. Bruce's scrupulous anxiety, though his heart is elsewhere engaged, to pay his debt of grateful love to kind Aurelia recalls the similar gratitude of Altophil in D'Avenant's *The Unfortunate Lovers*, of Clorinda in Carlell's *The Passionate Lovers*, and of Aglaura in Suckling's *Aglaura*. No lover could have addressed Aurelia more solicitously than Bruce, when he exclaims:

> Aurelia, why would you not let me know,
> While I had power to pay, the debt I owe?
> 'Tis now too late; yet all I can I'll do,
> I'll sigh away the breath I've left for you.[13]

---

[12] *The Comical Revenge, or Love in a Tub*, I, 4, p. 21.
[13] *Ibid.*, V, 1, p. 88.

Such lines exhibit Platonic idealism at its most extravagant pitch of devotion.[14]

The comic action of *The Comical Revenge* becomes resolved into three strands of adventure: (1) Sir Frederick's widow-wooing, (2) the cozenage of Cully, followed by the disgrace of the rascals who have gulled him, and (3) the farcical escapades of the French valet, Dufoy. The characterization of Sir Frederick Frolic, Palmer considers noteworthy, maintaining:

> The hero of *Love in a Tub* is the first of a line that culminated in Congreve's Mirabell. Almost as the curtain rose the audience must have felt that here was something new — no straw-splitting of 'humours,' but a gentleman that had walked into comedy from their midst, the image of their time and manner. He seized the immediate occasion, turning it to epigram. Each moment sufficed him, so long as it might be gracefully encountered. His first apology to Jenny for his conduct over-night sounded a new note in English comedy. 'Men are now and then subject to those infirmities in drink which women have when they're sober.' Here was an epigram of fine life, with fine life itself for company. . . .[15]

It is true that Sir Frederick reveals certain evidences of kinship with the more courtly gallants of Etherege's later comedies. Yet these revelations prove to be surprisingly few. Whatever conversational talents Sir Frederick may have possessed are persistently obscured through his preoccupation in a rollicking widow-wooing, an affair which is decidedly Elizabethan in character. The impudence with which he conducts the wooing and the palpable tricks by which he attempts to "fit" the not too squeamish lady of his choice revive memories of half a dozen or more of Fletcher's plays. His high-handed procedure is much like that of Valentine in *Wit without Money*, of Jacomo in *The Captain*, and of Ricardo in *The Widow;* and two of his tricks, the serenading for admission and the death feint, definitely parallel stratagems pursued in *Monsieur Thomas* and *The Woman's Prize*. Other interesting analogues may be observed in Brome's *A Mad Couple well Match'd*

---

[14] The pattern of these Platonic loves bears some resemblance to love relationships in Shirley's *The Changes* (cf. Summers, *op. cit.*, p. xviii).

[15] Palmer, *The Comedy of Manners*, p. 71.

and Killigrew's *The Parson's Wedding*. No more thoroughly Elizabethan adventure could have absorbed Sir Frederick's talents.

The cozenage of Cully by the rogues Wheedle and Palmer restores the atmosphere of Middleton's cony-catching plays, particularly of *Michaelmas Term*, where the plight of the Essex Gentleman, Easy, is very similar to that of Cully. Cully's cowardice on the duel-field allies him with Jonson's and Shirley's boastful but timorous fools, while his Puritan shortcomings are assailed in the spirit of Tatham, Wilson, and Sir Robert Howard. The disguising of Wheedle's whore as that gentleman's young sister recalls similar impostures in Middleton's *A Trick to Catch the Old One* and *A Chaste Maid in Cheapside*, and Brome's *The Northern Lasse*. Sir Frederick himself, in ultimately obliging Wheedle to wed his own courtesan and Palmer the courtesan's maid, revives Fitsgrave's decree for the cheating gallants in Middleton's *Your Five Gallants*. And the final gulling of Cully, through the match with a whore whom he supposed a young woman of birth and breeding, offers again the favorite solution of Shirley and Brome for the disposal of clownish lovers.

By a process of elimination, we are left with the adventures of Sir Frederick's French valet — Dufoy — as the only possible field of French influence in *The Comical Revenge*. Gosse was impressed by the kinship of Dufoy with the Mascarilles of Molière's first three plays, *L'Étourdi*, *Le Dépit Amoureux*, and *Les Précieuses Ridicules*,[16] and Nettleton has seconded Gosse's opinion.[17] In his conceit, his solicitude for his personal comfort, his submissiveness to a beating, his loyalty to his master, and his taste for conducting his own love affairs in the manner of his master, Dufoy may, indeed, be said to resemble the Mascarilles. But he certainly has little of the intelligence of these French valets. The Mascarilles of the plays listed above are clever, efficient fellows, who competently assume control of affairs. Of Du-

[16] Gosse, *op. cit.*, p. 267.   [17] Nettleton, *op. cit.*, p. 74.

foy, on the other hand, the comment has to be made that "he was Jack-pudding to a mountebank, and turned off for want of wit." [18] Dufoy is easily duped, obtuse, blundering, and becomes a laughing-stock. He is condescendingly indulged by Sir Frederick in much the same way as the foolish and devoted Irish Tegue is humored by his cavalier master in Sir Robert Howard's *The Committee.* In his stupidity, the absurdity of his broken English jargon, and his ridiculous scorn of English ways Dufoy resembles Monsieur le Frisk in Shirley's *The Ball,* Galliard in Newcastle's *The Varietie,* and Monsieur Raggou in Lacy's *The Old Troop;* and his kinship of spirit with these anglicized French clowns is far more marked than his relation to the type of clever servant made immortal by Molière.

On the whole, then, the case against the theory that the contemporaries of Etherege "had not yet seen a comedy upon the English stage in the least resembling *Love in a Tub*" [19] seems pretty strong. Of the four loosely-knit strands of plot in this comedy three, at any rate, appear deeply rooted in the Elizabethan tradition, and the farcical subplot, which gives the play its title, cannot be said to owe more than a slight debt to French influences. It is obvious that in this first play of his Etherege did not define, to any appreciable degree, the spirit of Restoration comedy. All that he attempted was an experimental fusion of certain familiar plot conventions of English comedy. The great success of the play was due perhaps to his audience's familiarity with these conventions and, in any case, could not have been the result of novelty of comic form.

Between the dates of *The Comical Revenge* and Etherege's second play, *She Would if She Could,* Dryden's new comedies are the only plays which challenge our interest. Several plays first acted in 1667 repeat with little variation Elizabethan moods and

[18] *The Comical Revenge,* III, 4, p. 51.
[19] Cf. p. 138, n. 5, of this volume.

manners. Inferior adaptations of two of Shakespeare's comedies appeared in Lacy's *Sawny the Scot* [20] and Dryden and D'Avenant's *The Tempest*.[21] In the Duke of Newcastle's *The Humorous Lovers*,[22] Fletcherian intrigue and Jonsonian humours are once more emphasized. But to 1667 also belong two important new comedies by Dryden, *Secret Love; or, the Maiden-Queen* and *Sir Martin Mar-all; or, The Feigned Innocence*. In the development of the Restoration comic mode, these two plays are far more significant than *The Comical Revenge*. Dryden takes pains to develop in both comedies, in the midst of other and somewhat hostile interests, the *précieuse* comic spirit of *The Wild Gallant*.

The grave and lifeless "heroic" action of *Secret Love* (March, 1667) [23] is much relieved by the comic courtship of Celadon and Florimel. The lively Celadon conducts various intrigues "only for the sweet sake of variety" [24] and in accordance with his comfortable philosophy that "we must all sin, and we must all repent, and there's an end on't." [24] Florimel makes his gay escapades mightily embarrassing for him by assuming active control of his affairs and, disguised as a young gallant, even courting his mistresses and winning over their affections. The two finally compromise on the "provisos" of an eccentric marriage contract. In the scene which Dryden boasted was "in the opinion of the best judges the most divertising of the whole comedy" [25] these most fickle lovers actually take oaths of inconstancy, to the mutual satisfaction of both and with a vast amount of mock dignity of language.

Celadon and Florimel exhibit a strong relationship, in the fashions of their courtship, to the inconstant Hylas and the coy Stelle of D'Urfé's *Astrée*. The "proviso" scenes in *Astrée* and in

[20] Pepys, *Diary*, VI, p. 249.   [21] *Ibid.*, VII, p. 176.
[22] *Ibid.*, VI, p. 233.
[23] *Ibid.*, VI, p. 192. See comment by Nicoll, *op. cit.*, pp. 215–216.
[24] *Secret Love; or, the Maiden-Queen* (*Works*, II), III, 1, p. 467.
[25] *Ibid.*, Preface, p. 240.

Secret Love are similarly prefaced. Hylas, debating with Sylvandre in an assemblage of shepherds, repudiates other attractive shepherdesses before acknowledging his preference for Stelle and making his covenant with her.[26] In *Secret Love* Celadon, in the rôle, for once, of Sylvandre proposes to Florimel the names of various mistresses whom he might marry, and Florimel, in the rôle of Hylas, disparages each in turn until she alone remains uncensured and Celadon is in a position to present his suit.[27]

The two "proviso" scenes have much in common. Celadon and Florimel "article" as follows:

Cel. One thing let us be sure to agree on, that is, never to be jealous.

Flo. No; but e'en love one another as long as we can; and confess the truth when we can love no longer.

Cel. When I have been at play, you shall never ask me what money I have lost.

Flo. When I have been abroad, you shall never inquire who treated me.

Cel. Item, I will have the liberty to sleep all night, without your interrupting my repose for any evil design whatsoever.

Flo. Item, Then you shall bid me good-night before you sleep.

Cel. Provided always, that whatever liberties we take with other people, we continue very honest to one another.

Flo. As far as will consist with a pleasant life.

Cel. Lastly, whereas the names of husband and wife hold forth nothing, but clashing and cloying, and dulness and faintness, in their signification; they shall be abolished for ever betwixt us.

Flo. And instead of those we will be married by the more agreeable names of mistress and gallant.

Cel. None of my privileges to be infringed by thee, Florimel, under the penalty of a month of fasting nights.

Flo. None of my privileges to be infringed by thee, Celadon, under the penalty of cuckoldom.[28]

When this contract is compared with that of Hylas and Stelle,

---

[26] *Astrée*, vol. III, bk. ix, pp. 663–664.

[27] *Secret Love* (*Works*, II), V, 1, p. 505. For citation of these parallel passages see my article, "D'Urfé's *Astrée* and the 'Proviso' Scenes in Dryden's Comedy," in *Philological Quarterly* (October, 1925), IV, pp. 304–305.

[28] *Ibid.*, V, 1, pp. 506–507. Compare with D'Urfé's scene, which is quoted in full, chap. IV, pp. 83–84, of this volume.

the correspondence of the various items appears striking. Both covenants agree in their essential regulations (1) prohibiting jealousy, (2) sanctioning inconstancy, (3) safeguarding liberty of speech and action, and (4) abolishing terms of endearment (terms of Platonic servitude in the one case, of marital affection in the other) between the contracting parties. The popularity of Dryden's "proviso" scene may be inferred from the fact that in James Howard's noisy farcical comedy *All Mistaken, or The Mad Couple* (September, 1667),[29] a similar contract between inconstant lovers [30] provides the most diverting episode of the play.

According to the testimony of Downes, Dryden composed his comedy *Sir Martin Mar-all* (August, 1667) [31] on the basis of a translation by the Duke of Newcastle of Molière's first comedy, *L'Étourdi*. It is evident that Dryden's play resembles *L'Étourdi* in its general scheme and in a few of its farcical incidents. An even closer resemblance may be traced between *Sir Martin Mar-all*, throughout the first four acts, and Quinault's *L'Amant Indiscret, ou Le Maître Étourdi*. Yet Dryden's alteration of the similar conclusions of both his sources suggests an essential distinction between the spirit of his comedy and the spirit of the two French plays.

Lélie, the hero of Molière's play, is an unusually clumsy representative of the typical sentimental, well-intentioned but decidedly unresourceful hero whom Molière portrays in his comedies. Clélie, Molière's heroine, is a nice young girl, also sentimental, who readily forgives her lover's many blunders and waits patiently for the lucky stroke of good fortune which finally effects their marriage. Quinault's Cleandre is more thick-headed, and is less sympathetically presented than Lélie; and Lucresse sometimes has doubts about his intelligence. But Lucresse, too, is

[29] Pepys, *Diary*, VII, p. 111.
[30] *All Mistaken, or The Mad Couple* (reprinted in Hazlitt's Dodsley, XV), II, pp. 347–350.
[31] Pepys, *Diary*, VII, pp. 64–65.

heartily in love with her blundering suitor and ultimately gives
him her hand, with genuine delight and with no real misgivings.
Dryden, on the other hand, had the temerity to portray Sir
Martin as a thorough-going fool and Millisent as an extremely
discerning young woman who, like most Restoration heroines,
has a wholesome contempt for fools. The spirited disposition
of the young English heroine is revealed in the remark
which she makes, apropos of her coming up to London, to Lady
Dupe:

> I came up, madam, as we country-gentlewomen use, at an Easter-term,
> to the destruction of tarts and cheese-cakes, to see a new play, buy a new
> gown, take a turn in the park, and so down again to sleep with my fore-
> fathers.[32]

Wit in a husband is his greatest attraction, to Millisent's way of
thinking, and when she becomes convinced that Sir Martin lacks
that, she "takes up" with his clever servant Warner, although
not before she has discovered that Warner was once a gentleman.
Dryden's hero nowhere exhibits that cautious docility as a servant which distinguishes Mascarille in *L'Étourdi* and which,
despite his inventive genius, keeps the latter contentedly in his
place. Warner plays a menial rôle with all the gracefulness of a
true Restoration gallant, and when Millisent rewards him with
her love, one more triumph has been won for a comic standard
which recognizes wit through all disguises and which greets its
successes with fervent applause.

It was the belief of Etherege's contemporary Shadwell that
She Would if She Could (1668),[33] although it had been much
impaired by being badly acted, was a comedy of unusual distinction. He commented on it in the preface to his *The Humourists*
as a play "which I think (and I have the Authority of some

---

[32] *Sir Martin Mar-all; or, The Feigned Innocence (Works*, III), I, 1, p. 10.
[33] Pepys saw the play in February, 1668, and expressed disgust at the
inferior acting. Cf. Pepys, *Diary*, VII, p. 287.

of the best Judges in England for't) is the best Comedy, that has been written since the Restauration of the Stage." [34] Modern critics, since Gosse re-discovered Etherege, have ordinarily been in sympathy with such a view. John Palmer expresses the consensus of opinion in declaring: "*She Would if She Could* is the first finished example of the new comedy of manners." [35] That the influence of Molière is conspicious in this comedy, no critic except Gosse [36] has affirmed. Miles records no Molière borrowings for the play, and Palmer warmly denies their existence.[37] Unfortunately, Etherege's critics have regarded with equal indifference the question of the relationship of *She Would if She Could* to preceding English comedy.

Perhaps in grace and ease of diction *She Would if She Could* reveals the influence of Molière's drama. In spirit the play is more akin to Dryden's earlier plays. Indeed, the *beau monde* of *She Would if She Could* is distinctly the *beau monde* of *The Wild Gallant* and *Secret Love*, depicted, at last, with perfect clarity, and released, in the main, from superfluous and confusing farcical entanglements. Etherege's people of fashion enact with unswerving devotion a social rôle which is amply commended by its artificial elegance. So supreme has the new social mode become that it energizes the entire action of the play.

The adventures of Courtal, Freeman, Ariana, and Gatty illustrate in considerable detail Etherege's conception of the Restoration standard of fashion. Love intrigues constitute the "weighty affairs" [38] of the gallants, and variety in these is all that makes life worth living. Courtal insists that "a single intrigue in love is as dull as a single plot in a play"; [39] and

---

[34] *The Humourists* (*Works*, I), Preface, p. 118.
[35] Palmer, *The Comedy of Manners*, p. 75.
[36] Gosse, *op. cit.*, p. 271, states that "the movement of *She Would if She Could* is founded upon a reminiscence of *Tartuffe.*"
[37] Palmer, *The Comedy of Manners*, p. 76.
[38] *She Would if She Could*, I, 1, p. 131.   [39] *Ibid.*, III, 1, p. 161.

although he and his fellow-adventurer are content to make the
affair with Ariana and Gatty their "main design," they are by
no means disposed to forego "some under-plots" in this "pleasant comedy." [39]   Even uninviting intrigues cannot be altogether
rejected, provided a lady is encouraging. Courtal has taken pains
to delay the climax of his affair with Lady Cockwood, but assures Freeman that he has "carried it so like a gentleman, that
she has not the least suspicion of unkindness." [40]   Constancy in
their amours, the gallants are persuaded, involves "forgetting
all shame." [41]   The artificial standards of Courtal and Freeman
are accepted by their young mistresses in entire good faith.
Ariana remarks: "The truth is, they can run and ramble here and
there and everywhere, and we poor fools think rather the better
of 'em." [42]   In their way, the girls behave with equal affectation.
They privately resolve that whatever they do they will be
"mighty honest." [42]   But their escapades in the Mulberry Garden
effectively conceal the real seriousness of their designs. They
jeer most keenly when they are most in love and in their raillery
are quite a match for their lovers.

The love intrigues conducted in *She Would if She Could* are
not as important in themselves as the manner in which they are
conducted. Witty conversation is the main test of social fitness.
With a few exceptions [43] the dialogue is not formally fashioned,
as in Suckling's plays, but its witty phrases exhibit a not dis-
similar studied precision. When Courtal and Freeman talk in
confidence, they are constrained to make clever remarks regarding their love intrigues. In pursuing these intrigues they
are never too busy to find comparisons and antitheses for con-
tinuing, all the while, the yet more absorbing conversational
game. In the courtship scenes raillery dominates the dialogue.

[40] *Ibid.*, I, 1, p. 130.   [41] *Ibid.*, II, 1, p. 143.   [42] *Ibid.*, I, 2, p. 137.
[43] See the similitude debate between Ariana and Gatty, *ibid.*, V, 1, p. 221.

The first encounter between the gallants and young ladies sets the key for all their subsequent fencing matches. The game begins thus:

Court. By your leave, ladies,

Gat. I perceive you can make bold without it.

Free. Your servant, ladies.

Aria. Or any other ladies that will give themselves the trouble to entertain you.

Court. Can you have so little good-nature to dash a couple of bashful young men out of countenance, who came out of pure love to tender you their service?

Gat. 'Twere pity to baulk 'em, sister.

Aria. Indeed, methinks they look as if they never had been slipped before.

Free. Yes, faith, we have had many a fair course in this paddock, have been very well fleshed, and dare boldly fasten.

[*They kiss their hands with a little force.*

Aria. Well, I am not the first unfortunate woman that has been forced to give her hand where she never intends to bestow her heart. . . .[44]

The young women assail masculine impudence; the gallants, in turn, foil these thrusts by ridicule of feminine pride, and the whole conversation assumes a neat symmetrical pattern.

The artificial life of these accomplished people of fashion is not without its embarrassments. Courtal's necessarily polite treatment of Lady Cockwood involves him in constant dilemmas. One smiles at his predicament when, as he conducts Lady Cockwood to her coach, the girls tease him by half exposing their intrigue with him, and he has to invent artful evasions and at the same time keep up an undercurrent of ceremonious compliment to Lady Cockwood herself.[45] But one smiles, not because Courtal is behaving in an ungentlemanly fashion, but because there exists at all a predicament which a little plain-dealing would have obviated. And at this point his trials are but just begun. Lady Cockwood later makes him appear in a false light

[44] *Ibid.*, II, 1, pp. 141–142.   [45] *Ibid.*, III, 1, pp. 166–167.

to the young ladies, exposes his schemes, keeps him ever in a state of affirming:

Anything to oblige you, madam,[46]

and at last frees him from her service only after he has told a "handsome lie" in her behalf.

The love affairs of Courtal and Ariana, Freeman and Gatty are similarly embarrassed by social convention. The girls fall in love with their gallants at first sight, but are obliged to rail furiously at them throughout the play, to the final interview, when Gatty turns to Freeman with the remark: "I hope you are not in so desperate a condition as to have a good opinion of marriage, are you?" [47] Gatty does yield sufficiently to propose to the gallants the test of a month's good behavior before marriage. Freeman, who has an equal horror of displaying sentimental lapses from good taste, retorts lightly: "A month is a tedious time, and will be a dangerous trial of our resolutions; but I hope we shall not repent before marriage, whate'er we do after." [48] As in *The Wild Gallant*, only now on a wider scale, the conduct of these polite lovers acquires comic vitality through the continually suggested opposition of artificial and real values.

With the fastidious pastimes of his true gentlemen of wit and pleasure Etherege contrasts the frolics of those social intruders, Sir Oliver Cockwood and Sir Joslin Jolley. The pair are well described in the words of Freeman: "They are harp and violin; Nature has so tuned 'em, as if she intended they should always play the fool in concert." [49] But the revels of the two harmonious fools hardly advance the action of the comedy. The rôle of awkward intruder in the fine world of fashion is much more strikingly played by Lady Cockwood, in whose characterization Etherege spares no pains.

[46] *Ibid.*, V, 1, p. 217.   [47] *Ibid.*, p. 228.
[48] *Ibid.*, p. 231.   [49] *Ibid.*, II, 1, p. 138.

Palmer has described Lady Cockwood as "the first of a long series of studies in fashionable virtue coquetting with fashionable vice." [50]   In view of the designs of Lady Bornwell in Shirley's *The Lady of Pleasure*, the Lady in Newcastle's *The Country Captaine*, and Lady Love-all in Killigrew's *The Parson's Wedding*, the statement is not strictly accurate.   Indeed, it is in contrast with these earlier amorous ladies of fashion, who carry on similar intrigues, that the full import of Lady Cockwood's characterization becomes most plainly discernible.   Etherege's title, *She Would if She Could*, which holds as strongly at the conclusion of his play as during its progress, well indicates the spirit in which the character of Lady Cockwood is conceived.   She is consistently judged by the only standard which the play enforces, the standard of compliance with the fashions of the age.   Like Lady Bornwell and Newcastle's Lady, she is an intruder in a society which she does not properly understand, and where she makes dangerous misjudgments.   Unlike those heroines, however, she is by no means a brand to be snatched from the burning.   She is subjected to social, but not, at the same time, moral discipline.   At the end of the play she observes, one suspects with a sigh, that she quite perceives "those dangers to which an aspiring lady must daily expose her honour," and is "resolved to give over the great business of this town."   And she concludes: "Certainly fortune was never before so unkind to the ambition of a lady." [51]

It is evident that the Restoration standard of fashion has nothing whatever to do with guilty consciences.   If Lady Cockwood could — with propriety — succeed in her intrigue, she would cease to be ridiculous.   As it is, judged by the standard of her age, she is a silly middle-aged woman, who labors too long under the delusion that she can be as popular with the town gallants as a girl of sixteen.   In *The Parson's Wedding* Killigrew

---

[50] Palmer, *The Comedy of Manners*. p. 76.
[51] *She Would if She Could*, V, 1, p. 233.

perceived the comic possibilities of a corresponding situation; but his Love-all is not a prominent personage and, like all his characters, is palely envisaged. In Lady Cockwood, Etherege achieved the first complete and brilliant portrayal of a woman of social pretensions whose attempted illicit amours are wrecked by the pressure of a social standard which she lacks intelligence to comprehend. Lady Cockwood appears particularly ludicrous in contrast with the sprightly Ariana and Gatty, who laugh at her without mercy and, as she knows in her heart, with justice.

The way had long been preparing for precisely this type of social drama. Already in *The Parson's Wedding* Killigrew had opposed, in the same manner, successful and unsuccessful social posing and had found in each case genuine cause for laughter. In *She Would if She Could* such comic contrast first becomes arresting, emphasized, as it is, with exceptional artistic and dramatic vigor. Etherege regards the standard of fashion as the one authoritative standard of conduct; by its terms he deftly defines and degrades folly and gives wisdom its due. He interprets this social standard with a charm and confidence in which no Restoration dramatist except Congreve excelled him.

The year 1668 is memorable in the history of Restoration comedy.[52] Etherege's second comedy was soon followed by three outstanding plays: Thomas Shadwell's first comedy, *The Sullen Lovers* (May, 1668),[53] Sir Charles Sedley's *The Mulberry Garden* (May, 1668),[54] and Dryden's *An Evening's Love, or The Mock Astrologer* (June, 1668).[55] The three plays are of only less importance in the Restoration tradition than *She Would if She Could*; they support Etherege's interpretation of the new social mode.

In the preface to *The Sullen Lovers*, Shadwell admitted that

---

[52] D'Avenant's last comedy, *The Man's the Master* (March, 1668: cf. Pepys, *Diary*, VII, p. 352), is a typical *capa y espada* comedy, adapted from two of Scarron's plays. It does not merit discussion.

[53] Pepys, *Diary*, VIII, p. 2.   [54] *Ibid.*, VII, p. 260.

[55] *Ibid.*, VIII, pp. 50–51.

he took the hint of the play from Molière's *Les Fâcheux*. He
claimed, at the same time, that the greater part of the work was
original and that he had added new complications of intrigue and
a greater variety of characters. Shadwell's readers soon discover
that *The Sullen Lovers* owes much to *Le Misanthrope* as well as to
Les Fâcheux. Stanford is a sort of "Alceste weakened to a mere
grumbler." [56] Lady Vaine resembles Arsinoé in *Le Misanthrope*,
and Sir Positive At-All, Ninny, Woodcock, and Huffe suggest
various combinations from among the bores of *Les Fâcheux* and
Célimène's affected guests in *Le Misanthrope*. In the "humours"
of the minor characters, Jonson's influence is also evident, an
influence which Shadwell himself felt pride in acknowledging.

Nevertheless, in spite of borrowings from Molière and Jonson,
The Sullen Lovers remains, like all of Shadwell's comedies, well
within the Restoration comic tradition. The most important
characters, Lovel and Carolina, are not "humours." Like Philinte and Éliante in *Le Misanthrope* they set a standard for the
play. But it is not a standard of good sense, such as that supported by Molière's staid and sensible lovers; it is a standard of
fashion. Lovel is a gay Restoration gallant, Carolina a Restoration coquette. Although in love with each other and contemplating marriage, the two never meet without a contest in raillery, in
which wit invariably triumphs over sentiment. Carolina assures
Lovel:

...I had rather hear a silenc'd Parson preach Sedition, than you talk
seriously of Love. . . . *My Love to you's as pure as the Flame, that burns
upon an Altar;* how scurvily it sounds! [57]

And she adds:

Besides, if we were marry'd, you might say, Faith, Carolina is a pretty
Woman and has Humour good enough, but a Pox on't she's my Wife;
no, no, I'll none of that. [57]

---

[56] Miles, *op. cit.*, p. 239.
[57] *The Sullen Lovers* (*Works*, I), II, p. 30.

The lively banter of these courtship scenes has clearly no precedent in Molière or in Jonson. It has a conspicuous precedent in
the comic mode of *précieuse* dialogue in Etherege's *She Would if
She Could*.

In Sedley's *The Mulberry Garden* the characters of the two
guardians are derived from Molière's *L'École des Maris*, although
the adventures of the English gentlemen are not paralleled in the
French source. To his friend and brother-wit, Etherege, Sedley
seems to have owed a much larger debt. In contrasting the love
adventures, set forth in heroic couplets, of two pairs of Platonic
lovers with the strictly comic action of his play, Sedley was probable influenced by the scheme of *The Comical Revenge*. As in *The
Comical Revenge*, the high-souled passions of the Platonic heroines
and the unselfish services of their lovers are emphasized with an
attempt at sober eloquence of style. There is a good deal of Platonic argument. Philander takes Eugenio to task for his jealousy
in a debate which reveals unmistakable echoes of Suckling's dialogue. Pleading his rights as a jealous lover, Eugenio ventures:

> A higher mark of love there cannot be,
> We doubt no lover, whom we jealous see.

But Philander remonstrates:

> So fevers are of life sure proofs we know,
> And yet our lives they often overthrow:
> Diseases, though well cur'd, our bodies mar,
> And fears, although remov'd, our loves impair:
> True love, like health, should no disorder know.[58]

The comic scenes of *The Mulberry Garden*, admirable in themselves though out of harmony with the romantic episodes, are
conceived in the spirit of rather similar scenes in *She Would if
She Could*. Sedley's gallants, Modish, Estridge, and Wildish,
with their taste for sprightly intrigues and for yet sprightlier

---

[58] *The Mulberry Garden* (*Works*, II), III, 1, p. 66. Cf. chap. III, pp. 70–71,
of this volume, where a similar description of jealousy is cited from Suckling's *Brennoralt*.

similitude sparring, and his merry coquette, Olivia, give the play all its life and color. Olivia undertakes her Park ramblings in the mood of Gatty, announcing:

. . . nothing venture, nothing win, and for my part I am resolv'd to allow all innocent liberty: this matrimony is a pill will scarce go down with a young man without gilding.[59]

Her railing wit encounters with Wildish parallel those of the modish young lovers in *She Would if She Could*. Neither Olivia nor Wildish can so disastrously sacrifice wit to sentiment as to indulge in a love confession. They play the graceful courtship game in which Courtal, Freeman, Ariana, and Gatty had been so dexterous. Like all witty Restoration lovers they are convinced, as Olivia avers, that —

. . . the great pleasure of gaming were lost, if we saw one another's hands; and of love, if we knew one another's hearts: there would be no room for good play in the one, nor for address in the other; which are the refin'd parts of both.[60]

Sedley's play was followed by Dryden's *An Evening's Love, or The Mock Astrologer*. In his preface to this comedy Dryden boasted of "our refining the courtship, raillery, and conversation of plays"[61] since the days of Jonson and Fletcher, and announced that repartee had at last rightly become "the greatest grace of comedy."[62] The chief value of the present comedy, Dryden wisely claimed,[63] lay in the wit encounters of Wildblood and Jacintha, which he had not derived from Calderon's *El Astrologo Fingido*, the Spanish source of his main plot.[64] Wildblood and Jacintha owe something, to be sure, to the lovers in Molière's *Le Dépit Amoureux*,[65] upon whose quarrel their own is modelled; but Dryden's claim to their originality is mainly correct. They are a

---

[59] *Ibid.*, III, 2, p. 68.   [60] *Ibid.*, I, 3, p. 43.
[61] *An Evening's Love, or The Mock Astrologer* (*Works*, III), Preface, p. 239.   [62] *Ibid.*, p. 245.   [63] *Ibid.*, p. 251.
[64] Alterations of Calderon's play were at this time accessible in *Le Feint Astrologue* by Thomas Corneille and *The Feign'd Astrologer* (anon., 1668).
[65] Langbaine, *op. cit.*, p. 131.

maturer Florimel and Celadon. Jacintha's disguises keep Wildblood in a state of perpetual perturbation, which he conceals
under a mask of polite composure. In the garb of a Turkish
maiden Jacintha wins his money at gaming; later she appears in
her own person and claims the sum he owes her. The bankrupt
Wildblood is unenlightened about the disguise but begins
promptly: "You make me happy by commanding me; To-
morrow morning my servant shall wait upon you with three
hundred pistoles." The payment, she insists, must be at once.
"Maskall, go and bring me three hundred pistoles immediately," [66] Wildblood hastens to command his servant, then scolds
the servant for losing the money. A clever gallant is not to be
shamed by a lady.

A recent critic of Dryden is of the opinion that in such courtship scenes as these, in which Dryden works more faithfully than
at other times in the manners tradition, the presence of "a certain passion and enthusiasm" [67] in his lovers still separates his
comedy from the comedy of Etherege. But, on the whole, the
contrast seems less striking than the resemblance. To Dryden's
credit, it must surely be remembered that the type of comic
effect achieved by him in the courtship scenes of his early plays
is quite the same as that upon which Etherege depended in similar scenes and which serves to distinguish Restoration comedy of
manners very clearly from other forms of comedy.

In the next five years, from 1669 to 1673, Restoration comedy
developed slowly but surely. Many of the comedies of this period are not strictly comedies of manners. On the other hand, few
plays were written in which some interest in manners is not discernible. Moreover, the best of the new plays may be termed
true comedies of manners, which leave no room for doubt as to
the nature of the type which they represent.

[66] *An Evening's Love* (*Works*, III), III, 1, p. 313.
[67] Nicoll, *op. cit.*, p. 185.

One persistent current of alien influence, not of itself in harmony with the Restoration social mode, was the influence of Molière. Lacy's *The Dumb Lady, or The Farrier Made Physician* (1669) [68] illustrates very well Molière's fate at the hands of uninspired adapters. Lacy lightly stirs together *Le Médecin malgré lui* and *L'Amour Médecin*,[69] liberally adds new episodes of a licentious sort, and sketches, besides, in a set of ludicrous adventures, the inevitable clownish suitor of English comedy. In *Sir Salomon: or, The Cautious Coxcomb* (1669) [70] John Caryl follows rather closely *L'École des Femmes*,[71] with some thefts in his secondary plot from *L'École des Maris*. For the character of Sir Arthur Addel, the country clown who goes a-wooing, Caryl, like Lacy, depends mainly upon English tradition. Edward Ravenscroft's first comedy, *The Citizen Turn'd Gentleman* (1671) [72] is an ingenious combination of *Le Bourgeois Gentilhomme* and *Monsieur de Pourceaugnac*, with borrowed hints, also, from *L'Avare*,[73] — "a most bewildering scrapbook farce" [74] in Ravenscroft's usual manner.[75]

Shadwell's *The Miser* (1671),[76] an adaptation of *L'Avare*, has the distinction of being the most original play of this group. Although not a dramatist of the first order, Shadwell was always more than a mere slavish imitator. Even in such a play as *The Miser*, the spirit of Etherege counts for something. Shadwell's hero is still a Restoration gallant, not a solemn fellow like Molière's Cléante. Cléante could never have been guilty of Theodore's reflection: "Pox o' this canting word Honour! it never did good yet." [77] And only a Restoration audience could appreciate

---

[68] Genest, *Some Account of the English Stage* I, p. 96.
[69] Cf. Miles, *op. cit.*, p. 229.   [70] Genest, *op. cit.*, I, p. 98.
[71] Miles, *op. cit.*, p. 237.   [72] Genest, *op. cit.*, I, p. 125.
[73] Miles, *op. cit.*, p. 234.   [74] *Ibid.*, p. 88.
[75] Among the adaptations from Molière, mention may be made of Betterton's *The Amorous Widow* (1670), an imitation of *George Dandin*, and Medbourne's *Tartuffe* (1670), translated from Molière's *Tartuffe*.
[76] Genest, *op. cit.*, I, p. 119.
[77] *The Miser* (*Works*, III), IV, p. 66.

the manner in which the cavalier friends deplore Theodore's marriage, yet take comfort in reminding him: "But 'tis but having a little Patience, and we shall have you amongst us again, as honest a Sinner as the best of us." [78] This infusion of Restoration sentiments deserves mention in a play in which the action was necessarily determined largely by the French source.

Not many of the new plays reverted wholly to Elizabethan fashions. Edward Howard, indeed, seems to have posed as a sort of second Jonson, who had come to deliver the stage from its addiction to miserable French farce. In *The Women's Conquest* (1671) and *The Six Days Adventure* (1671) [79] he revived Jonsonian humours in a feeble but pretentious manner. The Duke of Newcastle, in his last comedy *The Triumphant Widow, or The Medley of Humours* (produced by 1674),[80] imitates Jonson with the same painful fidelity. The majority of lesser Restoration dramatists preferred a more varied dramatic program.

Among the new plays comedies of intrigue appear to have been popular. These were commonly derived from Spanish sources or composed under the influence of Spanish stage conventions. Two of Dryden's comedies, *The Assignation; or, Love in a Nunnery* (1672) and *Marriage à la Mode* (1672),[81] have little interest aside from complications of intrigue. In the latter play, it is true, there are fragments of "proviso" contracts,[82] and one of the characters, the *précieuse* Melantha, suggests Congreve's Millamant without possessing any of Millamant's charm. The first two comedies of Mrs. Aphra Behn, *The Amorous Prince* (1671) [83] and *The Dutch Lover* (1673),[84] possess briskness of action, flavored at times with Restoration libertinism.

In Ravenscroft's *The Careless Lovers* (1673) [85] farcical intrigue

[78] *Ibid.*, V, p. 103.		[79] Cf. Summers, *op. cit.*, p. xvi.
[80] Nicoll, *op. cit.*, p. 203.
[81] Genest, *op. cit.*, I, pp. 135 and 133.
[82] *Marriage à la Mode* (*Works*, IV), II, 1, pp. 280-281, and V, 1, p. 356.
[83] Genest, *op. cit.*, I, p. 120.		[84] *Ibid.*, p. 154.		[85] *Ibid.*, p. 151.

of a very boisterous sort may be observed. Yet this play is related more closely than most of its type to the manners tradition. Borrowings from Molière are numerous [86] but do not occur in the best scenes. The plan of the minor action, which gives the play its title, is derived from Dryden's *Secret Love*,[87] with an addition of new features in what is certainly Ravenscroft's happiest manner. In the portrayal of his railing lovers, Careless and Hillaria,[88] Ravenscroft betrays, as he turns. temporarily from Molière, his genuine appreciation of the Restoration comic spirit.

Ravenscroft's Hillaria is even more spirited and imperious than Dryden's Florimel. She is the despair of her old-fashioned uncle, whom on one occasion she actually threatens with a cane, shouting: "Down on your Marry-Bones." [89] When the uncle begs her to marry Careless, whom she loves, she wavers, then retorts gaily:

Stay Uncle, now I think on't, you may take him with you. Marriage is quite out of Fashion, and I hate to be out of it, as much as you do to be in't; if he had Ten or Twelve Thousand a year would keep me a Coach and six Horses, and all things suitable to that Grandeur, I might admit him as a gallant, and all that — [90]

Presently, talking with Careless, she relents a little and concedes:

But you know what you must have first — a huge Estate; but because you brought us so handsomely off: There's my hand to Kiss, and I confer on you the Title of my Servant.[91]

Later on, like Dryden's Florimel, Hillaria disguises herself as a gallant, pursues her lover to a gaming-house, makes love to a couple of his courtesans, and humiliates him by other merry pranks.

[86] Miles, *op. cit.*, p. 226.
[87] Miles does not note this influence. He suggests Ravenscroft's indebtedness to *An Evening's Love*, a play from which the dramatist could not have made any very important borrowing.
[88] Ravenscroft's own predilection for these merry lovers is easy to guess. He removes them bodily to his later play, *The Canterbury Guests* (1694).
[89] *The Careless Lovers*, IV, p. 37.
[90] *Ibid.*, III, p. 29.   [91] *Ibid.*, p. 30.

The skirmishes of the pair end in a courtship scene in which the two lovers follow the example of Celadon and Florimel in their provisos regarding marriage. The stipulations are considerably more shameless than those in *Secret Love*, Hillaria going so far as to insist upon having a gallant and Careless making arrangements for his mistresses. The concluding articles deal with the problem of the names by which the lovers shall address each other.

> *Hil.* In Company, you shall never call me Wife, or Dear, or Sweetheart, but Madam.
>
> *Carel.* In Company you shall never call me Husband, or by my Christian Name, but Mr. Careless.
>
> *Hil.* In none of these particulars will I ever offend Mr. Careless.
>
> *Carel.* In none of these particulars will I ever offend you, Madam.[92]

The formality of the agreement Hillaria emphasizes by demanding of her uncle: "Uncle, pray con o're the Articles, for you are to be summon'd for a Witness upon occasion."[93] In the vivacity of this scene Ravenscroft seems to bring us one step nearer to Congreve's "proviso" covenant in *The Way of the World*.

The comic mode which could flourish in such unpromising soil as Ravenscroft's *The Careless Lovers* became more impressive in the work of dramatists who entertained a more serious view of their art. Shadwell and Wycherley make an ill-assorted pair. Both dramatists, however, understood the dramatic value of the Restoration tradition. Shadwell interpreted the current mode in a drab manner, although admiringly; Wycherley with vivid power, yet with increasing personal aversion.

To Shadwell Etherege's second comedy had given the great dramatic inspiration of his life. Throughout a long career, with patient, plodding devotion, Shadwell revived in comedy after comedy the dramatic scheme of *She Would if She Could*. As we have observed, Shadwell proclaims his esteem for Etherege in his

---

[92] *Ibid.*, V, pp. 76–77.   [93] *Ibid.*, p. 77.

preface to *The Humourists* (1670).[94] The same play, best known for its abundance of licentious detail, marks the beginning of Shadwell's actual discipleship. Etherege was never Shadwell's sole master. Jonsonian humours still decorate *The Humourists*. But even the humours are conceived in the new comic spirit. The false wit Drybob, for example, is comic because he apes the similitudes and other mannerisms of the true man of fashion. More noteworthy still is Shadwell's repetition in this play of the main intrigue of *She Would if She Could*. Lady Loveyouth, an amorous old woman who supposes herself a widow, endeavors with the aid of her maid to carry on an intrigue with Raymond, a young gallant. Raymond politely courts the old coquette in order to mask his affair with her niece Theodosia. With the triumph of Theodosia comes the aunt's final humiliation and her denunciation of the hero as "False and ungrateful Man!" [95] Lady Loveyouth, although she suffers by the comparison, is the genuine successor of Lady Cockwood.

Shadwell's fourth comedy, *Epsom Wells* (1672),[96] bears an even closer resemblance to *She Would if She Could*. The young gallants, Raines and Bevil, "men of wit and pleasure," correspond to Etherege's Freeman and Courtal; Lucia and Carolina, the sprightly girls whom they woo, are very like Gatty and Ariana; Bevil's intrigue with amorous Mrs. Woodly is conducted in practically the same fashion as that of Courtal with Lady Cockwood; and the marital hostilities between the Woodlys are patterned after the domestic quarrels of the Cockwoods. The parallelism extends to the letter forgery, the subsequent railing scenes between the girls and their suitors, the polite defense by her lover of the angry mistress' honor, and the same lady's provocation of the quarrel of her husband and lover, followed by her at-

94 Genest, *op. cit.*, I, p. 110.
95 *The Humourists* (*Works*, I), IV, p. 190.
96 Genest, *op. cit.*, I, p. 137.

tempt at a new amour with the latter's friend. The spirit of
Etherege's comedy is amply reënforced. Raines, like Bevil, has
two love affairs and believes that variety in love intrigues is essential to a life of pleasure.[97] Woodly, who is married, courts his
young cousin Carolina and justifies his action by explaining to
her: "Marriage is the last Engagement of all; for that only
points out where a Man cannot love."[98] Lucia and Carolina are
both heartily in love with their gallants and quite disposed to
marry them, yet Lucia scorns to offer the young gentlemen any
more encouraging declaration than:

> This is no Age for Marriage; but if you will keep your Distance, we
> will admit you for a couple of Servants, as far as a Country-Dance, or
> Ombre, or so.[99]

As usual, Shadwell felt obliged to round out his comedy with a
number of minor characters, whose humours divert, throughout
the play, all persons of a more refined taste. The vulgarity and
obviousness of these humours Etherege would surely have known
how to avoid. But in the relations of witty and witless personages and in his consequent achievement of two sorts of comic
effect Shadwell was following, though humbly, in the footsteps
of his greater contemporary.

It is with a sense of relief that we turn from Shadwell's labored comedies to William Wycherley's first plays, *Love in a
Wood, or St. James's Park* (1671)[100] and *The Gentleman Dancing-
Master* (1671?).[101] The former play owes a few features, though
only a few, to Molière's *L'École des Maris* and *L'École des
Femmes*.[102] Ranger, the most important character, is the typical
fine gallant of Restoration comedy. In his various adventures,
in the Park and elsewhere, he becomes involved in amusing

---

[97] *Epsom Wells* (*Works*, I), I, p. 206.
[98] *Ibid.*, II, pp. 210–211.   [99] *Ibid.*, V, p. 281.
[100] See the discussion of this date by W. C. Ward in Wycherley, *Works*,
pp. 3–5.   [101] *Ibid.*, pp. 126–127.
[102] Miles, *op. cit.*, p. 231.

predicaments, such as those experienced by Courtal in *She
Would if She Could*, from which he extricates himself through
his invariable politeness, affable flattery, and ingenious lying.
He is earnestly ceremonious with the too willing Lady Flippant,
cautious and wary in his dealings with the jealous Lydia, all ob-
sequiousness in his unwelcome wooing of the new mistress, Christina. His kinship with Courtal is revealed in his first words to
Christina:

> *Chris.* Sure, to my plague, this is the first time you ever saw me!
> *Ran.* Sure, to the plague of my poor heart, 'tis not the hundredth
> time I have seen you! For since the time I saw you first, you have not been
> at the Park, playhouse, Exchange, or other public place, but I saw you;
> for it was my business to watch and follow.
> *Chris.* Pray, when did you see me last at the Park, playhouse, or
> exchange?
> *Ran.* Some two, three days, or a week ago.
> *Chris.* I have not been this month out of this chamber.
>
> . . . .
>
> *Ran.* You'll pardon a lover's memory, madam. —. . .[103]

Christina's implication in this intrigue is warranted by the Restoration necessity for punishing Valentine's jealousy. At the close
of the play, Valentine and Christina, Ranger and Lydia pair off
in high spirits, Ranger still with words of flippant raillery on his
lips.

The play discloses Wycherley's "prentice work"[104] in its rather
grimly handled humours. Alderman Gripe, while recalling similar
figures in the comedy of Brome and Wilson, is satirized with
unique vehemence. Lady Flippant, the prudish "revenger" of
her sex, is drawn with a much heavier stroke than Lady Cockwood. The match-making bawd, Mrs. Joyner, is less ridiculous
than vicious. Even the fops, Addleplot and Dapperwit, are tedious and their folly a sober affair. Dapperwit claims a special
share of our interest because of the fact that he is in the tradition

[103] *Love in a Wood, or St. James's Park*, II, 2, p. 48.
[104] Palmer, *The Comedy of Manners*, p. 122.

of Cowley's Puny. His head is full of similitudes which he strings together, whenever he can get an audience, in a manner which he himself considers very "brisk" and engaging. Once Lydia is so good-humored as to hear him out on the various kinds of wits,[105] and he manages his *précieuse* argument with a propriety which the Duchess of Newcastle might well have applauded. Yet Dapperwit decidedly lacks the volatile gaiety and exuberant animation which effectively keep Cowley's Puny and Congreve's Witwoud from becoming insufferable bores. Indeed, Dapperwit's sobriety is a clear sign of Wycherley's divergence from the typical joyousness of mood of Restoration comedy.

The Gentleman Dancing-Master, a much livelier play, has been termed the "merriest"[106] of Wycherley's comedies. The play owes something to the scheme of *L'École des Maris*, a hint for the intrigue to Calderon's *El Maestro de Danzar*, and repeats some conventional humours. Its largest debt is to the Restoration comic tradition. Hippolita is as venturesome a young coquette as Gatty and at fourteen is prepared to "shift" for herself. She longs to "take the innocent liberty of the town."[107] As she assures her absurdly old-fashioned aunt, Mrs. Caution, she is convinced:

By what I've heard, 'tis a pleasant, well-bred, complaisant, free, frolic, good-natured, pretty age; and if you do not like it, leave it to us that do.[108]

She is young at coquetry but quick to learn the art, and manages her intrigue with Gerrard with commendable adroitness. Politely following her lead, Gerrard behaves, in embarrassing circumstances, as handsomely as a gallant gentleman can. His true wit is pleasantly contrasted, in accordance with the usual practice of Restoration comic dramatists, with the folly of his rival, Monsieur de Paris, who is only a "monsieur,"[109] and who himself ad-

---

[105] *Love in a Wood*, II, 1, pp. 40–41.
[106] Palmer, *The Comedy of Manners*, p. 126.
[107] *The Gentleman Dancing-Master*, I, 2, p. 140.
[108] *Ibid.*, I, 2, p. 141.   [109] *Ibid.*, I, 1, p. 132.

mits to Hippolita's father that "dere is not de least ribbon of my garniture but is as dear to me as your daughter, jarni!" [110] Paris poses as a yet finer gentleman of fashion than Gerrard, but is manifestly an impostor who provokes his own defeat.

Between Wycherley's first comedies and his last a break seems to occur. The note of depression apparent in *Love in a Wood* and only temporarily silenced in the farcical scenes of *The Gentleman Dancing-Master* finds expression, in *The Country Wife* (c. 1674 ?)[111] and *The Plain Dealer* (1675 or 1676),[112] in a serious indictment of the Restoration comic mode. The mode was stronger, of course, than the indictment. Wycherley was forced to acknowledge, in the heat of his attack, the stability of the social order that he assailed.

In *The Country Wife* and *The Plain Dealer* the influence of Molière acquired a new emphasis. The two plays are related, more closely than any other distinguished comedies of the Restoration period, to important comedies by Molière. *The Country Wife* owes its plot-scheme, with some alterations, and the initial inspiration for most of its characters to *L'École des Femmes*, "modified" [113] by *L'École des Maris*. The same sort of relationship exists between *The Plain Dealer* and *Le Misanthrope*, modified by *La Critique de l'École des Femmes*.[114]

In *The Country Wife* the pattern of the adventures of Pinchwife, Mrs. Pinchwife, and Horner is derived from *L'École des Femmes*. The Pinchwifes are related to Arnolphe and Agnes, and

[110] *Ibid.*, III, 1, p. 181.
[111] Nicoll, *op. cit.*, p. 226, is of the opinion that the play was not produced until January, 1675, for the performance at which date he cites (p. 307) a warrant from one of the documents in the Lord Chamberlain's department of the Public Record Office. G. B. Churchill, *The Country Wife and The Plain Dealer*, Introduction, p. xxv, argues that the play was acted at the Duke's Theatre between 1672 and 1674. It was published in 1675.
[112] Cf. Churchill, *op. cit.*, pp. xxv-xxvii. Nicoll, *op. cit.*, p. 308, notes a performance in December, 1676. We cannot be sure that this was the first performance. The play was published early in 1677.
[113] Cf. Miles, *op. cit.*, p. 227.   [114] *Ibid.*, p. 235.

Horner to Horace. *L'École des Maris* furnishes Wycherley with the framework of such important matters of intrigue as the surreptitious correspondence between the lovers and the disguise adopted by the young woman in the furtherance of her love affair. The rôle of Alithea recalls that of Léonor in *L'École des Maris*. In *The Plain Dealer* the relations of Manly and Olivia bear a general resemblance to those of Alceste and Célimène in *Le Misanthrope*. In both cases the lover is painfully disillusioned. Olivia exhibits in her temperament combined qualities of Célimène and Arsinoé in *Le Misanthrope* and of Élise and Climène in *La Critique de l'École des Femmes*. From the last-named play Wycherley borrows half of the second act of *The Plain Dealer*. Eliza owes much to Éliante in *Le Misanthrope* and something to Uranie in *La Critique de l'École des Femmes*. Freeman in his relations with Manly occupies the position of Philinte in his relations with Alceste in *Le Misanthrope*. Those who champion the indebtedness of Restoration comedy to Molière make much of these resemblances. It must be confessed that without the background of Molière's plots and characters it is impossible to imagine the existence of *The Country Wife* and *The Plain Dealer*.

While following Molière thus closely, Wycherley still employs, but with noticeable aversion, the conventional Restoration milieu. Sparkish in *The Country Wife* and Novel and Plausible in *The Plain Dealer* have even less exuberance of spirit than the earlier Dapperwit; not only have they no real enthusiasm for false wit in others, but also their applause of their own similitudes is stiff and formal. Much of the gaiety is forced. Horner's program of debauchery is undertaken in a spirit of scornful cynicism and yields no more gracious amusement than an affair with a "dear idiot." [115] Wycherley permits even his fools to satirize the social order to which they belong. Novel insists all too ironically: "railing is satire, you know; and roaring and making a

[115] *The Country Wife*, V, 4, p. 357.

noise humour." [116] Lady Fidget tranquilly assures Horner, in behalf of herself and her associates: "You would have found us
modest women in our denials only." [117] Manly's stern aphorisms
cut and wound the pretenses of the age with such injuries as
Etherege would never have dreamed of inflicting. Wycherley
makes for himself a place apart from the majority of contemporary English dramatists, who, on the whole, discovered an
agreeable propriety in Restoration society and who certainly had
no disposition to attack its foundations.

Are we to conclude, then, that Wycherley sympathized with
Molière's comic spirit? Or are we to suppose that these two
plays embody "standards of judgment peculiar to Wycherley"? [118] "Are not these comparisons otiose?", [119] asks Palmer and
reasonably concludes that Wycherley was "a Restoration gentleman, not born, but made." [120]

Comparisons are sometimes advisable and perhaps especially
so in Wycherley's case. If in following Molière Wycherley nevertheless readjusted his material, however unwillingly, to suit the
temper of Restoration society, the dominant authority of the
Restoration social mode becomes more convincing than ever.
The two plays give evidence of the fact that this was precisely
what Wycherley did.

In *The Country Wife* the striking figure of Horner, a Restoration rake in the most extravagant sense of the term, stands out in
clear relief against a Restoration background of silly, intriguing
women. Horner would have shocked Molière's gentle, love-sick,
and somewhat ineffectual Horace; but the Fidgets and Squeam-
ishes gratefully accept him, and admire his clever control of the
predicament of their social group. Pinchwife, the jealous, suspicious husband, must be cuckolded, not because like Arnolphe he

[116] *The Plain Dealer*, V, 2, p. 491.   [117] *The Country Wife*, V, 4, p. 350.
[118] G. B. Churchill, "The Originality of William Wycherley," in *Schelling Anniversary Papers*, p. 82.
[119] Palmer, *The Comedy of Manners*, p. 135.   [120] *Ibid.*, p. 94.

has been obtuse and short-sighted, but for the sake of social justice. Mrs. Pinchwife, with all her crudity and inexperience, is much less like Agnes, humbly desiring a husband who does not make himself ridiculous, than like Lady Cockwood, the too eager social pretender who cannot quite play the game. When Mrs. Pinchwife's schemes, like those of Lady Cockwood, come tumbling in ruins about her, she can only echo the rueful sentiments of all such Restoration social pretenders, past and to come, as she laments: "And I must be a country wife still too, I find; for I can't like a city one, be rid of my musty husband and do what I list." [121] In *The Plain Dealer* Manly's relations with his mistress present problems which any Restoration gallant might have to face, but which could never have been included in Moliére's scheme of things. Olivia is a mercenary, hypocritical, unscrupulous, wanton jilt, who violates the rules of the social game and is punished. Vernish is her fitting partner.

Alithea, Harcourt, Eliza and Freeman are thoroughly reasonable people; like the characters of Molière with whom they correspond, they acquire a special importance through setting a comic standard for the plays in which they appear. Like Molière's reasonable people they keep us sane and clear-headed, by their clarity of vision, in the midst of extraordinary exhibitions of social folly. The resemblance extends no farther. Molière's reasonable people are philosophers, sober incarnations of good sense, whereas Wycherley's are men and women of the world, intelligent compliers with Restoration fashions.

The good sense of Léonor in *L'École des Maris* is very different from the good sense of Alithea in *The Country Wife*. Léonor has a chance to enjoy freely all the pleasures of society, and, as her guardian had predicted, they do not turn her head. Society rather bores her. At the end of the play she deliberately chooses to give her hand in marriage to her prudent old guardian, whose

[121] *The Country Wife*, V, 4, p. 359.

judgment she respects and for whose devotion to her welfare she is duly grateful. One cannot imagine such a conclusion for Alithea's frivolities. Alithea's rôle is that of the intelligent woman of fashion and presumably will always be so. It is her delight to "take the innocent liberty of the town." [122] She is convinced that a husband's jealousy means for a woman —

... loss of her honour, her quiet, nay, her life sometimes; and what's as bad almost, the loss of this town; that is, she is sent into the country, which is the last ill-usage of a husband to a wife, I think.[123]

She is even ready, she fancies, to "marry a fool for fortune, liberty, or title." [124] But when Sparkish at last proves jealous, she agrees to a marriage with Harcourt, who shares her tastes and prejudices.

Eliza and Freeman in *The Plain Dealer* similarly champion "the naughty world." [125] Eliza differs from Éliante, whose common sense has nothing to do with a special society, but is to be interpreted in broadly human terms. Éliante has no illusions about conventions of any sort. She frankly explains to Philinte that she would be glad to see Célimène and Alceste happily married, but, if that may not be, she would be equally glad to become Alceste's second choice. Later, she sees Alceste in a somewhat different light and without the slightest ceremony offers her hand to Philinte, the prosaic but ever loyal friend. With Wycherley's Eliza conventions count for everything. The diversions of the *beau monde* absorb all her energies. To her mind "the world is but a constant keeping gallant, whom we fail not to quarrel with when anything crosses us, yet cannot part with't for our hearts." [126] Whenever she appears in *The Plain Dealer*, Eliza is on the defensive for the best ideals of Restoration society, and she plays her cards well.

---

[122] *The Country Wife*, II, 1, p. 266. [123] *Ibid.*, IV, 1, p. 309.
[124] *Ibid.*, V, 4, p. 346. [125] *The Plain Dealer*, V, 1, p. 480.
[126] *Ibid.*, II, 1, p. 395.

Freeman, in his easy-going compliance with social fashions, offers a sharp contrast to the sagacious philosopher Philinte. Philinte governs all his acts by a standard of reasonable conduct, based on a very charitable philosophy of life. In debate with Alceste he argues earnestly:

> Mon Dieu, des moeurs du temps mettons-nous en peine,
> Et faisons un peu grâce à la nature humaine;
> Ne l'examinons point dans la grande rigeur,
> Et voyons ses defauts avec quelque douceur.
> Il faut, parmi le monde, un vertu traitable;
> A force de sagesse, on peut être blamable;
> La parfaite raison fuit tout extrémité,
> Et veut que l'on soit sage avec sobriété.[127]

Freeman's philosophy, in contrast, is no deeper than that of the typical Restoration gallant who complies sensibly with the age. His gay widow-wooing, which occupies no small amount of his time and effort, could never have engaged the interest of a person like Philinte. Being hard-pressed for money, Freeman is quite prepared to carry through a most ridiculous marriage. His implicit faith in the social standard of his age is apparent in his remark to Manly: "Well, doctors differ. You are for plain dealing, I find: but against your particular notions, I have the practice of the whole world."[128]

The theory is sometimes advanced that Manly represents Wycherley's ideal hero,[129] assailing, with some necessary brutality, the vices of an ugly world. Unfortunately for this assumption, the conduct of Manly, through nearly all of *The Plain Dealer*, is not very far removed from that of a madman. He kicks his sailors and forces them to keep off visitors with drawn cutlasses; he cuffs on the ear a lawyer who tells him a lie; he takes by the nose an alderman who asks a favor of him; he

[127] *Le Misanthrope (Oeuvres*, V), I, 1, p. 452.
[128] *The Plain Dealer*, I, 1, p. 384.
[129] Cf. Miles, *op. cit.*, p. 113, and G. B. Churchill, "The Originality of William Wycherley," *Schelling Anniversary Papers*, pp. 82–84.

threatens to cut his mistress' throat and his boy's too, if the boy will not hold the door while he wreaks vengeance on the mistress. Furthermore, this man who has proudly boasted that he "can do a rude thing rather than an unjust thing" [130] commits a yet greater offense in weakness of judgment. Early in the play he insists that he "can have but one friend, for a true heart admits but of one friendship, as of one love." [131] Freeman suggests that this is a short-sighted judgment, and so it proves. Manly is at last obliged to concede that Freeman has had a clearer vision of the world than his own. Fidelia, of course, is partly responsible for Manly's conversion to the ways of the world. But Fidelia is a romantic intruder in this highly unromantic society and, save as fortune favors her, is quite powerless to cope with its problems. She is perhaps the only type of woman who could have convinced Manly's heart of the truth of feminine virtue and devotion. It is Freeman, however, who forces Manly to weigh and judge the worth of social values. As the play closes, Freeman stands by Manly's side, attentive, affable, master of the situation as he had been from the beginning, knowing well the heart of his friend. Freeman turns to Manly with a pleasant aphorism on his lips, to the effect that we quarrel with the world only because we cannot enjoy it as we would choose to do. And Manly, in his last speech, seconds Freeman's conclusion and makes his peace with the age.

It is true that Wycherley's reasonable people often fade into the background when we feel most need of their assurances. Social folly and hypocrisy are much closer realities to Wycherley than the social poise and integrity which make amends. In his most powerful scenes Wycherley devotes himself, with more bitterness than any of his contemporaries, to the unlovelier aspects of Restoration society. When other writers of Restoration comedy ridicule folly and vice, it is more lightheartedly and rarely

[130] *The Plain Dealer*, I, 1, p. 376.   [131] *Ibid.*, p. 381.

with corrective emphasis. On some occasions, Wycherley assails some of the most cherished ideals of the age, and even a gallant gentleman like Freeman winces under the assault. At such times — nor should we hesitate to make the admission — Wycherley is playing false to the tradition of Restoration comedy of manners; he confirms our suspicion that he was not "born" a Restoration gentleman. In the main, unable to reject its claims, he supports the Restoration comic standard of social compliance. His wisest characters accept its decrees and in so doing become distinguished from the foolish people in their midst. If we still find occasion to laugh at Wycherley's wise people, as well as his fools, we introduce another standard of judging, which has no weight within this society, but upon our perception of which Wycherley, like Etherege, though with a malice unknown to Etherege, relies for our diversion. Even in *The Plain Dealer*, where social pretensions are subjected to the repeated fire of Manly's dangerous charges, the social standard of the age is accorded an ultimate triumph.

Wycherley's sceptical mood was not repeated. With the conspicuous exception of Wycherley, Restoration dramatists accepted the leadership of Etherege. In *She Would if She Could* the main course of development of Restoration comedy had been determined. In *The Man of Mode* the general significance of the movement, thus far, was summed up with reassuring finality.

A small group of comedies dating 1675 and 1676 requires comment. Material from Molière's plays was again utilized in John Crowne's first comedy, *The Country Wit* (January, 1676),[132] and Thomas Rawlins' *Tom Essence: or, The Modish Wife* (September, 1676).[133] The latter play repeats in its main action,[134] with little originality, the plot of Molière's *Sganarelle*. *The Country Wit*

---

[132] Nicoll, *op. cit.*, p. 310.   [133] *Ibid.*, p. 204.
[134] The secondary plot (cf. Langbaine, *op. cit.*, p. 552) is based on Thomas Corneille's *Don Caesar D'Avalos*.

combines plot features from *Le Sicilien, Tartuffe, La Comtesse d'Escarbagnas,* and *Les Femmes Savantes.*[135] Crowne's play is not, however, a mere accumulation of borrowings. Like all adapters of Molière who brought to their task some measure of native endowment, Crowne concentrates, in his best scenes, on a study of Restoration manners. His hero, Ramble, is a witty, debonair gentleman, who cleverly conducts a number of hazardous intrigues, takes pains to be polite even to the troublesome Lady Faddle, extricates himself from dilemmas by exuberant lying, and brightly persuades the heroine that he is at all times a gallant fellow. The other characters in the play, especially the old-fashioned father who condemns "such a frolicsome age," [136] the amorous Lady Faddle, the debauched old Lord, and the clownish lover whose head is "as full of similes as the plays are," [137] appear, on investigation, to bear a much more convincing resemblance to their prototypes in Restoration comedy than to any characters in the plays by Molière which Crowne consulted for his plot.

Comedies of intrigue, bordering upon farce, continued to be popular. Mention may be made of *Love in the Dark, or The Man of Bus'ness* (1675) [138] by Sir Francis Fane, *The Town-Fop; or, Sir Timothy Taudrey* (September, 1676) [139] by Mrs. Behn, *The Wrangling Lovers, or The Invisible Mistress* (September, 1676) [140] by Ravenscroft, and *Madam Fickle or The Witty False One* (November, 1676) [141] by Thomas D'Urfey. All these plays illustrate, to a greater or less degree, the Restoration comic mode, although the claims of farcical intrigue are ordinarily paramount. D'Urfey's play suggests the future program of its author, one of the most indefatigable dramatic pilferers of the age. Already in *Madam*

---

[135] Miles, *op. cit.,* pp. 217–218.
[136] *The Country Wit (Works,* III), III, p. 63.
[137] *Ibid.,* IV, p. 85.   [138] Genest, *op. cit.,* I, p. 173.
[139] Nicoll, *op. cit.,* p. 255.   [140] *Ibid.,* p. 242.
[141] *Ibid.,* p. 261. D'Urfey's *A Fond Husband* (cf. Nicoll, p. 261, n. 3) was licensed for printing in June, 1676, but apparently was not acted until the following year.

Fickle D'Urfey manipulates in his characteristic easy-going, en-
tertaining manner the material which he has borrowed from a
variety of sources.[142]   It is a curious coincidence, if nothing more,
that the love affair of D'Urfey's Manly and Constantia parallels
that of Manly and Fidelia in Wycherley's *The Plain Dealer*.

With Shadwell's *The Virtuoso* (May, 1676) [143] we return to genuine comedy of manners.   Two gallants, Longvil and Bruce, wittily
woo Clarinda and Miranda, a couple of merry flirts.   Bruce also
conducts an intrigue with the girls' aunt, Lady Gimcrack, an
affected lady who protests her virtuous inclinations in the very
act of yielding readily to her lover's suit.   The relations of the
Gimcracks are copied from those of the Cockwoods.   Sir Nicho-
las, like Sir Oliver, is a ridiculously credulous husband, ever san-
guine as to his wife's "dear Truth." [144]

The courtship scenes between the girls and their gallants are
rich in artificial dialogue.   Similitude contests are more numerous
than in Shadwell's earlier comedies.   In one conversation the
lovers elaborately develop the theme of love as a money-lending
project; [145] in another, they compare love to a game; [146] in a
third, to music.[147]   The last of these encounters is here quoted,
not for its liveliness, alas, but for its faithful reproduction of the
most formal type of *précieuse* discussion:

> *Bruce.* But to us there is no Musick like Love, or Harmony like the
> consent of Lover's Hearts.
> *Miran.* But as Musick is improv'd by Practice, Love decays by it;
> and therefore I scarce dare talk on't.
> *Clarin.* Let what Harmony soever be between Lovers at first, in a short
> time it turns to scurvy jangling: and therefore can you blame us, if we
> divert so dangerous a thing any way? —
> *Long.* I confess, it may come to Discord; but 'tis as in Musick, if it be
> made good, it makes the following Concord better.

---

[142] Cf. Langbaine, *op. cit.*, p. 182.   [143] Nicoll, *op. cit.*, p. 194.
[144] *The Virtuoso* (*Works*, I), IV, p. 379.
[145] *Ibid.*, II, pp. 334–335.   [146] *Ibid.*, III, p. 351.
[147] *Ibid.*, IV, pp. 380–381.

Bruce. If they play upon one another, till they are out of Tune, they must needs jangle.

Long. In that case, they must lay by, and tune again, and then strike up afresh.

Miran. That Simile will never hold; for when Love grows once out of Tune, they may screw and keep a Coil, but 'twill never stand in tune again.

Clarin. 'Tis most certain: when Love comes once to bend, it breaks presently.

Bruce. But perhaps it may be set again, like a broken Limb, and be the stronger for't.

Miran. No; when Love breaks, 'tis into so many Splinters, 'tis never to be set again.[147]

With all such exhibitions of true wit and graceful affectation Shadwell contrasts the false wit and foppery of his usual retinue of coarse fools and triflers.

In Etherege's *The Man of Mode, or Sir Fopling Flutter* (March, 1676),[148] we become intimately acquainted, once more, with the most brilliant society which Restoration comedy has to offer us. Etherege's hero, Dorimant, superlatively well-bred, witty, engaging, is the finest of all fine gentlemen in Restoration comedy. We may perceive in the character of Dorimant the fine flowering of Restoration culture, a culture rooted in the curious artifices of *préciosité* and still controlled by its mannerisms.

Belinda may object (though not in her heart) that Dorimant is "a man of no principles." But his brother-gallant, Medley, is on the alert to rebuke her with the ironical reminder: "Your man of principles is a very fine thing indeed!"[149] Dorimant is, of course, inconstant. He exclaims: "Constancy at my years! 'tis not a virtue in season; you might as well expect the fruit the autumn ripens i' the spring."[150]

He is, of course, a dissembler. "Good nature and good manners," he admits, corrupt him, causing him even to "wilfully mistake art for nature," in order to "avoid offence."[150] His dis-

---

[148] Nicoll, *op. cit.*, p. 224.
[149] *The Man of Mode, or Sir Fopling Flutter*, III, 2, pp. 290–291.
[150] *Ibid.*, II, 2, p. 277.

sembling stands him repeatedly in good stead. In a clever disguise, he makes Lady Woodvil, who has always been horrified at the mere mention of his wicked name, fall absurdly in love with his charms. He knows how to soothe Belinda artfully into a good humor. When she reproaches him for his cruelty to Mrs. Loveit, he protests eagerly: "Nothing is cruel to a man who could kill himself to please you." [151] He contrives their intrigue with uniform dexterity and politeness, although it involves him in some decidedly embarrassing situations. The jealous fury of Mrs. Loveit makes his intrigue with her rather more difficult to manage gracefully. On one occasion he is rendered speechless while, seconded by Belinda, Loveit lashes him with her tongue, and the best that he can do is to shout as he "flings off": "You were never more mistaken in your life, and so farewell." [152]

After all, Dorimant, like Courtal, and for precisely the same reason, is not proof against comic ridicule, sympathetic though that ridicule may be. The joke about Dorimant is that he is "obliged to complaisance." [153] In all his busy intrigues, he "can never quietly give over when he's weary." [153] He may pledge Harriet his honest devotion, but in another moment he must be bowing to Belinda and saying pretty things to her, which, as Belinda herself knows, have no heart in them. Greeting his discarded mistress, Dorimant smilingly insists: "We must meet again." "Never," announces Belinda indignantly. "Never?", [154] echoes Dorimant. And that episode closes. The incident manifests Dorimant's polite allegiance to good manners, at the cost of all else.

Dorimant's really serious affair with Harriet, who charms him through being so "wild, witty, lovesome, beautiful, and young," [155] makes possible, in the progress of their railing courtship, a trium-

[151] *Ibid.*, III, 2, p. 292.　　　[152] *Ibid.*, V, 1, p. 354.
[153] *Ibid.*, III, 2, p. 293.　　　[154] *Ibid.*, V, 2, p. 367.
[155] *Ibid.*, III, 3, p. 314.

phant exhibition of both his wit and hers. The two become acquainted by means of a formal wit encounter, in which they exchange similitudes, quite in the fashion of Suckling's characters. They elaborately compare love intrigues to gaming, Dorimant taking his cue for the beginning of the conversation from a remark which he has overheard Harriet make to Young Bellair.

Dor. You were talking of play, madam; pray what may be your stint?

Har. A little harmless discourse in public walks, or at most an appointment in a box barefaced at the playhouse; you are for masks and private meetings where women engage for all they are worth, I hear.

Dor. I have been used to deep play, but I can make one at small game when I like my gamester well.

Har. And be so unconcerned you'll ha' no pleasure in it.

Dor. Where there is a considerable sum to be won the hope of drawing people in makes every trifle considerable.

Har. The sordidness of men's natures, I know, makes 'em willing to flatter and comply with the rich, though they are sure never to be the better for 'em.

Dor. 'Tis in their power to do us good, and we despair not but at some time or other they may be willing.

Har. To men who have fared on this town like you 'twould be a great mortification to live on hope, could you keep a Lent for a mistress?

Dor. In expectation of a happy Easter, and though time be very precious, think forty days well lost to gain your favour.

Har. Mr. Bellair! let us walk, 'tis time to leave him; men grow dull when they begin to be particular.[156]

The acquaintance thus artificially begun soon ripens into love. By the third interview Harriet finds herself unable to look Dorimant in the face, for, as she explains in an aside: "My love springs with my blood into my face, I dare not look upon him yet."[157] Still not looking at him, she jeers at him as gaily as ever, urging him to "play the dying fop"[157] for her diversion. At last, begging her to read his secret in his eyes, Dorimant has a chance to observe her face, and swears then the sincerity of his love "by the inimitable colour"[158] in her cheeks. Her love is re-

---

[156] *Ibid.*, III, 3, pp. 303–304. [157] *Ibid.*, V, 2, p. 350.
[158] *Ibid.*, p. 360.

vealed, but not by verbal confession; and she rails on to the end
of the interview. Later, she explains to her maid that her "sense
of modesty" [159] enforced all this fine acting, and adds: "May he
hate me — a curse that frights me when I speak it — if ever I
do a thing against the rules of decency and honour!" [159] Her
comment betrays the principle which animates all such graceful courtship scenes in Restoration comedy.

Dorimant, Harriet, and the young people of fashion among
their friends enforce their own wit at the expense of the fools of
the play. These discerning young persons are quite of the opinion
announced by Lady Townley:

> 'Tis good to have an universal taste; we should love wit, but for variety
> be able to divert ourselves with the extravagancies of those who want it. [160]

Among those who "want" wit, according to Lady Townley's
standard, are Lady Woodvil and Old Bellair, both of whom make
themselves ridiculous in exhibiting old-fashioned notions about
society, the madly jealous mistress, Loveit, and, most important
of all, that "pattern of modern foppery," [161] Sir Fopling Flutter.

The "sophisticate dulness" [162] of Sir Fopling, which can pass
for wit only with "the tasteless multitude," [162] is an especial
source of delight to Dorimant and his circle, and is encouraged
by them as generously as possible. Sir Fopling belongs to the
fraternity of affected fops that Wycherley also exposed to ridicule through his portrayal of Monsieur de Paris in *The Gentleman
Dancing-Master*. Dorimant briskly sketches Sir Fopling's character in the remark: "He went to Paris a plain bashful English
blockhead, and is returned a fine undertaking French fop." [163]

Sir Fopling's pet affectations, regarding the fineness of his
clothes, the brightness of his wit, and his talent for courtship,
obviously recall similar traits in the Mascarille of *Les Précieuses*

[159] *Ibid.*, p. 362.
[161] *Ibid.*, I, 1, p. 256.
[163] *Ibid.*, IV, 1, p. 327.

[160] *Ibid.*, III, 2, p. 294.
[162] *Ibid.*, III, 1, p. 299.

Ridicules. But if Etherege copied from Mascarille certain features of Sir Fopling's portrait, the use which he made of the character was a quite different one. In *Les Précieuses Ridicules* Mascarille is no more absurd than the romantic young women who rapturously commend his charms; and the dramatist's satire is directed against affectation as a general folly. Sir Fopling, on the other hand, enhances by contrast the attractiveness of Dorimant. We laugh at Sir Fopling because he so clumsily parodies social fashions which Dorimant interprets with unfailing grace and distinction. We laugh at Dorimant because his assumed affectation admits of so poor and incomplete an expression of an attractive and vigorous personality.

Every fresh reading of *The Man of Mode* leaves with us a renewed sense of the importance of the *précieuse* influence in Etherege's comedy. Where Etherege led the way, his contemporaries followed. Wycherley could never effectually oppose a social habit, distasteful to himself, which had grown thus firmly into English comic tradition. Dryden, in spite of wandering interests, wrote his most charming scenes in the *précieuse* manner. Shadwell sturdily repeated the pattern of *She Would if She Could*, with a realistic emphasis on contemporary manners which, to some extent, redeems his dulness. Even the greatest plagiarists of the period, who drew heavily upon French and Spanish sources for their decidedly heterogeneous productions, in their happiest moments found inspiration in the Restoration mode, and from that source derived whatever vitality their plays possess.

CHAPTER VII

CONGREVE

B Y 1676 the dramatic mode of Restoration comedy of manners had become so authoritative that all comic dramatists felt the pressure of its unwritten laws. Our specific purpose in tracing the development of this mode has been accomplished. The history of later seventeenth century comedy affords fresh examples, merely, of well-established dramatic fashions. Yet if we may be permitted to illustrate in the case of one of the later dramatists the persistence of the *précieuse* tradition, a discussion of the work of William Congreve will not appear unseasonable. The greatest master of Restoration comedy, Congreve was also, as one of his best critics reminds us, the "natural and perfect heir" of the Restoration dramatists who preceded him and to whom his relationship may be stated in the phrase *finis coronat.*[1]

Seventeen years had elapsed between the completion of Etherege's work and the beginning of Congreve's. During this period Shadwell had been the only dramatist of any distinction at all who attempted to save for true comedy an age which, as Shadwell lamented, was running mad after farces.[2] From Shadwell alone of the comic dramatists whose plays mark these seventeen years, Congreve, from time to time, made noteworthy borrowings. But Congreve's comedy is again clear and brilliant like Etherege's, not confused and inartistic like Shadwell's; and the freshness of Congreve's renewal of the Restoration mode seems to belie the passage of years between Etherege's plays and his own.

---

[1] Palmer, *The Comedy of Manners*, p. 141.
[2] *The Squire of Alsatia* (*Works*, IV), Dedication, pp. 5–6.

Critics of Restoration comedy have naturally been much attracted to Congreve the man as well as to Congreve the dramatist. Despite his unfailing allegiance to the rigid forms of Restoration manners, Congreve appears to have manifested in all the relationships of his life a most gracious and most lovable personality. He once wrote to a friend: "You know me enough to know I feel very sensibly and silently for those whom I love." [3] In this one phrase is concentrated that quiet depth of feeling betrayed by the dramatist in his most memorable comic scenes. Students of his drama take pleasure in recognizing Congreve as the ideal Restoration gentleman, whose humanity does not suffer through his polite sympathy with the social conventions of his age.

It is not difficult to agree with Palmer that contemporary social life must have strongly influenced Congreve's dramatic work. On the other hand, his plays convince us that Congreve, like Etherege, was a faithful student of earlier English drama. We may reasonably suppose that the Restoration comic mode developed in excellent harmony with the actual temper of Restoration society. In any case, it is evident that Congreve entered in the fullest possible manner into his legitimate dramatic inheritance.

Investigation of Congreve's literary sources has been far too limited. Congreve's indebtedness to Molière has been studied in some detail,[4] yet quite without reference to the English dramatist's more vital connections with English comedy. The influence of the Elizabethan dramatists upon Congreve is generally recognized, but beyond occasional parallels the precise nature of that influence has not been indicated. Regarding Congreve's indebtedness to *préciosité*, a few general comments have been deemed sufficient. Gosse, for example, observes of that "charming

[3] Gosse, *Life of William Congreve*, p. 168.
[4] Cf. the subsequent discussion of the comparisons cited by Miles.

young blue-stocking," Lady Froth: "Twenty years earlier she might have been supposed to be a study of Margaret, Duchess of Newcastle." [5] It becomes our task to examine carefully these various literary influences and to determine the relative importance of each in Congreve's richly reminiscent drama.

A large claim has been made regarding the influence of Molière on Congreve. It has been asserted by Miles that Congreve "studied Molière for suggestions, absorbed the Frenchman's manner, and adopted his dramatic method," [6] and that "Congreve is nearer Molière in his attitude toward his material than any other writer of comedy." [7] In support of his claim, Miles has conveniently listed Congreve's definite borrowings from Molière in matters of plot and characterization.

In the case of *The Old Bachelor* (1693) [8] Miles has cited [9] a number of apparent borrowings from Molière which are of rather minor interest. Sharper's trick for securing money from Wittol (II, 1) may have been suggested to Congreve by the similar course of action of Scapin in *Les Fourberies de Scapin* (II, 7) or of Éraste in *Monsieur de Pourceaugnac* (I, 4). The relations of Setter and Lucy (III, 2) parallel, in a general way, those of the two servants, Lubin and Claudine, in *George Dandin* (II, 1). Laetitia's deception of Fondlewife (IV, 6) may be compared with Angélique's treatment of her husband in *George Dandin* (II, 8) and Isabelle's artful management of Sganarelle in *L'École des Maris* (II, 9).[10] All these comparisons concern relatively unimportant episodes. Among Congreve's characters in the same play, Heartwell may owe something to Sganarelle in *Le Mariage Forcé*, although the old bachelor who foolishly decides upon matrimony is not an un-

---

[5] Gosse, *Life of William Congreve*, p. 43.

[6] Miles, *op. cit.*, p. 203.   [7] *Ibid.*, p. 206.

[8] Genest, *op. cit.*, II, p. 44.

[9] For all the citations for this play see Miles, *op. cit.*, pp. 234–235.

[10] Miles fails to note an amusing parallel between Bellmour's surreptitious love-making in the same scene and Sganarelle's courtship of Jacqueline in *Le Médecin malgré lui* (II, 2).

common figure in English comedy. A more important resemblance may be observed between the relations of Belinda and Araminta (II, 2) and those of Armande and Henriette in *Les Femmes Savantes* (I, 1). In each case a *précieuse* who affects a fine scorn of marriage is contrasted with a sensible young woman who has no such aversion. Yet Congreve would not have been obliged to search beyond Wycherley's contrasted portraiture of Olivia and Eliza in *The Plain Dealer* (II, 1) for the originals of his two heroines.

In *The Double-Dealer* (1693) [11] Congreve owed an obviously larger debt to Molière.[12] The resemblance between the intrigue of Congreve's Maskwell and that of Tartuffe in *Tartuffe* may well be emphasized. Maskwell has Tartuffe's gift for securing blindly devoted friends. Lord Touchwood is like Orgon in his attachment to Maskwell. As Orgon promises his daughter, Touchwood promises his niece to the villainous intriguer. And at the moment when Maskwell's treachery would have been confirmed to anyone who had eyes to see, Touchwood rashly disinherits his nephew and makes Maskwell his heir (V, 1), as Orgon, at a similar crisis, disinherits his son and places his fortune at the disposal of Tartuffe (III, 7). On the other hand, Maskwell's love intrigue with Lady Touchwood does not parallel that of Tartuffe with Elmire. The prudent Elmire, with her fine dignity and her reticent composure, respected and loved by her step-children and ordering her household by admirably harmonious methods, is, indeed, a type of woman never to be met with in Restoration comedy. Elmire has no notion of playing the only rôle open to a step-mother in Restoration comedy, the rôle of cuckolding her husband. In her place we have three intriguing wives, who divert a considerable portion of the action of *The Double-Dealer* into channels of intrigue unknown to Molière. Maskwell himself and the melodramatic Lady Touchwood with

[11] Genest, *op. cit.*, II, p. 50. [12] Cf. Miles, *op. cit.*, p. 228.

her stormy passions and her threatened dagger-thrusts introduce an atmosphere strangely opposed to the usual temper of Restoration comedy. Lady Plyant and Lady Froth do much to restore the comic balance. Even for these characters prototypes have been discovered in Molière's comedy. Miles assures us that Congreve's affected ladies are copied from similar affected characters in *Les Femmes Savantes*. The resemblances, we perceive, are not marked. Furthermore, the comic contrasts in the two plays are not at all the same. Molière treats his *précieuses* as a ridiculous little coterie that may be easily laughed to scorn by all the wise people of the world. Congreve's Lady Plyant and Lady Froth and their following constitute three-fourths of Restoration society and exhibit, though with false exaggeration, the affectation in which all that society has its roots. Molière's problem is to oppose folly and sanity, Congreve's to oppose false and true social affectation.

Possible borrowings from Molière [13] in *Love for Love* (1695) [14] are limited in number and do not deserve much consideration. Valentine's treatment of his troublesome creditor Trapland (I, 1) is practically the same as Don Juan's treatment of Dimanche in *Don Juan* (IV, 3). The episode is trivial. The relations between Valentine and his father may have been suggested by those between father and son, who are also rivals in love, in *L'Avare*. At the same time, Valentine's lack of sympathy with his father illustrates a type of unfilial attitude often exhibited in Restoration comedy.

In *The Way of the World* (1700) [15] the rôle of Waitwell bears a general resemblance to that of Mascarille in *Les Précieuses Ridicules*.[16] Waitwell's courtship of Lady Wishfort is much more condensed than Mascarille's similar exploit. Lady Wishfort's pert maid Foible seems to be in the tradition of Molière's saucy wait-

---

[13] *Ibid.*, p. 232.
[15] *Ibid.*, I, p. 206.

[14] Genest, *op. cit.*, II, p. 67.
[16] Miles, *op. cit.*, pp. 240–241.

ing-women.[17] Such minor similarities are worth noting only in the absence of more vital resemblances.

We have still to consider Congreve's alleged indebtedness to Molière in "dramatic method." Miles has been impressed by the fact that in *The Double-Dealer* and *The Way of the World* the hero and his confidant open the action, as in *Le Misanthrope*, and in *Love for Love* the hero and his servant, as in *Le Dépit Amoureux*; by the fact that in *The Old Bachelor* and *The Way of the World* the entrance of the heroine is deferred until the second act, as in *Le Misanthrope*; by the fact that there are soliloquies in Congreve's second and last plays, as in *L'École des Femmes* and *L'École des Maris*; and by the fact that some of Congreve's realistic interiors, as Valentine's lodgings in *Love for Love* and the chocolate house in *The Way of the World*, recall interiors in Molière's comedies, as Orgon's home in *Tartuffe* and Célimène's drawing-room in *Le Misanthrope*.[18] But it must not be forgotten that Congreve might have drawn abundantly upon English comedy for just such expedients. We might urge as convincingly, for instance, that Congreve planned the beginning of *The Double-Dealer* or *The Way of the World* on the model of Shadwell's *The Virtuoso* or *A True Widow* (1679).[19] We might as well insist that in writing the first scene of *Love for Love* Congreve had in mind Shadwell's *The Sullen Lovers*, where Stanford and his servant Roger, the latter very much like Jeremy in the quality of his wit, open the action, or Shadwell's *Bury Fair* (1689)[20] or *The Scowrers* (1690),[21] where the action is similarly opened. The delay in the introduction of Belinda and Araminta and of Millamant might

[17] Miles does not note the similarity between Foible's clever way of getting even with Lady Wishfort (III, 1) and Maître Jacques' manner of plain-speaking with Harpagon in *L'Avare* (III, 1). He also overlooks the resemblance between the relations of the unsophisticated Peg and her mistress (III, 1) and the relations of Andrée and the Countess in *La Comtesse d'Escarbagnas* (I, 2).

[18] Miles, *op. cit.*, pp. 201–203.

[20] *Ibid.*, I, p. 472.

[19] Genest, *op. cit.*, I, p. 265.

[21] Cf. Nicoll, *op. cit.*, p. 197.

have been suggested to Congreve by Shadwell's common habit of deferring the appearance of his heroines until the second act of his plays, a device employed in *The Sullen Lovers*, *The Humourists*, *The Virtuoso*, *A True Widow*, *Bury Fair*, and *The Scowrers*, or Wycherley's like method in *Love in a Wood* and *The Country Wife*. The use of soliloquies, which Congreve seems to have found particularly serviceable for the presentation of Maskwell, Congreve himself, in his dedication to *The Double-Dealer*, commented upon as a device "that does not relate in particular to this play, but to all or most that have been written." [22] And we are under no necessity of searching for the setting of Congreve's plays outside the limits of the large number of Restoration plays with similar backgrounds preceding his own work.

It appears, then, rather futile to attempt to support more than a very moderate claim for Congreve's indebtedness to Molière. Congreve's one important experiment with a plot derived from Molière, in *The Double-Dealer*, served to weaken rather than strengthen the comic effectiveness of the scenes involved. For the most part, Congreve's borrowings are slight and occasional and become harmoniously related to a comic program foreign to Molière's taste.

A more conspicuous and fundamental influence in Congreve's comedy is the influence of the Elizabethan tradition. Most writers of Restoration comedy fell back at times, with a sense of relief, upon Elizabethan plots and humours. But Congreve was in this respect even more conservative than the majority of his fellow-dramatists. All that is best in the Restoration continuance of Elizabethan dramatic conventions may be illustrated in Congreve's plays.

In *The Old Bachelor*, written while the author was still a very young man, the Elizabethan influence is naturally stronger than in Congreve's later work. Heartwell, the character who gives the

[22] *The Double-Dealer*, Dedication, p. 99.

play its title, is plainly an Elizabethan "humour." He barely escapes a disgraceful marriage with a designing courtesan, a fate which actually befalls the usurer Hoard in Middleton's *A Trick to Catch the Old One* and the country justice Clodpate, an Elizabethan survival, in Shadwell's *Epsom Wells.* Like Sir Arnold Cautious in Brome's *The Sparagus Garden* and Snarl in Shadwell's *The Virtuoso,* Congreve's old bachelor has a cynical contempt for matrimony, yet is easily beguiled by a clever mistress. Heartwell is finally rescued by a compassionate young friend, as foolish Belfond Senior, another Elizabethan survival, is saved from a similar plight by his younger brother in Shadwell's *The Squire of Alsatia* (1688).[23]

The trick played by the young wife Laetitia and the young gallant Bellmour on the doting but jealous old husband, Fondlewife, recalls similar intriguing in Fletcher's *The Spanish Curate* and Middleton's *A Mad World, My Masters.* In the last-named play a feigned illness allays the husband's suspicions, as in *The Old Bachelor.* The "little language" with which the old alderman sugars his discourse with Laetitia is like that used by similar characters in Brome's *The New Academy* and *The Northern Lasse,* in Howard's *The Committee,* and in Shadwell's *Epsom Wells* and *The Scowrers.* Laetitia, like her prototypes in these earlier plays, humors her ridiculous husband but watches her chance to shame him.

Still a third intrigue in *The Old Bachelor,* the adventures of the braggarts Sir Joseph Wittol and Captain Bluffe, including their cozenage by two scheming cheats, is derived unmistakably from Elizabethan sources. The partnership of Wittol and Bluffe has a celebrated precedent in that of Bobadill and Matthew in Jonson's *Every Man in His Humour.* Like Matthew, Wittol fervently admires his martial friend and is only a little doubtful whether the latter should have yielded so readily to a beating. Bluffe resembles Bobadill closely in his wholesome contempt for

[23] Genest, *op. cit.,* I, p. 459.

all military leaders prior to himself, his boasted predisposition for "pinking" people's flesh and, withal, the tameness with which he submits to being beaten. Gildon [24] notes Bluffe's further resemblance to Bounce in William Mountfort's *Greenwich Park* (1691)[25] and Hackum in Shadwell's *The Squire of Alsatia*. In the latter play the rôle of Belfond Senior corresponds to that of Wittol.[26] Bluffe and Wittol likewise recall Bilboe and Titere Tu in Wilson's *The Cheats*. The unfortunate marriages of Congreve's braggarts enforce the usual penalty for bullies and clowns in the comedies of Jonson and Shirley. The cheats, Sharper and Setter, who substitute a whore and her maid for the ladies whom Wittol and Bluffe have designed to marry, are of the order of the cheats in Jonson's *The Alchemist*, in Middleton's cony-catching plays, and in Etherege's *The Comical Revenge*.

In *The Double-Dealer* one character, Sir Paul Plyant, completely illustrates an Elizabethan type.[27] Sir Paul is a timid, uxorious husband. His wife makes him an allowance and keeps him quite under her thumb, as Mistress Otter does her submissive captain in Jonson's *Epicoene*. Sir Paul tries as hard and often as vainly to fulfill Lady Plyant's caprices as Deliro strives to please an exacting wife in *Every Man out of His Humour*. Like Camelion in Brome's *The New Academy*,[28] Sir Paul grants his lady the first perusal of all letters and scolds the boy who commits the shocking offense of delivering a letter to him instead of to her. He seconds her judgments as meekly as Saleware seconds those of Alicia in Brome's *A Mad Couple well Match'd*. Gentle-

[24] Langbaine's *The Lives and Characters of the English Dramatic Poets*, continued by Charles Gildon, p. 25.

[25] Genest, *op. cit.*, II, p. 11.

[26] Wittol's favorite phrase, "By the Lord Harry," is also a pet phrase with Major-General Blunt in Shadwell's *The Volunteers*.

[27] Lord Touchwood's name and temper were perhaps suggested by Touchwood in Brome's *The Sparagus Garden*.

[28] Cf. *The New Academy (Works*, II), II, 1, p. 24, and *The Double-Dealer*, III, 2, p. 142.

men of a similar disposition had been popular with Congreve's immediate predecessors. The type is exhibited in Etherege's Sir Oliver Cockwood in *She Would if She Could* and in Shadwell's Bisket in *Epsom Wells*, Maggot in *The Scowrers*, and Hackwell Senior in *The Volunteers* (1693).[29]

The outline of the main plot of *Love for Love* Congreve apparently derived largely from Fletcher's *The Elder Brother*. In both plays a father tries to make an older brother give up his inheritance in the interests of a foolish younger brother. The older brother at first agrees, then refuses, and ultimately contrives to outwit his father and brother. Fletcher's Charles does not, like Valentine, feign madness, but has pedantic obsessions, and insists on talking astrology while his father eagerly and impatiently, but futilely, presses him to sign the deed. Charles and Valentine have, too, the same motive for wishing to keep their estates, for both are in love and cannot marry if disinherited. Charles' rival in love is his brother, Valentine's his father.[30] Both heroes have devoted servants who help to restore their fortunes. Some of the details of Valentine's madness Congreve may have borrowed from Shakespeare's *Hamlet*.[31] Valentine's father is impressed by the fact that his son "talks sensibly in his madness," [32] as Polonius is impressed by the "method" [33] in Hamlet's similar ravings. Again, Valentine's cryptic sayings to Angelica in disparagement of her sex [34] are very like those of

[29] Cf. Nicoll, *op. cit.*, p. 198.

[30] The title of Congreve's play may have been suggested by Charles' query to Angelina, *The Elder Brother* (*Works*, X), III, 5, p. 252: " Can you love for love, and make that the reward? "

[31] There is a definite verbal parallel between Valentine's address to his father, *Love for Love*, IV, 2, p. 272:
Aha, old truepenny! sayst thou so?
and Hamlet's address to the ghost, *Hamlet*, I, 5, p. 114:
Ah, ha, boy! sayst thou so? art thou there true-penny?

[32] *Love for Love*, IV, 2, p. 269.

[33] *Hamlet* (ed. H. H. Furness), II, 2, p. 152.

[34] *Love for Love*, IV, 3, p. 282.

Hamlet to Ophelia.[35]   In the plot development of Congreve's play, Fletcher's influence is, of course, more decisive than Shakespeare's.

There are two outstanding Elizabethan "humours" in *Love for Love*. The credulous old Foresight is related to Elizabethan imposters who profess mastery of the occult science of astrology. He particularly resembles Weatherwise in Middleton's *No Wit, No Help like a Woman's*. Weatherwise and Foresight both study the almanac with meticulous care, in order to discover signs for the minute details of daily conduct.   Both are afraid of being cuckolded and are suspiciously alert to detect celestial conjunctions indicating such disaster.   In his quackery Foresight also resembles Mopus in Wilson's *The Cheats*, and in his methodical habits, Lump in Shadwell's *A True Widow*.   The character of the foolish younger brother Ben is presented in a somewhat novel fashion, owing to his "sea-wit"; yet Ben, too, is an old-school "humour." His clownish manners, especially his clumsy, conceited habits in courtship, ally him with all the country gulls from Jonson through Shirley and with those numerous Shallows, Softheads, and Addels who carry on the ludicrous type in earlier Restoration comedy.

The Way of the World revives in a subplot which has important bearings, however, on the main action, a phase of the intrigue in Jonson's *The Devil is an Ass*.   Fitzdottrel and Fainall both treat their wives unfairly and are disposed to desert them for other women.   Both wives have lovers who champion their interests and who reduce the husbands to a state of financial dependence on these abused mates.   In Jonson's comedy Wittipol secures Fitzdottrel's estate for Frances by causing the unsuspecting Fitzdottrel to convey it in trust to Manly, Wittipol's good friend.   In *The Way of the World* Mrs. Fainall has had the foresight to give her estate in trust to Mirabell, previous to her mar-

[35] *Hamlet*, III, 1, pp. 216–221.

riage with Fainall. Toward the close of each play the husband is suddenly informed of the financial authority with which the signing of the deed has invested his wife, and the wife's security in this matter brings about the husband's surrender and effects a satisfactory dénouement for all parties. The Elizabethan influence is also apparent, in this play, in the characterization of Sir Wilfull Witwoud, the country suitor, and Waitwell in his disguise. Both characters are variations of the type illustrated by Ben in *Love for Love*.

Elizabethan tradition had at least more influence than Molière's drama on the spirit of Congreve's plays. When Congreve imitated Elizabethan humours and incidents, he did so with a painstaking concern for detail which is not evident in his borrowings from Molière. *Love for Love* is actually dominated by its Elizabethan plot. Congreve's three remaining comedies, on the other hand, emphasize in their major situations interests which neither the influence of Elizabethan tradition nor the influence of Molière can satisfactorily explain.

Certain close resemblances in Congreve's dramatic methods in *The Old Bachelor*, *The Double-Dealer*, and *The Way of the World* afford definite enough evidence that the influence of *préciosité* is really the supreme influence in Congreve's comedies. In the case of *Love for Love* we are forced to conclude that for once Congreve "turned aside from the natural development of his style." [36] Even in this play Restoration youth is pitted against "the old Elizabeth" conservatism. But the *précieuse* influence is largely overshadowed by the claims of a strictly Elizabethan program of intrigue. In the three other comedies the evidences of Congreve's preference for the *précieuse* mode are abundant and convincing. The theme of the main intrigues of these three plays may be stated in a single phrase: The honest love affair of a couple of worthy young lovers is impeded and all but wrecked by the

[36] Palmer, *The Comedy of Manners*, p. 189.

hero's unfortunate relations with some other woman or women. In each of the plays, the hero is involved in such perilous relations simply because the sort of gallantry prescribed by the age places him more or less at the mercy of affected, intriguing women. In just such terms might be stated the central theme of Etherege's last two plays, of Wycherley's first play, and of the majority of those comedies with which Shadwell had been bridging the gap between the dates of production of *The Man of Mode* and *The Old Bachelor*. The central intrigues of *The Old Bachelor*, *The Double-Dealer*, and *The Way of the World* could never have existed without the dominance of the type of social affectation fostered by *préciosité*.

The predicaments of Vainlove, Mellefont, and Mirabell are the natural consequences of artificial habits of conduct, which make intrigues the main business of life and continually exalt all varieties of graceful love-making for fashion's sake. Because Vainlove in *The Old Bachelor* had once been all complaisance with Sylvia, this abandoned mistress, in a fury of jealousy, forges a letter from his new mistress and makes a violent effort to hinder the success of his new amour. Youth and good will triumph in the end, but it is a slow battle. In *The Double-Dealer* the intrigue is heightened by the fact that two intriguing women claim the hero, as in *The Man of Mode*. In *The Way of the World* the hero's fate is largely in the hands of three women, one of whom, however, aids him in his serious love suit. In this last play it requires considerable patience on the reader's part to disentangle the confused strands of Mirabell's most complicated affairs. For plot-making Congreve seems to have had little natural aptitude. He repeats intricately, but with surprisingly little variation, the most popular plot conventions of Restoration comedy.

In this *précieuse* scheme of life, familiar character types of Restoration comedy are again opposed. The young people who wisely interpret the affectations of the age are contrasted, as

Etherege had contrasted such persons, with false wits and with meddling fools. Of the wise, wit is the greatest attribute and is more insisted upon by Congreve than by any of his predecessors. It is a thoroughly conventional, although unusually brilliant, variety of wit, just as the false wit of Congreve's fools is a thoroughly conventional, although unusually brilliant, variety of false wit.

We become acquainted with Congreve's clever young lovers chiefly through similitude debates and contests in raillery of the type popularized by Suckling. Other Restoration comic dramatists had, of course, employed such artificial dialogue, though not with the precision and graceful symmetry achieved by Congreve. In the first and only extended conversation between Vainlove, Bellmour, Araminta, and Belinda in *The Old Bachelor*, a formal love pleading is engaged in by the gentlemen, and proceeds almost entirely by the interchange of similitudes. The conversation is as follows:

Bell. So, fortune be praised! — To find you both within, ladies, is —
Aram. No miracle, I hope.
Bell. Not o' your side, madam, I confess. — But my tyrant there and I are two buckets that can never come together.
Belin. Nor are ever like. — Yet we often meet and clash.
Bell. How, never like! marry, Hymen ·forbid! But this it is to run so extravagantly in debt; I have laid out such a world of love in your service, that you think you can never be able to pay me all; so shun me for the same reason that you would a dun.
Belin. Ay, on my conscience, and the most impertinent and trouble-some of duns. — A dun for money will be quiet, when he sees his debtor has not wherewithal; but a dun for love is an eternal torment that never rests.
Bell. Till he has created love where there was none, and then gets it for his pains. — For importunity in love, like importunity at court, first creates its own interest, and then pursues it for the favour.
Aram. Favours that are got by impudence and importunity, are like discoveries from the rack, when the afflicted person, for his ease, sometimes confesses secrets his heart knows nothing of.
Vain. I should rather think favours so gained, to be due rewards to indefatigable devotion. — For as Love is a deity, he must be served by prayer.

Belin. O gad, would you would all pray to Love then, and let us alone!

Vain. You are the temples of Love, and 'tis through you our devotion must be conveyed.

Aram. Rather poor silly idols of your own making, which, upon the least displeasure, you forsake, and set up new. — Every man, now, changes his mistress and his religion as his humour varies or his interest.

Vain. O madam!

Aram. Nay, come, I find we are growing serious, and then we are in danger of being dull.[37]

This rather taxing discourse, with all its transitions as distinct and perfect as those in similar dialogue passages in Suckling's plays, is followed immediately by a less formal railing contest, which concludes the scene. The subsequent conversations of the lovers are hurried and interrupted. Bellmour tries to tempt Belinda to marry him by suggesting the similitude: "Alas! courtship to marriage, is but as the music in the playhouse till the curtain's drawn; but that once up, then opens the scene of pleasure." And Belinda demurs with the rejoinder: "Oh, foh! no; rather courtship to marriage, is as a very witty prologue to a very dull play." [38]

The characterization of Araminta and Belinda is not altogether successful. It is evident that Congreve intended to contrast Belinda's silly affectations with Araminta's laudable good sense. Like Olivia in Wycherley's *The Plain Dealer*, Belinda feigns disgust with society, yet derives all her pleasure from social diversions and is never so happy as when poking fun at ill-mannered people. The intended contrast between Belinda and Araminta is not consistently enforced. Belinda is sometimes ridiculed, but both young women are rewarded with equally desirable husbands, and Belinda's eventual triumph is quite as notable as that of her cousin.

The only conversations between the lovers, Mellefont and Cynthia, in *The Double-Dealer* are formal similitude contests,

---

[37] *The Old Bachelor*, II, 2, pp. 31–32.   [38] *Ibid.*, V, 4, p. 85.

much like those in Suckling's *Aglaura*.[39] In the first of these love is compared to a game:

> *Cyn.* . . . . 'Tis an odd game we're going to play at; what think you of drawing stakes, and giving over in time?
>
> *Mel.* No, hang't, that's not endeavoring to win, because it's possible we may lose; since we have shuffled and cut, let's e'en turn up trump now.
>
> *Cyn.* Then I find it's like cards; if either of us have a good hand, it is an accident of fortune.
>
> *Mel.* No, marriage is rather like a game at bowls; Fortune indeed makes the match, and the two nearest, and sometimes the two farthest are together; but the game depends entirely upon judgment.
>
> *Cyn.* Still it is a game, and consequently one of us must be a loser.
>
> *Mel.* Not at all; only a friendly trial of skill, and the winnings to be laid out in an entertainment.[40]

The second encounter [41] of the two is of precisely the same nature. Now love is compared to a hunting expedition, and the process of comparison leads Cynthia to the happy conclusion: "nothing has been between us but our fears." She is still capricious, however, and refuses to accept Mellefont until he has afforded her an exhibition of his wit. To these two scenes his wit seems largely confined. He suffers as the dupe of Maskwell and the victim of Lady Touchwood's lies. At times, he shows a seriousness of spirit not exactly in keeping with the character of a Restoration gallant, as when he assures Lady Touchwood: "You have been to blame — I like those tears, and hope they are of the purest kind — penitential tears." [42] Cynthia is more clearly envisaged through the few quiet comments and pertinent asides in which she reveals her sane judgment and good-humored tolerance of the fools in whose company she ordinarily moves.[43] Her best wit, too, is reserved for her lover.

[39] Cf. Chap. III, pp. 73–77, of this volume.
[40] *The Double-Dealer*, II, 1, pp. 122–123.
[41] *Ibid.*, IV, 1, pp. 150–151.   [42] *Ibid.*, IV, 5, p. 169.
[43] In these relationships Cynthia recalls Gertrude in Shadwell's *Bury Fair*. Of the foolish people by whom she is surrounded Cynthia observes indulgently (III, 3, p. 149):

In *Love for Love* the love interest is for once largely obscured by other issues; hence it is not strange that similitude debates do not occur between the young lovers. To be sure, Angelica assures Valentine, in the usual mood of Restoration heroines: " Never let us know one another better: for the pleasure of a masquerade is done, when we come to show our faces." [44] But the brief masquerading encounters of the pair are in no way memorable. Angelica is usually exhibited in her rather farcical relations with two foolish old men, Foresight and Sir Sampson Legend.[45] Valentine, who has some taste for similitudes,[46] languidly indulges his servant Jeremy's fluent *précieuse* wit. Congreve takes no pains to distinguish Valentine himself, in special excellence of wit, from the common run of Restoration gallants. His own careless estimate of his hero reads: "as the world goes, he may pass well enough for the best Character in a Comedy." [47]

In *The Way of the World* the encounters of Mirabell and Millamant may be said to dominate the action in a peculiarly significant manner. Mirabell and Millamant had been presaged, of course, in Shakespeare's Beatrice and Benedick in *Much Ado about Nothing* and in Shirley's Carol and Fairfield in *Hyde Park*. Under the influence of the *précieuse* mode, courtship wit of a more ambitious sort had been developed in Suckling's *Aglaura* and elaborated in the "closet drama" of the Duchess of Newcastle. In Restoration comedy, the *précieuse* impulse persisting, the relations of witty

---

. . . Why should I call 'em fools? the world thinks better of 'em; for these have quality and education, wit and fine conversation, are received and admired by the world: — if not, they like and admire themselves, — And why is not that true wisdom, for 'tis happiness?

Compare with this Gertrude's reflection in *Bury Fair* (II, p. 148):

These Fops are very happy: For if an Archangel should tell 'em they were Fops, they would not believe it.

[44] *Love for Love*, IV, 3, p. 286.

[45] Angelica's encouragement of Sir Sampson resembles Elvira's treatment of her lover's old father Bernado in Shadwell's *The Amorous Bigot* (1690).

[46] Cf. *Love for Love*, IV, 3, p. 287.

[47] Congreve, *Amendments of Mr. Collier's Citations*, p. 89.

lovers, especially of railing lovers, were still further conventionalized. The most striking Restoration courtship scenes, preceding
Congreve's, will be readily recalled. In *Secret Love* and *Amphitryon* (1690) [48] Dryden made a special feature of "proviso"
bargaining; in *She Would if She Could* and *The Man of Mode*
Etherege placed emphasis on sex duels; in *Epsom Wells*, *The
Virtuoso*, and *Bury Fair* Shadwell followed Etherege's example,
returning also in *The Virtuoso* to the older *précieuse* habit of
similitude argument. In *The Way of the World* Congreve made
happy use of the most admirable features of these courtship conventions and, by the added pressure of his own genius, created in
Mirabell and Millamant the finest of Restoration railing lovers.

When Mirabell and Millamant first meet, Mirabell announces
his mistress' entry in the words employed by Wildblood regarding
Jacintha on a similar occasion in Dryden's *An Evening's Love*: [49]
"Here she comes, i' faith, full sail." [50] A rapid game in similitudes follows, in which Millamant and Witwoud, who entered with
her, engage in some very adroit fencing:

Mir. (to Mrs. Millamant) You seem to be unattended, madam — you
used to have the *beau monde* throng after you; and a flock of gay perukes
hovering round you.

Wit. Like moths about a candle. — I had like to have lost my comparison for want of breath.

Mrs. Mil. O I have denied myself airs to-day, I have walked as fast
through the crowd.

Wit. As a favourite just disgraced; and with as few followers.

Mrs. Mil. Dear Mr. Witwoud, truce with your similitudes; for I'm
as sick of 'em —

Wit. As a physician of a good air. — I cannot help it, madam, though
'tis against myself.

Mrs. Mil. Yet, again! Mincing,[51] stand between me and his wit.

Wit. Do, Mrs. Mincing, like a screen before a great fire. — I confess I
do blaze to-day, I am too bright.

---

[48] Genest, *op. cit.*, I, p. 489.
[49] *An Evening's Love* (*Works*, III), II, 1, p. 273.
[50] *The Way of the World*, II, 2, p. 344.
[51] Mrs. Fainall and Millamant's maid Mincing are also of the party.

Mrs. Fain. But, dear Millamant, why were you so long?

Mrs. Mil. Long! Lord, have I not made violent haste; I have asked every living thing I met for you; I have inquired after you, as after a new fashion.

Wit. Madam, truce with your similitudes. — No, you met her husband, and did not ask him for her.

Mrs. Mil. By your leave, Witwoud, that were like inquiring after an old fashion, to ask a husband for his wife.

Wit. Hum, a hit! a hit! a palpable hit! I confess it. . . . [52]

Mirabell presently assails his mistress' vanity, and she disparages his conceit. Another rapid fire of similitudes, in which Mirabell also joins, ensues. Then Mrs. Fainall "draws off" Witwoud, leaving the two lovers alone.

Mirabell undertakes, at this juncture, to give Millamant some wholesome advice, and she laughs at him. Like Wildish in *Bury Fair*,[53] and as vainly, he entreats his lady to be a little more "serious." Millamant rejoins:

What, with that face? no, if you keep your countenance, 'tis impossible I should hold mine. Well, after all, there is something very moving in a love-sick face. Ha! ha! ha! — well, I won't laugh, don't be peevish — Heigho! now I'll be melancholy, as melancholy as a watch-light. Well, Mirabell, if ever you will win me woo me now. — Nay, if you are so tedious, fare you well. . . .[54]

She now hastens to conclude the interview:

Mir. Can you not find in the variety of your disposition one moment —

Mrs. Mil. To hear you tell me Foible's married and your plot like to speed; — no.

Mir. But how came you to know it?

Mrs. Mil. Without the help of the devil, you can't imagine; unless she should tell me herself. Which of the two it may have been I will leave you to consider; and when you have done thinking of that, think of me.[54] [*Exit.*

Millamant's final sally recalls a similar leave-taking of Jacintha's in *An Evening's Love.* Jacintha merrily parts with Wildblood,

[52] *Ibid.,* II, 2, pp. 344–345.
[53] *Bury Fair* (*Works*, IV), IV, p. 193.
[54] *The Way of the World*, II, 2, pp. 348–349.

exclaiming: "Adieu; and when you have a thought to throw away, bestow it on your servant Fatima." [55]

In subsequent scenes Millamant is shown off in the company of the false wits, Witwoud and Petulant, the half-witted Sir Wilfull, and jealous Mrs. Marwood. The latter hints that Mirabell's secret is out and concludes pleasantly: "You are nettled." Millamant, tearing her fan, replies: "You're mistaken. Ridiculous !" [56] In the remarks that follow, the younger woman, as always in such cases, wins out. As Harriet exposes Loveit in *The Man of Mode* [57] and Shadwell's numerous young heroines expose the affected older women who are their unequal rivals in love,[58] so Millamant thrusts through Mrs. Marwood's weak defense. Mrs. Marwood asserts that she "detests" Mirabell. Millamant quickly agrees:

O madam, why so do I — and yet the creature loves me, ha! ha! ha! how can one forbear laughing to think of it. — I am a sibyl if I am not amazed to think what he can see in me. I'll take my death, I think you are handsomer — and within a year or two as young — if you could but stay for me, I should overtake you — but that cannot be. — Well, that thought makes me melancholic. — Now I'll be sad.[56]

Mrs. Marwood's only revenge for such jeering is in the way of continued underhanded intrigue, in which she is doomed to failure.

A final contest of wits between Mirabell and Millamant occurs in the scene in which the two draw up provisos regarding marriage.[59] This famous scene is simply a modernized version of the "proviso" covenant between D'Urfé's Hylas and Stelle recorded, three quarters of a century before, in *Astrée*. It is not improbable that Congreve knew D'Urfé's scene at first hand; at

[55] *An Evening's Love* (*Works*, III), III, 1, p. 310.
[56] *The Way of the World*, III, 3, p. 362.
[57] *The Man of Mode*, V, 2, p. 370.
[58] Cf. especially *The Humourists* (II, pp. 153–155) and *The Virtuoso* (II, p. 339).
[59] *The Way of the World*, IV, 1, pp. 377–381.

any rate, he knew it at second hand through the "proviso" scenes of Dryden. In the contract of Mirabell and Millamant echoes from Dryden abound, reënforced, perhaps, by recollections from the Elizabethan "proviso" scenes and from Ravenscroft's *The Careless Lovers.*

Millamant insures her "dear liberty," [60] as concerns doing and saying exactly what she pleases, in carefully detailed provisos. She resembles Melantha [61] in *Marriage à la Mode* in her request: "Let us never visit together, nor go to a play together." [62] Like Isabelle [63] in *The Wild Gallant,* she describes most of her articles as mere "trifles." She does not, like Florimel, threaten inconstancy, although she insists on the privilege of paying and receiving visits at her pleasure and of writing and receiving letters "without interrogatories and wry faces" [62] on Mirabell's part. Terms of conjugal affection she condemns as emphatically as Celadon and Florimel.[64] She declares that she abhors such names "as wife, spouse, my dear, joy, jewel, love, sweetheart, and the rest of that nauseous cant, in which men and their wives are so fulsomely familiar." [62] Mirabell, like Isabelle's lover, finds her first terms reasonable enough but her later "bill of fare" somewhat alarming. Mirabell's own provisos are fairly original and voice a "sententious" sobriety unknown to the wayward Celadon. Yet, like Celadon, Mirabell is still jealous of his rights and refuses' to allow his mistress to test his constancy. Mirabell phrases his provisos with all the formality displayed in corresponding scenes in *Secret Love* and in *Amphitryon.* Each of his articles is introduced with the conventional "imprimis" or

[60] *Ibid.,* p. 378.
[61] *Marriage à la Mode (Works,* IV), II, 1, p. 281. Melantha observes to Palamede: "Then, we will never make visits together, nor see a play, but always apart."
[62] *The Way of the World,* IV, 1, p. 379.
[63] *The Wild Gallant (Works,* II), III, 1, p. 75.
[64] *Secret Love (Works,* II), V, 1, p. 506.

"item." Concluding his statements, he observes with dignity: "These provisos admitted, in other things I may prove a tractable and complying husband." [65] With due ceremony he begs leave to kiss Millamant's hand upon the contract. At this moment Mrs. Fainall enters, and Mirabell claims her, as Hillaria in *The Careless Lovers* had claimed her uncle, as a witness to the sealing of the deed. To the end Millamant remains in control of the situation. Quite appropriately she departs from established custom in having her own very characteristic last word:

> . . . well, you ridiculous thing you, I'll have you — I won't be kissed, nor I won't be thanked — here kiss my hand though. — So, hold your tongue now, don't say a word.[66]

It is probably safe to assert that Millamant is the most admirably portrayed heroine in Restoration comedy. Her triumph is all the more noteworthy because she never violates the essential restrictions of the Restoration mode. A temporary whim in the career of Shakespeare's Beatrice becomes conventionalized into the governing temper of Millamant's life; and for that reason, any serious comparison of the two heroines is unfair to both. Millamant could not exist in society without her affectations. Her most piquant charm is permanently embodied, as she very well knows, in the artificial rôle that she plays. But despite her conventionality, we are thoroughly aware of the gracious power of her nature. Like Meredith's Diana, wherever she goes "she makes everything in the room dust round a blazing jewel." [67] Meredith himself has paid her the just and fine tribute:

> Millamant is an admirable, almost a lovable heroine. It is a piece of genius in a writer to make a woman's manner of speech portray her. . . . An

---

[65] *The Way of the World*, IV, 1, p. 381. See Isabelle's similar conclusion in *The Wild Gallant*, III, 1, p. 75: "These trifles granted me, in all things of moment, I am your most obedient wife and servant, Isabelle."

[66] *The Way of the World*, IV, 1, p. 382.

[67] Meredith, *Diana of the Crossways* (published by Charles Scribner's Sons, 1906), p. 19.

air of bewitching whimsicality hovers over the graces of this comic heroine, like the lively conversational play of a beautiful mouth.[68]

Other personages in Restoration comedy, even Dorimant, have elusive personalities. Although it is apparent that many of these people have warm hearts and generous sympathies, the social mask obscures their best impulses. But through all her subterfuges and evasions we know intimately the real Millamant, or, at least, we boldly fancy so.

Millamant's personality is not exhibited simply through sparkling rejoinders, inspired, from moment to moment, by the wit of her associates. Unlike other characters in Restoration comedy, she has a gift for interpreting a situation as a whole and moulds her caprices to suit the temper of the occasion, of which she at once assumes full control. She has an advantage over Mirabell in possessing an alert sense of humor, which enables her to laugh at his "love-sick face" [69] and sententious phrases and gaily expose the weak spots in his lover's self-conceit. She begs of him in merry concern: "Ha! ha! ha! what would you give, that you could help loving me?" And poor Mirabell can only reply: "I would give something that you did not know I could not help it." [69]

Millamant's very flippancies are charged with meaning. It is plain that her excessive gaiety is forced. She talks very fast and is afraid of pauses, fearful lest the realities of love may somehow rudely intrude upon the pretty decorum of this *beau monde*. The social mode makes no allowance for the sympathies of lovers. In those inarticulate silences that check now and again the flashing current of her raillery, Millamant is wistfully pleading with Mirabell to accept her love without the shame of a confession and to permit her to remain in appearance imperious, brilliant, heartless, the finest of fine ladies.

[68] Meredith, *An Essay on Comedy*, pp. 101–102.
[69] *The Way of the World*, II, 2, p. 348.

We are so vividly assured of Millamant's personality that the comic contrast between her real and her artificial self becomes remarkably distinct and thought-provoking. One recalls Meredith's wise aphorism:

You may estimate your capacity for comic perception by being able to detect the ridicule of them you love without loving them the less; and more by being able to see yourself somewhat ridiculous in dear eyes, and accepting the correction their image of you proposes.[70]

In the light of the first half of Meredith's aphorism we estimate Millamant. By relying upon this type of friendly laughter, Congreve and other comic dramatists of his age are able to cherish and protect their ideal characters.

The type of laughter evoked by Millamant is obviously not called forth by the majority of Congreve's characters. For one Millamant and one Cynthia we have a host of Froths and Witwouds. Millamant and Cynthia themselves laugh at the Froths and Witwouds, because the latter, when judged by the best Restoration standards, are guilty of false wit and false affectation. In contrasting true people of fashion and these pretenders to fashion, Congreve continually emphasizes the double standard of Restoration comedy.

No doubt Congreve has been justly censured because his false wits by accident often seem to display true wit, and "are permitted to stumble on too many brilliants." [71] Congreve takes an intellectual pleasure in developing their witticisms, and at times too much intellect and too little nonsense mark the results of his labor. His false wits may be partially vindicated, however, through their legitimate possession of "scraps of other folks' wit." [72] They fulfill a literary tradition which confirms their agility in the use of witty comparisons. Brisk and Witwoud, for instance, simply carry on, with a distinction of speech which

[70] Meredith, *An Essay on Comedy*, p. 133.
[71] Nettleton, *op. cit.*, p. 130.
[72] *The Way of the World*, I, 2, p. 326.

Congreve, could not help giving them, the mode established by Puny in Cowley's *The Cutter of Coleman-Street* and already familiar in the language of Cowley's day.

In *The Double-Dealer*, the first of these false wits appear in Lord Froth and Brisk. As Cynthia explains, the former affects formality, the latter pertness.[73] Lord Froth resembles Puny in his fastidious attempts to avoid vulgarity. He has an incurable propensity for raillery. His own wit frequently overcomes him, yet he has sufficient complaisance to let other people finish his comparisons and to applaud the joint product. Brisk is much more diverting and more sympathetically portrayed. Like Puny and Dapperwit, he is immensely proud of his wit, especially of his gift for similitudes, and he has all of the joyous complaisance of the former and none of the dullness of the latter. Once he borrows a similitude from Suckling's rich storehouse,[74] and in so doing illustrates the importance of Suckling's pioneer work in this *précieuse* tradition. Brisk's indulgence of Lady Froth is really generous and as good-tempered as Congreve's own might have been. He agrees to make notes to her heroic poem, insisting that he is "proud of the vast honour, let me perish!"[75] On another occasion, when she asks him what he thinks she is laughing at, he suggests promptly: "Me, egad, ha! ha!"[76] At such moments the sharp edge of his conceit is softened, and he acquires, as an individual, an interest which his more coldly conventionalized predecessors fail to arouse.

In *Love for Love* false wit has only a restricted triumph in the similitudes of Valentine's servant Jeremy, who in such tastes recalls Roger in *The Sullen Lovers*, and in the "sea-wit" of Ben. Jeremy is but a "rogue" and quite at the mercy of his master, and Ben excels more in obtuseness than in *préciosité*. Tattle and

---

[73] *The Double-Dealer*, II, 2, p. 119.
[74] Cf. Chap. IV, p. 92, n. 39, of this volume.
[75] *The Double-Dealer*, III, 3, p. 147.   [76] *Ibid.*, IV, 2, p. 160.

Scandal to some extent take the places of Froth and Brisk in the preceding play. They are utilized for scenes of social raillery such as that directed by Olivia and supported by Novel and Plausible in *The Plain Dealer*.[77] Yet Tattle has little individuality, and Scandal contradicts his fondness for social gossip and for Restoration intrigue by playing the additional rôle of a cynical plain dealer who lashes the age that supports him.

The relations of Witwoud and Petulant in *The Way of the World* resemble those of Cutter and Worm in *The Cutter of Coleman-Street*. All four are "detracting fops," and each one disparages his friend in a burst of confidence to a third party. Cutter privately assures Lucia that Worm is "a good ingenious fellow, that's the truth on't, and a pleasant Droll when h'as got a Cup o'Wine in his pate"[78] but is not to be trusted in serious matters. In a similar confession, Worm explains to Lucia that Cutter is an unreliable fellow, only "he has some wit (to give the devil his due) and that 'tis makes us endure him."[79] In the same spirit, Witwoud confides to Mirabell:

... Petulant's my friend, and a very honest fellow, and a very pretty fellow, and has a smattering — faith and troth, a pretty deal of an odd sort of a small wit: nay I'll do him justice, I'm his friend, I won't wrong him neither. — And if he had any judgment in the world, he would not be altogether contemptible. Come, come, don't detract from the merits of my friend.[80]

And Petulant pays Witwoud back in his own coin by thus describing him to Mirabell: "Now he's soft you know; . . . he's what you call a — what-d'ye-call-'em, a fine gentleman; but he's silly withal."[81] In spite of repeated hostilities, Congreve's fops could not exist without their frequent contests in raillery. Witwoud, in particular, is eager and effusive in his wit, like Brisk, and his similitudes blaze forth in lavish abundance to the very end.

Congreve's studies in feminine social folly are not in all cases

[77] Cf. *The Plain Dealer*, II, 1.
[78] *The Cutter of Coleman-Street*, I, 6, p. 279.
[79] *Ibid.*, p. 281.
[80] *The Way of the World*, I, 2, p. 327.
[81] *Ibid.*, p. 333.

memorable. Silvia and Belinda in *The Old Bachelor* are slightly sketched, and the latter's contrast to Araminta, as we have commented, is not emphasized with sufficient clearness. Lady Touchwood in *The Double-Dealer* is, as far as the comic interest is concerned, "out of the picture." [82] In *Love for Love*, Mrs. Foresight and Mrs. Frail are not given rôles of much consequence, and Prue, recalling Gertrude in Shadwell's *A True Widow* and her namesake, Hippolita's maid, in *The Gentleman Dancing-Master*, is a farcical character. Mrs. Marwood in *The Way of the World* renews again the vehement intensity of Maskwell's nature, too stern for manners comedy, and Mrs. Fainall is pale and ineffectual. In opposition to such sketches, Congreve has drawn three remarkable full-length portraits of extravagantly affected *précieuses*, Lady Froth and Lady Plyant in *The Double-Dealer* and Lady Wishfort in *The Way of the World*. These three character studies manifest powers of penetration and insight in which Congreve easily outstripped earlier Restoration dramatists.

Lady Froth is a sort of feminine counterpart of Brisk. But in saying that we leave much unsaid. She has been termed "one of the best and most complex characters that Congreve has created." [83] Congreve's success was extraordinary in portraying so extremely silly a woman in such a fashion that she becomes positively attractive. It is intended that we shall join with Cynthia in laughing at Lady Froth. And so we do. We laugh at her pedantic pretensions, her egotism regarding her absurd verses, her romantic idealization of that solemn coxcomb, her husband, her ecstatic raptures over her "adored Mr. Brisk." [84] Yet her unfailing good humor and eager enthusiasms enlist our sympathies in her behalf, her naïve confidences disarm our ridicule, her parental pride in the small Sappho who at the tender age of nine months

---

[82] Palmer, *The Comedy of Manners*, p. 180.
[83] Cf. p. 184, n. 5, of this volume.
[84] *The Double-Dealer*, IV, 2, p. 160.

"has a world of wit, and can sing a tune already" [85] quite warms our hearts. Some of the finest scenes in *The Double-Dealer* are those in which Lady Froth, in her encounters with Brisk, brings all these qualities into play and assures us in her own picturesque way of her very human reality.

The character of Lady Plyant in the same play is thus sketched by Mellefont: "She's handsome, and knows it; is very silly, and thinks she has sense, and has an old fond husband." [86] The type which she represents was singularly popular with Shadwell. Lady Vaine in *The Sullen Lovers*, Mrs. Woodly in *Epsom Wells*, and Lady Gimcrack in *The Virtuoso* suggest Lady Plyant in their loud vindications of their "honour" and their ill-concealed alacrity in participating, all the while, in dishonorable intrigues. Lady Gimcrack is much like Lady Plyant in her affected irresolution between "honour" and "opportunity." The former explains to Bruce:

... I swear, I am in earnest, and were I not sure of my Honour, that never fail'd me in a doubtful Occasion, I would not give you this Opportunity of tempting my Frailty; not but that my virtuous Inclinations are equal with any Lady's; But there's a prodigious Witchcraft in Opportunity. But Honour does much; yet Opportunity is a great thing, I swear, a great thing.[87]

Similarly, Lady Plyant encourages the amazed Mellefont by observing:

... I know love is powerful, and nobody can help his passion: 'tis not your fault, nor I swear it is not mine. — How can I help it, if I have charms? and how can you help it if you are made a captive? I swear it is pity it should be a fault. — But my honour, — well, but your honour too — but the sin! — well, but the necessity —. . . .[88]

Lady Plyant's later intrigue with Careless also parallels Lady Gimcrack's intrigue with Longvil. The *précieuse* effusiveness of speech with which Lady Plyant dignifies this second venture

[85] *Ibid.*, III, 3, p. 149. [86] *Ibid.*, I, 1, p. 109.
[87] *The Virtuoso (Works, I)*, III, p. 353.
[88] *The Double-Dealer*, II, 1, p. 128.

recalls, besides, Lady Maggot's fervent tribute to Wildish in *The Scowrers*. Lady Maggot informs Wildish:

> But you shall find, noble Sir, that she who can to Extravagance be sensible of Affronts and Injuries, can with as much zeal and Ardency resent the generous Favour you have loaded her with . . .
> And I'll assure you, Sir, there is not a Person living, who can be more grateful to a Person, that obliges any Person, than I shall shew myself to your noble Person.[89]

In like manner, Lady Plyant with many circumlocutions assures Careless:

> Mr. Careless, if a person that is wholly illiterate might be supposed to be capable of being qualified to make a suitable return to those obligations which you are pleased to confer upon one that is wholly incapable of being qualified in all those circumstances, I'm sure I should rather attempt it than anything in the world; [*Curtsies.*] for I'm sure there's nothing in the world that I would rather. [*Curtsies.*]

And again:

> . . . I know my own imperfections. — But at the same time you must give me leave to declare in the face of the world, that nobody is more sensible of favours and things; for with the reserve of my honour, I assure you, Mr. Careless, I don't know anything in the world I would refuse to a person so meritorious. — You'll pardon my want of expression.[90]

Lady Plyant's portrait is nevertheless idealized, as Shadwell's studies in the type never are. Her naïveté is never mean and calculating, but is merely very impulsive and indiscreet. Congreve indulges her with that kindly urbanity and good temper whereby he so often humanizes social folly.

Lady Wishfort is the *précieuse* grown old, as old and as ugly as Love-all in Killigrew's *The Parson's Wedding*. Her name and tastes recall Loveit in *The Man of Mode* and Lady Loveyouth in *The Humourists*. Shadwell had created a whole gallery of such portraits. When Lady Wishfort hastily represses her fastidiousness and encourages the grotesque wooing of Sir Wilfull, her behavior resembles Belliza's treatment of the vulgar Bernado in

---

[89] *The Scowrers* (*Works*, IV), III, p. 342.
[90] *The Double-Dealer*, III, 2, pp. 140–141.

The Amorous Bigot. Her pride in the refined education of her daughter, who, however, sadly shames her, parallels Lady Fantast's satisfaction in her ridiculous training of a similar daughter in *Bury Fair.* But Lady Wishfort's characterization is more well-rounded than that of persons resembling her in earlier comedy. Congreve displays her in as wide a variety of moods as possible. He elaborates her spirited relations with her maids, her patronizing indulgence of and final disgust with her untutored nephew, her ardent romantic friendship with Mrs. Marwood. His ridicule of Lady Wishfort's elderly caprices Congreve spices with a touch of contemporary satire, recording the fact that her closet-library contains Prynne and *The Short View of the Stage,*[91] and emphasizing her horror of "filthy plays" and "obscene play-books." [92] At all times, with his usual good humor, Congreve contrives to soften the conventional follies of the old coquette. He endows her with abundant animation, a gift of shrewd, cutting irony, and a keen sense of humor which extends even to a perception of her own decayed charms, her "arrant ash-colour" [93] complexion and her painted face cracked "like an old peeled wall." [94] At best, the portrait is revolting. "Female frailty!" comments Mrs. Fainall, "we must all come to it, if we live to be old." [95] Even for Millamant, alas, as for all Restoration coquettes, the gray future holds this inheritance in store. It is no wonder that Dryden's Florimel, contemplating this common destiny, announces a resolution to enjoy life until she is forty, and then "slip out of the world with the first wrinkle, and the reputation of five-and-twenty." [96]

We need not hesitate to affirm that Congreve's most characteristic work supports the Restoration *précieuse* tradition. In *The Old Bachelor* the progress of the central love intrigue is impeded

[91] *The Way of the World,* III, 1, p. 354.
[92] *Ibid.,* V, 2, p. 399.   [93] *Ibid.,* III, 1, p. 352.
[94] *Ibid.,* p. 356.   [95] *Ibid.,* II, 2, p. 344.
[96] *Secret Love (Works,* II), III, 1, p. 465.

by a young gallant's *précieuse* adventure with a jealous mistress. The leading characters confidently display their skill in formal argument. In *The Double-Dealer* the *précieuse* influence is still stronger. The discourse of the young lovers is limited to similitude contests. The hero's relations with affected, intriguing women are very complicated. The play includes, besides, some of Congreve's finest studies in characters whose extravagant *préciosité* constitutes a travesty of the social mode. In *Love for Love* Congreve is less faithful to Restoration conventions than elsewhere. Yet Restoration wit and gallantry, as exemplified by Valentine and Angelica, win a partial triumph over Elizabethan conservatism and bad manners, as exemplified by Foresight, Sir Sampson, and Ben, and over Restoration social folly, as exemplified by Mrs. Foresight, Mrs. Frail, Prue, and Tattle. The play becomes a true Restoration comedy of manners so far, and only so far, as this *précieuse* influence serves as a unifying dramatic force. In *The Way of the World* Congreve returns emphatically to the type of intrigue which he had stressed in *The Double-Dealer*. Extravagances of conduct are opposed with even greater clarity than in *The Double-Dealer* to the harmoniously tempered social attitudinizing of persons of excellent taste and refinement. The comedy owes its chief distinction to the courtship scenes between Mirabell and Millamant, scenes which serve to crystallize imperishably the Restoration comic mode at its highest point of development.

The plays of Congreve present a brief, authentic record of the *précieuse* movement in comedy. With studious zeal Congreve examined the earliest dramatic models of *précieuse* dialogue in the drama of Suckling and Cowley, and in not a few instances derived from these sources the pattern of his own carefully planned dialogue. He likewise utilized the best developments within the Restoration tradition attained by such predecessors as Etherege, Dryden, and Shadwell, borrowing from these dramatists his program in comic intrigue and in character contrasts. The Restoration *beau monde* which Etherege had described so vividly in *The Man of Mode*, Congreve describes and interprets with new power in *The Double-Dealer* and *The Way of the World*. With Congreve this *beau monde* is more indulgently idealized than with Etherege, more thoughtfully refined in "wit," less careless in its joyousness, richer in its humanity.

CHAPTER VIII

CONCLUSION

EVEN to the casual reader, the comedy of Etherege and Congreve inevitably suggests questions as to the literary origin of this type of drama. It has been the object of the foregoing chapters to attempt an answer to such questions. Through its representation of a peculiarly specialized society, divided into two distinct groups, which must be evaluated by two distinct comic standards, Restoration comedy of manners may be defined in terms so definite that they may serve as a legitimate test of comparison for the purpose of relating this drama to earlier forms of comedy. The terms of definition are fundamentally opposed, it is clear, to the terms in which Molière's comedy, with its larger world, interpreted by a single standard, is to be defined.

In the comedy of Etherege the fashions of this specialized society are illustrated with a precision which seems to indicate that Etherege was not responsible for their first intrusion into English comedy. It has been our contention that the work of Etherege and his contemporaries may be best explained in terms of earlier English dramatic tradition. We have, therefore, reviewed the various developments in English realistic comedy from the time of Jonson to the time of Etherege and his group, hoping thus to reveal whatever elements had been most vital in the literary inheritance of the Restoration comic dramatists.

We have observed that the comedy of Jonson, which in certain matters of dramatic technique exerted so powerful an influence on later dramatists, maintains a decidedly unsocial point of view, strikingly opposed to the spirit of Restoration comedy. Jonson was primarily interested in the problem of securing an equable balance of mental powers in the individual, not at all in the problem of the individual's adjustment to society. Nevertheless, as early as Jonson's time, a new social consciousness was developing, which found expression in the drama of a number of his contemporaries. Fletcher was aware of significant unifying forces at work in contemporary upper-class society and with careless grace achieved occasional sketches of this society, sketches never very well sustained and frequently abandoned in the interests of unique and surprising vicissitudes of intrigue. Middleton discovered a new source of comic effect in the interrelations of various social groups and especially in the restless trafficking of rich and ambitious tradesmen with impoverished members of the landed gentry. Brome studied middle-class life still more critically and excelled in portraying the citizen and the citizen's wife aping mannerisms of a higher society, whose social code was becoming all the while more highly specialized and more authoritative. The mannerisms which Brome caricatured, Shirley, on the other hand, exhibited with sympathetic approval in a few memorable portraits of people of fashion. The immoralities of fashionable gallantry Shirley frankly condemned, but its frivolities he regarded with good-humored complaisance and a polite faith in their propriety.

To an already quite sophisticated English court Henrietta Maria, the French bride of Charles I, opportunely introduced the elaborate fashions of French *préciosité*, in which she herself had been educated. She pronounced D'Avenant court interpreter of the *précieuse* cult of Platonic love, and in spite of ·personal cynicism in the matter, D'Avenant gallantly set forth the appropriate doctrines in a number of plays designed to meet the requirements of a novelty-loving courtly audience. To the queen's delight, the cult become a court fad, practiced in a most spectacular manner with all outward seriousness and decorum. Henrietta's own intellectual enthusiasm for *précieuse* gallantry was never, it is true, very satisfactorily communicated to her English subjects.

From the first, many of the English courtiers privately ridiculed the idealism of the "new religion" and exploited its ceremonies, taking advantage, whenever possible, of the generally more romantic Platonic sympathies of court ladies. Yet the forms of the *précieuse* system indisputably offered an attractive way of life. Its speech conventions brilliantly enriched conversation and encouraged a new type of social pastime. Every one admired the *précieuse* wit of Suckling, and presumably every one admired its graceful expression in his plays. Other dramatists, too, for example Carlell, and the promising young university scholar, Cartwright, devoted their dramatic talents to a serious interpretation of the popular cult. Society became thoroughly adjusted to an artificial mode of life, of which wit and gallantry were the great realities.

While the queen's authority continued to exert a sobering influence upon all literary expressions of the new cult, comedy had little chance to assert its verdict upon the social situation. At the outbreak of the civil war all court festivities were concluded. The romantic splendors of Platonism were extinguished, not again to be restored. Yet Platonic formalities still survived in cavalier society, and under their moulding influence the new comedy developed. In the new comedy *précieuse* dialogue was still elaborated, although it no longer had serious arguments to phrase. *Précieuse* gallantry was still gracefully enforced, but it now signified only a conventional habit of courtship. This now thoroughly conventionalized social mode was discovered to have manifestly comic aspects, both when awkwardly misinterpreted, and when completely fulfilled through personalities to which, however, it could not give complete expression. Killigrew announced the new comic program in *The Parson's Wedding*, shortly before the overthrow of the royalist party, and confirmed it in *Thomaso*, shortly after the royalist Restoration.

During the interregnum this comic spirit was simply silenced, not destroyed. The wit that was "banished with the Cavaliers" flourished again upon their return home. To divert a Restoration audience, Dryden ingeniously developed the most picturesque features of *précieuse* comedy. Etherege enlarged the scope of such drama, finding its type of "wit" and its pattern of artificial love intrigue admirably expressive of social habits of his day. Contemporary playwrights readily followed the example of Etherege. Foreign plots, especially those of Molière, were frequently adapted for the Restoration stage, but borrowed material was, for the most part, revised and altered in such a way as to enhance the authority of the courtly mode. In the last decade of the century, *précieuse* comedy reached its highwater mark in the plays of Congreve.

Beyond the art of Congreve, Restoration comedy of manners could not advance. Its essential excellences and its essential limitations were completely realized in his work. In brilliant dialogue, in vivid contrasts of social types, in the expression of that eager, yet formal urbanity of temper which characterized Restoration society at its best, Congreve triumphed over all other comic dramatists of his age. It was his further distinction to reveal clearly how inexpressive such comedy must be of the realities of character, how profound must be its silences concerning human passions, how restrained and stereotyped must remain its rule of life. It is not strange that this drama broke down in conflict with the reactionary forces of eighteenth century sentimentalism. It is not strange that its fashions have been regarded with hostility by large groups of people sympathetic with other habits of thought. To certain limited audiences, however, Restoration comedy of manners will continue to appeal. It will appeal to them not only as a picturesque literary phenomenon of a special era, but also as an interpretation of a type of comic predicament perpetually recurring in civilized society, whenever the lives of men and women become dominated by artificial standards of social discipline.

BIBLIOGRAPHY

A. DRAMATIC TEXTS

BEAUMONT, FRANCIS, AND FLETCHER, JOHN. *The Works of Beaumont and Fletcher*, edited, with notes and a biographical memoir, by Alexander Dyce. London, 1843–1846. 11 vols.

BEHN, APHRA. *The Plays, Histories, and Novels of the Ingenious Mrs. Aphra Behn*. London, 1871. 6 vols.

BERKELEY, SIR WILLIAM. *The Lost Lady. A tragi-comedy.* Reprinted in Dodsley's *Select Collection of Old English Plays*, ed. W. Carew Hazlitt, XII, pp. 536–627. London, 1875.

BROME, RICHARD. *The Dramatic Works of Richard Brome, containing fifteen comedies now first collected.* London, 1873. 3 vols.

CALDERON DE LA BARCA, PEDRO. *Las Comedias de D. Pedro Calderon de la Barca*, ed. Juan Jorge Keil. Leipsique, 1827. 4 vols.

[CARLELL, LODOWICK.] *Arviragus and Philicia. As it was acted at the Private House in Black-Fryers by his Majesties Servants. The first and second Part.* London, 1639.

CARLELL, LODOWICK. *The Deserving Favourite. A tragi-comedy.* Reprinted by Charles H. Gray, in *Lodowick Carliell*, pp. 70–162. Chicago, 1905.

CARLELL, LODOWICK. *The Passionate Lovers. A tragi-comedy. The First and Second Parts.* London, 1655.

CARLELL, LODOWICK. *Two New Playes, viz. 1. The Fool Would Be a Favourit: or The Discreet Lover, and 2. Osmond, the Great Turk: or The Noble Servant. As they have been often acted by the Queen's Majesty's Servants, with great applause.* London, 1657.

CARTWRIGHT, WILLIAM. *Comedies, Tragi-Comedies, with Other Poems.* London, 1651.

[CARYL, JOHN.] *Sir Salomon: or, The Cautious Coxcomb: A Comedy. As it is Acted at His Royal Highness the Duke of York's Theatre.* London, 1671.

CONGREVE, WILLIAM. *William Congreve*, ed. Alex. Charles Ewald. (Mermaid Series) London, 1887.

CORNEILLE, P[IERRE]. *Oeuvres de P. Corneille*, par M. Ch. Marty-Laveux. Paris, 1862. 12 vols.

CORNEILLE, T[HOMAS]. *Poèmes dramatiques de T. Corneille.* Paris, 1722. 5 vols.

COWLEY, ABRAHAM. *Essays, Plays and Sundry Verses*, ed. A. R. Waller. Cambridge, 1906.

COWLEY, ABRAHAM. *The Works of Mr. Abraham Cowley*. . . . London, 1707–1708. 3 vols.

CROWNE, JOHN. *The Dramatic Works of John Crowne*, edited, with prefatory memoir and notes, by James Maidment and W. H. Logan. (Dramatists of the Restoration) Edinburgh and London, 1873–1874. 4 vols.

D'AVENANT, SIR WILLIAM. *The Dramatic Works of Sir William D'Avenant*, edited, with prefatory memoir and notes, by James Maidment and W. H. Logan. (Dramatists of the Restoration) Edinburgh and London, 1872–1874. 5 vols.

DAY, JOHN. *The Works of John Day*, edited, with an introduction and notes, by A. H. Bullen. [London,] 1881.

DEKKER, THOMAS, CHETTLE, HENRY, AND HAUGHTON, WILLIAM. *Patient Grissil: A Comedy. Reprinted from the Black-Letter Edition of 1603*. (Shakespeare Society Publications) London, 1841.

[DESMARETS DE SAINT SORLIN, JEAN.] *Les Visionnaires, Comédie*. Paris, 1637.

DIGBY, GEORGE, EARL OF BRISTOL. *Elvira, or The Worst Not Always True. A Comedy.* Reprinted in Dodsley's *Select Collection of Old English Plays*, ed. W. Carew Hazlitt, XV, pp. 1–107. London, 1876.

DRYDEN, JOHN. *The Works of John Dryden*. . . . ed. Sir Walter Scott, Bart. Revised and corrected by George Saintsbury. Edinburgh, 1882–1893. 18 vols.

D'URFEY, THOMAS. *Madam Fickle or The Witty False One. A Comedy. As it is Acted at His Royal Highness the Duke's Theatre*. London, 1682.

ETHEREGE, SIR GEORGE. *The Works of Sir George Etheredge*, edited, with critical notes and introduction, by A. Wilson Verity. London, 1888.

FANE, SIR FRANCIS. *Love in the Dark, or The Man of Bus'ness. A Comedy: Acted at the Theatre Royal by His Majesties Servants*. London, 1675.

The Feign'd Astrologer. A Comedie. London, 1668.

GLAPTHORNE, HENRY. *The Plays and Poems of Henry Glapthorne, now first collected with illustrative notes and a memoir of the author*. (Pearson's reprint) London, 1874. 2 vols.

HABINGTON, WILLIAM. *The Queen of Arragon. A tragi-comedie.* Reprinted in Dodsley's *Select Collection of Old English Plays*, ed. W. Carew Hazlitt, XIII, pp. 321–409. London, 1875.

[HOWARD, EDWARD.] *The Six Days Adventure, or The New Utopia. A Comedy. As it is Acted at His Royal Highness the Duke of York's Theatre.* London, 1671.

H[OWARD], E[DWARD]. *The Women's Conquest. A Tragi-comedy. As it was Acted by His Highness the Duke of Yorks Servants.* London, 1671.

HOWARD, JAMES. *All Mistaken, or The Mad Couple. A Comedy.* Reprinted in Dodsley's *Select Collection of Old English Plays,* ed. W. Carew Hazlitt, XV, pp. 321–397. London, 1876.

HOWARD, SIR ROBERT. *The Dramatic Works of Sir Robert Howard.* . . . London, 1722.

JONSON, BEN. *The Works of Ben Jonson,* ed. W. Gifford, with introduction and appendices by F. Cunningham. London, 1875. 9 vols.

KILLIGREW, THOMAS. *Comedies and Tragedies.* London, 1664.

KILLIGREW, SIR WILLIAM. *Four New Playes, viz.: The Seege of Urbin, Selindra, Love and Friendship, tragy-comedies, Pandora, a comedy.* Oxford, 1666.

LACY, JOHN. *The Dramatic Works of John Lacy, Comedian,* edited, with prefatory memoir and notes, by James Maidment and W. H. Logan. (Dramatists of the Restoration) Edinburgh and London, 1875.

LYLY, JOHN. *The Complete Works of John Lyly,* edited, with introduction, essays, and notes, by R. Warwick Bond. Oxford, 1902. 3 vols.

MARMION, SHAKERLEY. *The Dramatic Works of Shackerley Marmion,* edited, with prefatory memoir and notes, by James Maidment and W. H. Logan. (Dramatists of the Restoration) Edinburgh and London, 1875.

MASSINGER, PHILIP. *Philip Massinger,* edited, with an introduction and notes, by Arthur Symons. (Mermaid Series) London, 1887–1889. 2 vols.

M[AYNE], J[ASPER]. *Two Plaies. The City Match. A Comoedy. And The Amorous Warre. A Tragy-comoedy.* Oxford, 1658.

MIDDLETON, THOMAS. *The Works of Thomas Middleton,* ed. A. H. Bullen. Boston and New York, 1885–1886. 8 vols.

MOLIÈRE [JEAN BAPTISTE POQUELIN]. *Oeuvres de Molière,* ed. Eugène Despois et Paul Mesnard. Paris, 1873–1893. 11 vols.

MONTAGUE, W[ALTER]. *The Shepheard's Paradise. A Comedy. Privately Acted before the Late King Charls by the Queen's Majesty, and Ladies of Honour.* London, 1629. (*This date is a misprint for 1659.*)

MOUNTFORT, [WILLIAM]. *Six Plays.* . . London, 1720. 2 vols.

NEWCASTLE, [MARGARET CAVENDISH], DUCHESS OF. *Plays Written by the Thrice Noble, Illustrious, and Excellent Princess, The Lady Marchioness of Newcastle.* London, 1662.

NEWCASTLE, [MARGARET CAVENDISH], DUCHESS OF. *Plays, Never before Printed.* London, 1668.

[NEWCASTLE, WILLIAM CAVENDISH, DUKE OF.] *The Country Captaine, and The Varettie; Two Comedies, Written by a Person of Honor. Lately presented by His Majesties Servants, at the Black-Fryars.* London, 1649.

NEWCASTLE, [WILLIAM CAVENDISH], DUKE OF. *The Humorous Lovers. A Comedy. Acted by His Royal Highnes's Servants.* London, 1677.

NEWCASTLE, [WILLIAM CAVENDISH], DUKE OF. *The Triumphant Widow, or The Medley of Humours, A Comedy. Acted by His Royal Highness' Servants.* London, 1677.

ORRERY, ROGER BOYLE, [1ST] EARL OF. *The Dramatic Works of Roger Boyle Earl of Orrery.* London, 1739. 2 vols.

QUINAULT, [PHILIPPE]. *Le Théatre de Monsieur Quinault.* . . . Paris, 1739. 5 vols.

RAVENSCROFT, EDWARD. *The Careless Lovers, A Comedy. Acted at the Duke's Theatre.* London, 1673.

RAVENSCROFT, EDWARD. *The Citizen Turn'd Gentleman: A Comedy. Acted at the Duke's Theatre.* London, 1672.

RAVENSCROFT, EDWARD. *The Wrangling Lovers, or The Invisible Mistress. A Comedy. Acted at the Dukes-Theater.* London, 1677.

[RAWLINS, THOMAS.] *Tom Essence: or, The Modish Wife. A Comedy. As it is Acted at the Duke's Theatre.* London, 1677.

SCARRON, [PAUL]. *Théatre complet, précédée d'une notice biographique,* par M. Édouard Fournier. . . . Paris, 1879.

SEDLEY, SIR CHARLES. *The Works of the Honourable Sir Charles Sedley, Bart. In Prose and Verse.* . . . London, 1776. 2 vols.

SHADWELL, THOMAS. *The Dramatick Works of Thomas Shadwell, Esq.* London, 1720. 4 vols.

SHAKESPEARE, WILLIAM. *A New Variorum Edition of Shakespeare,* ed. Horace Howard Furness. Philadelphia, 1871–1919. 19 vols.

SHIRLEY, JAMES. *The Dramatic Works and Poems of James Shirley,* edited, with notes by William Gifford, Esq. and additional notes and biography by Alexander Dyce. London, 1833. 6 vols.

SUCKLING, SIR JOHN. *The Poems, Plays and Other Remains of Sir John Suckling,* ed. W. Carew Hazlitt. London, 1892. 2 vols.

TATHAM, JOHN. *The Dramatic Works of John Tatham,* edited, with prefatory memoir and notes, by James Maidment and W. H. Logan. (Dramatists of the Restoration) Edinburgh and London, 1879.

TUKE, SIR SAMUEL. *The Adventures of Five Hours. A Tragi-comedy.* Reprinted in Dodsley's *Select Collection of Old English Plays,* ed. W. Carew Hazlitt, XV, pp. 185–320. London, 1876.

WILSON, JOHN. *The Dramatic Works of John Wilson*, edited, with prefatory memoir and notes, by James Maidment and W. H. Logan. (Dramatists of the Restoration) Edinburgh and London, 1874.

WYCHERLEY, WILLIAM. *William Wycherley*, ed. W. C. Ward. (Mermaid Series) London and New York [1876].

B. NON-DRAMATIC TEXTS, BIOGRAPHICAL AND
CRITICAL WORKS

ADAMS, JOSEPH QUINCY, editor. *The Dramatic Records of Sir Henry Herbert, Master of the Revels, 1623–1673.* New Haven and London, 1917.

ADAMS, JOSEPH QUINCY. *Shakespearean Playhouses. A History of English Theatres from the Beginnings to the Restoration.* Boston, New York, Chicago [1917].

[ADDISON, JOSEPH, AND STEELE, RICHARD.] *The Spectator*, ed. Henry Morley, London [1868].

ANDREWS, CLARENCE EDWARD. *Richard Brome: A Study of his Life and Works.* (Dissertation, Yale) New York, 1913. (Yale Studies in English, XLVI.)

[BAKER, DAVID ERSKINE.] *The Companion to the Playhouse: or An Historical Account of all the Dramatic Writers (and their Works) that have appeared in Great Britain and Ireland, from the Commencement of our Theatrical Exhibitions, down to the Present Year 1764.*· . . . London, 1764.

BAKER, GEORGE PIERCE. "Richard Brome," in Gayley's *Representative English Comedies*, III, pp. 417–429. New York and London, 1914.

BALZAC, [JEAN LOUIS GUEZ, SEIGNEUR DE]. *Letters of Monsieur de Balzac. . . . Translated out of French into English. By Sir Richard Baker Knight, and Others.* London, 1654.

BAYNE, RONALD. "Lesser Jacobean and Caroline Dramatists," in *Cambridge History of English Literature*, ed. A. W. Ward and A. R. Waller, VI, pp. 210–240. Cambridge, 1910.

BERGSON, HENRI. *Laughter. An Essay on the Meaning of the Comic*, tr. Cloudesley Brereton and Fred Rothwell. New York, 1921.

BETTERTON, THOMAS. *The History of the Stage, English from the Restauration to the Present Time.* . . . London, 1741.

BIRCH, THOMAS. *The Court and Times of Charles the First.* London, 1849. 2 vols.

BONAFOUS, NORBERT. *Études sur L'Astrée et sur Honoré d'Urfé.* Paris, 1846.

BRUNETIÈRE, FERDINAND. *Études critiques sur l'histoire de la littérature française, Deuxième série.* "La Société précieuse au XVIIᵉ siècle," pp. 1-26. Paris, 1893.

CAMPBELL, O[SCAR] J[AMES]. "Some Influences of Meredith's Philosophy on His Fiction," in *University of Wisconsin Studies in Language and Literature*, No. 2, 1918, pp. 323-339.

CANBY, HENRY SEIDEL. "Congreve as a Romanticist," in *Publications of the Modern Language Association of America*, XXXI, 1916, pp. 1-23.

CANFIELD, DOROTHEA FRANCES, see Fisher.

CAREW, THOMAS. *The Poems of Thomas Carew*, ed. Arthur Vincent. London and New York, 1899.

CHAMBERS, [SIR] E[DMUND] K. *The Elizabethan Stage*. Oxford, 1923. 4 vols.

CHARLANNE, L[OUIS]. *L'Influence française en Angleterre au XVIIᵉ siècle.* . . . (Dissertation, Paris) Paris, 1906.

CHASE, LEWIS NATHANIEL. *The English Heroic Play.* (Dissertation, Columbia) New York and London, 1903.

CHURCHILL, GEORGE B., editor. *The Country Wife and The Plain Dealer by William Wycherley.* Introduction, pp. v-lxiii. Boston, New York, Chicago, London, 1924.

CHURCHILL, GEORGE B. "The Originality of William Wycherley," in *Schelling Anniversary Papers*, pp. 64-85. New York, 1923.

COLLIER, JEREMY. *A Short View of the Immorality and Profaneness of the English Stage.* . . . London, 1698.

COLLIER, JEREMY. *A Defence of the Short View of the Profaneness and Immorality of the English Stage.* . . . London, 1699.

COLLIER, JEREMY. *A Second Defence of the Short View of the Profaneness and Immorality of the English Stage.* . . . London, 1700.

[CONGREVE, WILLIAM.] *Amendments of Mr. Collier's False and Imperfect Citations.* . . . London, 1698.

[COTGRAVE, JOHN.] *Wits Interpreter, The English Parnassus.* . . . London, 1655.

COUSIN, VICTOR. *La Société française au XVIIᵉ siècle d'après le Grand Cyrus.* Paris, 1886. 2 vols.

COWLEY, ABRAHAM. *Poems* . . . ed. A. R. Waller. Cambridge, 1905.

CRANE, THOMAS FREDERICK, editor. *La Société française au XVIIᵉ siècle; an account of French society in the XVIIᵗʰ century from contemporary writers.* New York and London, 1889.

CYRANO DE BERGERAC, [SAVINIEN]. *Oeuvres comiques, galantes et littéraires* . . . par P. L. Jacob. Paris [1858].

DIBDIN, [CHARLES]. *A Complete History of the English Stage.* . . . London [1800]. 5 vols.

DIGBY, SIR KENELM. *Private Memoirs of Sir Kenelm Digby.* . . . London, 1827.

DOBRÉE, BONAMY. *Restoration Comedy, 1660–1720.* Oxford, 1924.

DONNE, JOHN. *The Poems of John Donne,* ed. Herbert J. C. Grierson. Oxford, 1912. 2 vols.

DOWNES, JOHN. *Roscius Anglicanus, or an Historical Review of the Stage, from 1660 to 1706. A Facsimile Reprint of the Rare Original of 1708.* With an historical preface by Joseph Knight. London, 1886.

DU BLED, VICTOR. *La Société française du XVIe siècle au XXe siècle,* vols. 1–4. Paris, 1903–1910.

D'URFÉ, HONORÉ. *L'Astrée de Me sire Honoré d'Urfé.* . . . Rouen, 1646–1647. 5 vols.

EVELYN, JOHN. *The Diary and Correspondence of John Evelyn.* . . . ed. William Bray. London, 1870. 4 vols.

FANSHAWE, [ANNE (HARRISON)], LADY. *Memoirs of Lady Fanshawe,* . . . with an introduction by Beatrice Marshall. London and New York, 1905.

FIRTH, C[HARLES] H[ARDING]. "The Suppression of the Drama during the Protectorate and Commonwealth," in *Notes and Queries,* VII Series, VI, 1888, pp. 122–123.

[FISHER], DOROTHEA FRANCES (CANFIELD). *Corneille and Racine in England.* New York, 1904.

FITZMAURICE-KELLY, JAMES. *A History of Spanish Literature.* New York, 1898.

FLEAY, FREDERICK GARD. *A Biographical Chronicle of the English Drama, 1559–1642.* London, 1891. 2 vols.

FLETCHER, JEFFERSON BUTLER. *The Religion of Beauty in Woman and Other Essays on Platonic Love in Poetry and Society.* New York, 1911.

FORSYTHE, ROBERT STANLEY. *The Relations of Shirley's Plays to the Elizabethan Drama.* New York, 1914.

FORSYTHE, ROBERT STANLEY. *A Study of the Plays of Thomas D'Urfey,* Part I. *Western Reserve University Bulletin,* XIX, No. 5, 1916.

GAYLEY, CHARLES MILLS, editor. *Representative English Comedies.* "A Comparative View of the Fellows and Followers of Shakespeare in Comedy" (Part Two), III, pp. xi–xcvii. New York and London, 1914.

[GENEST, JOHN.] *Some Account of the English Stage, from the Restoration in 1660 to 1830.* Bath, 1832. 10 vols.

GERMA, BERNARD. *L'Astrée d'Honoré d'Urfé. Sa Composition — Son Influence.* Toulouse, Paris, 1904.

[GILDON, CHARLES.] *The Lives and Characters of the English Dramatic Poets.
. . . . First begun by Mr. Langbain, improv'd and continued down to
this Time by a Careful Hand.* London [1699].

GOSSE, [SIR] EDMUND. *Life of William Congreve.* London, 1924.

GOSSE, [SIR] EDMUND. *Seventeenth Century Studies.* . . . New York, 1897.

GRAY, CHARLES H. *Lodowick Carliell. His Life, a Discussion of His Plays,
and The Deserving Favourite, a Tragi-comedy Reprinted from the
Original Edition of 1629.* (Dissertation, Chicago) Chicago, 1905.

GREG, WALTER W. *Pastoral Poetry and Pastoral Drama.* London, 1906.

HABINGTON, WILLIAM. *Castara. The Third Edition of 1640,* . . . ed.
Edward Arber. London, 1870.

HAMILTON, ANTHONY, [COUNT]. *Memoirs of Count Grammont by Anthony
Hamilton,* ed. Sir Walter Scott. New York, 1889.

HARRISON, JOHN SMITH. *Platonism in English Poetry of the Sixteenth and
Seventeenth Centuries.* New York, 1915.

HARTMANN, CYRIL HUGHES. *The Cavalier Spirit and its Influence on the Life
and Work of Richard Lovelace (1618–1658).* London, 1925.

HATCHER, ORIE LATHAM. *John Fletcher. A Study in Dramatic Method.*
(Dissertation, Chicago) Chicago, 1905.

HAZLITT, WILLIAM. *The Collected Works of William Hazlitt,* ed. A. R.
Waller and Arnold Glover. London, 1902–1904. 12 vols.

HAZLITT, W[ILLIAM] CAREW. *A Manual for the Collector and Amateur of
Old English Plays.* London, 1892.

HENRIETTA MARIA. *Letters of Queen Henrietta Maria.* . . . ed. Mary Anne
Everett Green. London, 1857.

HERBERT, EDWARD, [1ST BARON] HERBERT OF CHERBURY. *The Poems,
English and Latin of Edward Lord Herbert of Cherbury,* ed. G. C.
Moore Smith. Oxford, 1923.

HERFORD, C[HARLES] H. AND SIMPSON, PERCY, editors. *Ben Jonson.* Vols. I
and II, *The Man and His Work.* Oxford, 1925.

HILL, HERBERT WYNFORD. *La Calprenède's Romances and the Restoration
Drama.* (Dissertation, Chicago) Chicago, n. d.

HOWELL, JAMES. *The Familiar Letters of James Howell, Historiographer
Royal to Charles II,* ed. Joseph Jacobs. London, 1892. 2 vols.

HUME, MARTIN. *Spanish Influence on English Literature.* London, 1905.

HUNT, [JAMES HENRY] LEIGH, editor. *Dramatic Works of Wycherley, Congreve,*

Vanbrugh, and Farquhar, with biographical and critical notices. London and New York, 1866.

JOHNSON, SAMUEL. *Lives of the English Poets*, ed. George Birkbeck Hill. Oxford, 1905. 3 vols.

KERR, MINA. *Influence of Ben Jonson on English Comedy, 1598–1642.* New York, 1912.

LAMB, CHARLES. *The Works of Charles and Mary Lamb*, ed. E. V. Lucas. London, 1903–1905. 7 vols.

LANCASTER, HENRY CARRINGTON. *The French Tragi-comedy, its Origin and Development from 1552 to 1628.* Baltimore, 1907.

LANGBAINE, GERARD. *An Account of the English Dramatick Poets.* . . . Oxford, 1691.

LIVET, CH[ARLES] L[OUIS]. *Précieux et précieuses: caractères et moeurs littéraires du XVIIᵉ siècle.* Paris, 1895.

LOVEDAY, R[OBERT]. *Lovedays Letters. Domestick and Forrein.* . . . London, 1659.

LOVELACE, RICHARD. *Lucasta. The Poems of Richard Lovelace, Esq.*, ed. W. Carew Hazlitt. London, 1864.

LYNCH, KATHLEEN M. "D'Urfé's *Astrée* and the 'Proviso' Scenes in Dryden's Comedy," in *Philological Quarterly*, IV, 1925, pp. 302–308.

MACAULAY, G[EORGE] C[AMPBELL]. "Beaumont and Fletcher," in *Cambridge History of English Literature*, ed. A. W. Ward and A. R. Waller, VI, pp. 107–140. Cambridge, 1910.

MACAULAY, [THOMAS BABINGTON, 1ST BARON]. *Critical and Historical Essays*, ed. F. C. Montague. "Leigh Hunt," III, pp. 3–48. London, 1903.

MAGNE, ÉMILE. *Voiture et les origines de l'Hôtel de Rambouillet, 1597–1635.* Paris, 1911. 2 vols.

MARKS, JEANNETTE. *English Pastoral Drama from the Restoration to the Date of the Publication of the "Lyrical Ballads" (1660–1798).* London [1908].

MARSAN, JULES. *La Pastorale dramatique en France à la fin du XVIᵉ et au commencement du XVIIᵉ siècle.* Paris, 1905.

MCAFEE, HELEN. *Pepys on the Restoration Stage.* New Haven and London, 1916.

MEREDITH, GEORGE. *An Essay on Comedy and the Uses of the Comic Spirit*, ed. Lane Cooper. New York, Chicago, Boston [1918].

MILES, DUDLEY HOWE. *The Influence of Molière on Restoration Comedy.* (Dissertation, Columbia) New York, 1910.

[MORRIS], ELISABETH (WOODBRIDGE). *Studies in Jonson's Comedy.* Boston, New York, and London, 1898. (Yale Studies in English, V.)

NASON, ARTHUR HUNTINGTON. *James Shirley, Dramatist. A Biographical and Critical Study.* New York, 1915.

NETTLETON, GEORGE HENRY. *English Drama of the Restoration and Eighteenth Century.* New York, 1914.

NEWCASTLE, MARGARET CAVENDISH, DUCHESS OF. *The Lives of William Cavendishe, Duke of Newcastle, and of his Wife, Margaret Duchess of Newcastle,* . . . edited, with a preface and notes, by Mark Antony Lower. London, 1872.

NICOLL, ALLARDYCE. *A History of Restoration Drama, 1660–1700.* Cambridge, 1923.

ODELL, GEORGE C. *Shakespeare from Betterton to Irving.* "The Age of Betterton," I, pp. 3–212. London, 1921.

ORRERY, [ROGER BOYLE, 1ST] EARL OF. *Parthenissa, That most Fam'd Romance, The Six Volumes Compleat.* London, 1676.

PALMER, JOHN. *Comedy.* London [1914].

PALMER, JOHN. *The Comedy of Manners.* London, 1913.

PARLIN, HANSON T. *A Study in Shirley's Comedies of London Life. University of Texas Bulletin,* No. 371, Humanistic Series, No. 17, Studies in English, No. 2, 1914.

PAYNE, F. W. "The Question of Precedence between Dryden and the Earl of Orrery with Regard to the English Heroic Play," in *The Review of English Studies,* I, 1925, pp. 173–181.

PEPYS, SAMUEL. *The Diary of Samuel Pepys,* . . . ed. Henry B. Wheatley. London, 1893–1899. 9 vols.

PERRENS, F[RANÇOIS] T[OMMY]. *Les Libertins en France au XVIIe siecle.* Paris, 1921.

PERROMAT, CHARLES. *William Wycherley. Sa Vie — Son Oeuvre.* Paris, 1921.

PERRY, HENRY TEN EYCK. *The Comic Spirit in Restoration Drama.* New Haven and London, 1925.

PERRY, HENRY TEN EYCK. *The First Duchess of Newcastle and Her Husband, as Figures in Literary History.* Boston and London, 1918.

PETIT DE JULLEVILLE, L[OUIS], editor. *Histoire de la langue et de la littérature française des origines à 1900.* "L'Hôtel de Rambouillet. — Balzac. — Voiture. — Les Précieuses," par M. Bourciez, IV, pp. 82–134. Paris, 1897–1898.

[PHILIPS, KATHERINE (FOWLER).] *Letters from Orinda to Poliarchus.* London, 1705.

RERESBY, SIR JOHN. *The Memoirs and Travels of Sir John Reresby, Bart.* . . . . London, 1813.

RETZ, [JEAN FRANÇOIS PAUL DE GONDI], CARDINAL DE. *Memoirs of the Cardinal de Retz. . . . Translated from the French.* London, 1896.

REURE, O[DON] C[LAUDE]. *La Vie et les oeuvres de Honoré d'Urfé.* Paris, 1910.

ROEDERER, P[IERRE] L[OUIS], COMTE. "Mémoire pour servir à l'histoire de la sociéte polie en France," in *Oeuvres du Comte P. L. Roederer*, II, pp. 393–545. Paris, 1853.

ROLLINS, HYDER E. "A Contribution to the History of the English Commonwealth Drama," in *Studies in Philology*, XVIII, 1921, pp. 267–333.

ROLLINS, HYDER E. "The Commonwealth Drama: Miscellaneous Notes," in *Studies in Philology*, XX, 1923, pp. 52–69.

RUDMOSE-BROWN, THOMAS B., editor. *La Galerie du Palais. Comédie par Pierre Corneille.* Introduction, pp. xi–liii. Manchester, 1920.

SAINT-AMANT, [MARC ANTOINE GERARD, SIEUR DE]. *Oeuvres complètes de Saint-Amant*, par. M. Ch. L. Livet. Paris, 1855. 2 vols.

SAINTSBURY, GEORGE, editor. *Minor Poets of the Caroline Period.* . . . Oxford, 1905–1921. 3 vols.

SCHELLING, FELIX E. *Elizabethan Drama, 1558–1642.* . . . Boston and New York, 1908. 2 vols.

SCHELLING, FELIX E. "The Restoration Drama" (I), in *Cambridge History of English Literature*, ed. A. W. Ward and A. R. Waller, VIII, pp. 115–145. Cambridge, 1912.

SCHMID, D[AVID]. "William Congreve, sein Leben und seine Lustspiele," in *Wiener Beiträge zur englischen Philologie*, VI, pp. 1–179. Wien und Leipzig, 1897.

SCUDÉRY [MADELEINE DE]. *Artamenes, or The Grand Cyrus, an Excellent New Romance, Written by that famous Wit of France, Monsieur de Scudéry.* . . . London, 1653–1655. 2 vols.

SCUDÉRY, [MADELEINE DE]. *Clelia, an Excellent New Romance: The Whole Work in Five Parts.* . . . London, 1678.

SMITH, G[EORGE] GREGORY. *Ben Jonson.* (English Men of Letters) London, 1919.

SMITH, HOMER. "Pastoral Influence in the English Drama," in *Publications of the Modern Language Association of America*, New Series, V, 1897, pp. 355–460.

SOMAIZE, [ANTOINE BAUDEAU,] SIEUR DE. *Le Dictionnaire des précieuses*, ed. Ch. L. Livet. Paris, 1856. 2 vols.

[SOREL, CHARLES.] *Le Berger Extravagant.* . . . Rouen, 1646. 2 vols.

SPENCE, JOSEPH. *Observations, Anecdotes, and Characters of Books and Men*, ed. Edmund Malone, Esq. London, 1820.

STRAUSS, LOUIS A., editor. *A Discourse upon Comedy, The Recruiting Officer and The Beaux Stratagem by George Farquhar.* Introduction, pp. xiii–lvi. Boston and London [1914].

SUMMERS, MONTAGUE, editor. *Restoration Comedies, The Parson's Wedding, The London Cuckolds, and Sir Courtly Nice, or It Cannot Be.* Introduction, pp. xiii–xlvi. Boston [1922].

SYMONS, ARTHUR. "Middleton and Rowley," in *Cambridge History of English Literature,* ed. A. W. Ward and A. R. Waller, VI, pp. 58–80. Cambridge, 1910.

[TEMPLE], DOROTHY (OSBORNE), [LADY]. *Letters from Dorothy Osborne to Sir William Temple, 1652–1654,* ed. Edward Abbott Parry. London and Manchester, 1903.

THORNDIKE, ASHLEY H. "Ben Jonson," in *Cambridge History of English Literature,* ed. A. W. Ward and A. R. Waller, VI, pp. 1–28. Cambridge, 1910.

UPHAM, Alfred H. *The French Influence in English Literature, from the Accession of Elizabeth to the Restoration.* New York, 1911.

[VIAU], THÉOPHILE [DE]. *Oeuvres complètes de Théophile.* . . . par M. Alleaume. Paris, 1855–1856. 2 vols.

VOITURE, [VINCENT]. *Oeuvres de Voiture,* par M. A. Ubicini. Paris, 1855. 2 vols.

WALLER, EDMUND. *The Works of Edmund Waller, Esq., in Verse and Prose,* ed. [Elijah] Fenton. London, 1730.

WARD, [SIR] ADOLPHUS WILLIAM. "Dryden," in *Cambridge History of English Literature,* ed. A. W. Ward and A. R. Waller, VIII, pp. 1–57. Cambridge, 1912.

WARD, [SIR] ADOLPHUS WILLIAM. *A History of English Dramatic Literature to the Death of Queen Anne.* London and New York, 1899. 3 vols.

WHIBLEY, CHARLES. "The Restoration Drama" (II), in *Cambridge History of English Literature,* ed. A. W. Ward and A. R. Waller, VIII, pp. 146–177. Cambridge, 1912.

WOODBRIDGE, ELISABETH, see Morris.

[WRIGHT, JAMES.] *Historia Histrionica. An Historical Account of the English Stage.* . . . *In a Dialogue of Plays and Players.* London, 1699. Reprinted in Dodsley's *Select Collection of Old English Plays,* ed. W. Carew Hazlitt, XV, pp. 399–431. London, 1876.

INDEX

Important references, relating to the chief discussion of authors and their work, are indicated by italics.

C

Calderon de la Barca, Pedro, translations and adaptations of his plays, 121 n., 157, 166.

Canfield, Dorothea Frances, *see* Fisher.

Canterbury Guests, The (Ravenscroft), 161 n.

Capon, John, 110.

Captain, The (Fletcher), 142.

Careless Lovers, The (Ravenscroft), *160–162*, 202, 203.

Carew, Thomas, 112; his poetry, 54–55, 87.

Carey, Patrick, his poetry, 113.

Carlell, Lodowick, 67, 216; his Platonic drama, *62–65*, 122, 141.

Cartwright, William, 89, 94, 123, 216; his Platonic drama, *66–69;* anti-Platonic moods in his drama, 88; influence of, on Mrs. Philips, 113, 115.

Caryl, John, *Sir Salomon*, 159.

Castara (Habington), 54.

Célidée (Rayssiguier), 51.

Chambers, Sir Edmund K., 15 n., 21 n., 22 n., 26 n.

Changes, The (Shirley), 142 n.

Charles I, court of, 43, 94, 102, 107 215.

Charles II, court of, 43, 140; Dryden's tribute to, 139.

Chaste Maid in Cheapside, A (Middleton), *27–28*, 143.

Cheats, The (Wilson), 121, 190, 192.

Chriséide et Arimant (Mairet), 51.

Churchill, George B., 167 n., 169, 172 n.

Citizen Turn'd Gentleman, The (Ravenscroft), 159.

City Madam, The (Massinger), 84 n.

City Match, The (Mayne), 94.

City Wit, The (Brome), *31–32*.

Claracilla (Thomas Killigrew), 66.

Clélie (Madeleine de Scudéry), 117.

Cléopâtre (La Calprenède), 118.

Cockpit Theater, 108, 109.

Collier, Jeremy, his attack on Restoration comedy, 3.

Comedy, Elizabethan, general influence of, on Restoration comedy, 11, 42, 188, 214–215; influence of, on Etherege's drama, 142–143; on Congreve's drama, 183, *188–193*.

Comedy of humours, general influence of, on Restoration comedy, 14, 19; Jonson's theory of humours, *15–16;* influence of Jonson's humours on Elizabethan dramatists, 20, 24, 29, 35; revival of Jonsonian humours by minor Restoration dramatists, 121, 145, 160; by Shadwell, 155, 163, 164; by Wycherley, 165; by Congreve, 189–190, 192.

Comedy of intrigue, Restoration, 160, 175–176.

Comedy of manners, Restoration, general sources of, 1–2, 8–10, *214–217;* immorality of, assailed by critics, 2–5; definition of, *6–8;* artistic excellence of, 217.

Comic standard, double in Restoration comedy defined, *7–9;* single in Molière's comedy, *8–9,* 214; unsocial emphasis of Jonson's, 16–19, 214–215; Shirley's anticipation of Restoration, 37–38, 42; Restoration illustrated by Killigrew, 106, 131; by Dryden, 135; by Etherege, 152, 154, 181; by Wycherley, 174; by Congreve, 194–195, 205, 212.

Comical Revenge, The (Etherege), 107, 126, 137, 138, *140–144*, 156, 190.

Committee, The (Sir Robert Howard), 121, 144, 189.

Committee-Man Curried, The (Sheppard), 110.

Comtesse d'Escarbagnas, La (Molière), 175, 187 n.

Congreve, William, 3, 6, 8, 35, 38, 79, 84, 106, 136, 166, 214; his theory of comedy, 8; influence of Suckling on, 77–78, 92–93, 94; influence of